FAMILY WHISPERING

FAMILY WHISPERING

The Baby Whisperer's Commonsense
Strategies for Communicating
and Connecting with the People You Love
and Making Your Whole Family Stronger

MELINDA BLAU
AND TRACY HOGG

ATRIA BOOKS
New York   London   Toronto   Sydney   New Delhi

ATRIA BOOKS

A Division of Simon & Schuster, Inc.
1230 Avenue of the Americas
New York, NY 10020

First Atria Books hardcover edition February 2014

ATRIA BOOKS and colophon are trademarks of Simon & Schuster, Inc.

For information about special discounts for bulk purchases,
please contact Simon & Schuster Special Sales at
1-866-506-1949 or business@simonandschuster.com.

The Simon & Schuster Speakers Bureau can bring authors to your live event.
For more information or to book an event, contact the Simon & Schuster Speakers
Bureau at 1-866-248-3049 or visit our website at www.simonspeakers.com.

Designed by Akasha Archer

Manufactured in the United States of America

10   9   8   7   6   5   4   3   2   1

Library of Congress Cataloging-in-Publication Data

Blau, Melinda.
    Family whispering : the baby whisperer's commonsense strategies for communicating and connecting with the people you love and making your whole family stronger / by Melinda Blau and (the late) Tracy Hogg. — First Atria Books hardcover edition.
        pages   cm
    Includes index.
    1. Parenting.   2. Parent and child.   3. Families.   I. Hogg, Tracy.   II. Title.
    HQ755.8.B593   2014
    306.85—dc23   2013009358
ISBN 978-1-4516-5446-2
ISBN 978-1-4516-5451-6 (ebook)

To
Henry, Sam, and Charlie
with love and awe

CONTENTS

FAMILY WHISPERING

FAMILY MATTERS
The Coauthors Reflect

We might not have it all together, but together we have it all.
—AUTHOR UNKNOWN

The first section of this prologue was written before Tracy Hogg lost her painful and courageous battle against cancer. She was forty-four. Although she didn't live to see the publication of The Baby Whisperer Solves All Your Problems, *published in January 2005, she spent several months planning and talking about "the family book," as this project was then called.*

Sherman Oaks, California, August 2004.

Doctors tell me that my cancer is back. A book about family now seems more important than ever. I don't know what I'd do without my family. Family is the one thing we can count on. Or at least, that's how it should be. Lucky for me, that's how it is. My family and others who feel like family are helping me cope. *Family matters.*

I'm a baby whisperer, not a family therapist. I don't have a degree in psychology. But I've been let into many people's homes. They welcome me into their lives. I sleep in their guest rooms or nurseries. I eat at their dinner tables. I join them on shopping trips to the local market. I'm invited to happy occasions, such as a baby naming, a baptism, or a bris (the Jewish celebration of circumcision, which is not so much fun for the little boy, I'm afraid). I'm also on hand when things go haywire: The flummoxed new mum snaps at her husband for buying the wrong kind of cottage cheese or blows up at her own mum for "just trying to help" by tidying up the linen closet.

I've heard and seen it all. And although I stand up for the baby, I've always warned new parents that it's not just about *the baby*. Once an adult or a couple brings a child into the world, they become *a family*. In my earlier books, I talked about my "whole family" approach—making your baby or toddler a *part* of your family, not King Baby. Children shouldn't become the parents' only focus, nor should they run the household. When decisions are made—whether it's to give little Johnny singing lessons or move him to another school—the *whole* family should be taken into consideration.

And yet parents often don't think about *the whole family*. Instead, they become overfocused on the children and on their role in shaping them. When the baby or toddler doesn't meet a particular challenge or difficulty, they think it's their "fault." And then the guilt sets in. They fret about what they did or didn't do or what they should have done. Trust me, luv, guilt doesn't do anyone any good. It only keeps you from being a good problem solver. You're so busy feeling rotten about yourself that you tend to miss what's right in front of you. Guilt also makes life more stressful, and heaven knows, parents today don't need more stress.

And here's the most important news flash, Mum and Dad: You alone do not control how your child "turns out." Of course, parenting matters. Why else would I have taken the time to write three books about it? But we also have to connect the dots. Parenting isn't the only reason Johnny bops Carlos on the head with a truck or Clarissa starts wearing lipstick in fifth grade or sweet fourteen-year-old Adam suddenly turns "mardy," as we say in Duncaster. How they act also has to do with their personalities and their friends and everything else happening in their lives.

This book is about connecting the dots. I don't think of it as a parenting book, although it will, I'm sure, be read mostly by parents. If your family is young,* all the better. That's when the most important groundwork is laid—and when most parents are more likely to open themselves to new ideas. But if you're farther along the road, not to worry. It's never

---

*By "young," I mean your *family's* age—the time you've been together as a group—not how old you or your children are. They don't necessarily go together. Some stepfamilies, for example, are very young, and yet they have kids who are much older and parents who've been 'round the block.

too late—and it's always a good idea—to shift your focus to the whole family.

What do I hope you'll get from this book? At the very least, you'll start to see the whole along with its parts. I hope you'll begin to pay attention to the daily minute-by-minute little stuff that you might otherwise overlook—conversations, nods, and gestures. In those everyday moments, you'll find clues about your family and about who each of you is. These bits of information will help you make better choices and deal with whatever your family has to face. I also hope that the whole-family lens will help you let go of the guilt.

I promise you, though, that the goal is not to have a "perfect" family—heavens, no! It's to have a family that supports you and yours and whatever circumstances *you* have to handle. Some days, you'll feel brilliant (that's Yorkshire for "great"). Other days, you'll wonder if you've done anything right!

Even if you do everything I suggest (and face it, luv, you won't), life will be unpleasant or difficult at times. Hard things and bad things happen to all families—even to good families—things that take us by surprise and knock our knickers off. But as my Nan always told me, it's not what happens to you in life that matters, it's what you *do* with it. If you have family whose members are there for one another, it makes the going a bit easier.

As you read through these pages, please this keep in mind:

Any group consisting of parents and children living together in a household qualifies as "a family."

Whether you're a biological parent, a stepparent, a single parent, a foster parent, a grandparent living with your adult child, or an aunt raising your brother's children, know that when I say "the parents," I mean you. I consider you and your children "a family," no matter what. Same-sex couples with children are families. Second marriages create various flavors of blended families. Even when parents don't live together, they are still a family—a "family apart," the term Melinda coined for co-parenting households after divorce.

Yes, I've seen it all. I've been at Thanksgiving dinners with exes and steps and half-sibs at the same table—and God bless them for being able to pull it off! I've also been in homes where three generations lived under one roof—parents, children, and grandparents. In fact, I myself grew up in what might be considered an "untraditional" arrangement. I was raised by my Nan and Granddad. My mother, Hazel, also grew up with her grandparents. And when I began to work in the U.S., she took care of my girls. It all seemed "normal" to us. None of us is quite sure where our "immediate" family ends and the "extended" clan begins. But there's always a lot of love to go around. Aunts, uncles, cousins—everyone gets into the act. And that makes all of us stronger.

This is the fourth book of the baby-whispering series and, in some ways, our most important. For babies and toddlers, family *is* the whole world. And as children grow up and begin to see what the world has to offer, having a strong family makes *them* strong, so they can handle life. That goes for the adults, too. We all need someone in our corner. That's why this book can't be just about the children. It has to be about the whole family.

—Tracy Hogg

Northampton, Massachusetts, January 2013.

I was Tracy's left brain. This was evident from the first time we met in 1999. I had flown out to California from the East Coast, so she could meet and judge "the writer." I was auditioning her, too, and skeptical about the hype. Her Hollywood clients raved, but I'd interviewed tons of parenting experts before. How different—and how much better—could *she* be?

The moment I arrived, I found out. Straight from the airport, she whisked me to a house in the Valley, where we were greeted by a desperate mother and her wailing three-week-old son.

"Give me him, luv," she said. Within moments, Tracy had calmed the baby and comforted the mother, who was also crying. I tagged along on other consults over the next ten days and, in between visits, listened to her phone conversations with mothers. In our work sessions, I asked tons of questions. "How did you come up with *that*?" or "Why do you think this works?" It was a challenge to take notes, because Tracy knew so much and rarely stayed on topic. In the midst of explaining breast-feeding, she'd veer off into a discussion of sleep.

The babies thrived. The mothers adored her—and why not? Here was a real-life Mary Poppins who could swoop down on a family and, somehow, leave them changed. She was sweet and supportive, funny and warm. People opened up to her—and rightfully so. She was a great listener and an even better problem solver. When she spoke of "my babies," it wasn't just because she took care of those children. It was because she had developed a *relationship* with them and their families.

On our ninth day together, I sat across from her in her office, taking notes and doodling, as I tend to do when listening. As she rattled on about the importance of establishing a structured routine ("You see, luv, babies are like us. They start their day by eating . . ."), I absently scribbled a big *E* in the margin. She went on ("The problem is, parents sometimes try to put them to sleep then, when they should be encouraging an activity, even if it's just a look out the window . . ."). I drew a big *A* next to the *E* (". . . and *then* they can put them down to sleep"), followed by an *S*, and bingo! The EASY method was born. (The *Y* was tagged on later, to stand for something every new mother needs: time for You.)

And so it began. In work sessions over the next six years, on the phone and via email, as well as in person, I extracted a life's worth of experience and knowledge from Tracy and shaped it with my own thinking. It was the best kind of collaboration, one in which both parties realize that there is no book without each other.

Tracy and I were passionate about the idea of extending her philosophy into the realm of family, the bigger unit of which babies and toddlers are a part. It was a natural place to go, especially at a time when so many parents seemed *over*focused on their children. After years of taking the child's perspective, Tracy knew it was time to shine a light on the family.

More than our first three projects, which were harvested almost exclusively from her experience, this one also tapped into my writing and research. Between us, we had hundreds of stories. She had lived with families; I had interviewed countless parents and spent almost my entire career focusing on relationships. We told each other our own family stories and knew each other's family. Tracy helped my daughter through the birth of her first son. I spent time with her daughters, Sara and Sophie, and had conversations with her mother, sister, and brother and, best of all, her beloved Nan, who is ninety-five at this writing and still going strong, the family's own Queen Mum.

Tracy's and my roots and issues were quite different, but we knew, from both personal and professional experience, that family, though complicated, is where it all begins and ends. Back in 2004, our intention was to go beyond babies and children, to apply the principles of baby whispering to this larger entity and to arm readers with simple, practical, and sometimes counterintuitive advice that would support and strengthen the whole family. A decade later, the idea is more important than ever.

"Family whispering," as I now think of it, is fundamentally about tuning in and staying connected, just as baby whispering was. But here we shine light on everyone, not just the baby. The first half of this book will help you "see" differently, to focus on the whole family. The second half will help you apply this new perspective—"family-think"—to everyday challenges and whatever unexpected changes your family has to face.

To help you figure out what's right for *your* family, we've peppered this book with lots of questions. Tracy was all about asking the right questions. The ones in these pages are designed to help you see what your particular family is made of, how it functions, its strengths and weaknesses, and what you can do to make it a place of safety and support for all its members.

You'll get more out of this book if you take the time to keep a "Family Notebook" in which you actually write down your answers to the various questions. Whenever you see the symbol **FYN**—"for your notebook"—reach for a paper notebook or an electronic tablet on which you can save your answers and later print them out. We've also provided a "Notes" page at the end of each chapter. Use it to jot down ideas, too. The act of writing will heighten your awareness, which will make it easier to troubleshoot and, if necessary, change course.

Another benefit of keeping a notebook is that you create a unique document about *your* family—a little insight here, some information there—which becomes a living record of your family's growth and change and eventually ends up showing you something new about yourselves. If you have a partner, answer the questions together, or go solo and compare notes later.

The ideas in these pages are drawn from recent social-science research

---

Keep a Family Notebook

Whenever Tracy visited a new family, whether she was there to establish a routine or solve a problem, she always urged parents to write down their observations. It isn't just a matter of helping you keep track. It's about increasing your awareness of patterns. To get the most out of this book, we suggest that you keep a "Family Notebook" in which you:

- Answer questions posed throughout the book.
- Record observations and "aha" moments that occur as a result of tuning in to your family.
- Set goals and reminders about trying something different or making a slight change of course.

The act of writing sets your intention and makes it more likely that you'll move in a new direction, as opposed to staying "stuck."

and, perhaps more important, from "the trenches," Tracy's favorite source of wisdom. Notably, some of our interviewees were already familiar with baby whispering. We talked to parents on the online forum that survived Tracy's original website and also to former clients, parents of babies and toddlers Tracy once cared for. These veterans of family life, many of whom have children who are now approaching adolescence, shared how Tracy's ideas and strategies served their families as their children grew up, how they bettered their lives and their relationships. Even when parents didn't embrace all of Tracy's techniques, they all applauded her "whole family" approach, because it honored everyone's needs.

For example, one of Tracy's former clients, Viola Grant,* a Hollywood producer Tracy worked for when her first son was born, recalled that Tracy's advice about family was a huge relief after a severe scolding from her pediatrician. "I had an open house a few days after Simon's birth, and the doctor heard about it from one of my friends who was also his patient. He told me, 'You should be in bed, bonding with your baby.'

"By the time I met Tracy for the first time a few days later, I was flipping out. I told her I was struggling with his advice. I didn't want my baby to get sick, but I'm a very social person, and I didn't want to change my life. Staying in bed wasn't me. I was excited for people to come see my first child. Tracy said to me, 'Don't worry, luv. This baby will adjust to the life *you* lead. If this is how your house runs, your baby will be fine. You can go to restaurants, and your baby will be fine. If you feel good and your home feels good to him, he'll be happy.' And she was right. My kids are now ten and thirteen, and they can hold their own with adults. They have been raised to be an integral part of the family—not the stars of the family but members of it."

Invariably, talks like these included discussion about how much of an impact Tracy had made in her too-short life and how much we all missed her. Certainly, I will forever have her unique Yorkshire burr in my head. Every day, I rely on her commonsense ideas in my own life and have passed them on to my daughter, who now has three sons. However,

---

*This and most names are pseudonyms, but the stories are true. In some cases, details have been changed. A few anecdotes have been cobbled together from multiple interviews, but all have been inspired by real-life circumstances. Also, we assume that our readers are women and men who might have sons, daughters, or both. To avoid awkward constructions such as "he or she" or "his or her" whenever we use a generic example, we alternate, "he" and "she" throughout as nongender-specific pronouns.

without Tracy at my side, it no longer feels right for me to write *as* Tracy. In the past, I managed to capture her "voice" on paper, in part by using her favorite British expressions, like "mum" and "codswallop," and by peppering the pages with her trademark sense of humor. Now the journalistic "we" seems more appropriate.

Be assured, though: Everything in these pages is built on the foundation of baby whispering, principles that go beyond babies and toddlers, and for which we will always have Tracy Hogg to thank.

—*Melinda Blau*

ONE

SHIFT YOUR FOCUS
From Parent-Think to Family-Think

*A family is a unit composed not only of children but of men,
women, an occasional animal, and the common cold.*
—OGDEN NASH

When her first child was born fifteen years ago, Sara Green, now forty-nine, intuitively knew that having a baby meant more than simply becoming a parent. "I was super aware, from the moment Katy was born, that Mike, Katy, and I were a *family*," she recalls. "It was a completely new relationship. And I knew I wanted to protect it."

For the first several days, Sara turned everyone away. She wanted to put the rest of the clan on hold, so that she and Mike could begin to define *their* family. Soon enough, she knew, they would interact with their parents and siblings and various members of their extended family, not to mention doctors, teachers, coaches, fellow parents, clergy, and numerous others who would influence the three of them. But she didn't want anyone's comments or advice just yet.

"That caused some problems with our relatives. They didn't understand why we would even want to do that." Sara stood her ground, and it paid off. "There were three of us, and we had to figure out where everyone fit in and what everyone needed. That way, when people started coming and asking what they could do, I could tell them."

To her credit, Sara had all the instincts of a baby whisperer. (If you're a new reader, or want a quick refresher, see the sidebar on page 10.) That is, Sara was respectful, took the time to tune in to Katy's needs. She never referred to Katy as "the baby." Rather, she talked about "Katy" the person and viewed this newest member of the family as a unique individual. Sara didn't rush in to "fix" Katy when she was crying. Instead, she took a breath,

The Baby Whisperer's Top Ten

If you're not familiar with baby whispering, here are the key principles on which it is built. They are equally applicable to "family whispering."

1. Be respectful.
2. Be patient.
3. Be conscious—pay attention.
4. Accept and embrace the child you have.
5. Let everyone in the family matter.
6. Slow down.
7. Listen and observe.
8. Allow for mistakes, and learn from them.
9. Have a sense of humor.
10. Don't chase perfection—there's no "right" way.

slowed down, and gave herself a moment to pay attention. Within a short time, Sara began to recognize what Katy's cries meant. And when she didn't, she learned from her mistakes and moved on. As all baby whisperers do, Sara soon got better at reading Katy's signals, better at understanding who her baby daughter was.

This fascinating little person whom Sara and Mike would get to know even better in the months and years to come was the focus of everyone's attention at first. But even as she was busy tending to her baby's needs and learning how to be a mother, Sara also knew that Katy couldn't—shouldn't—occupy center stage forever. A bigger and more complex question was, how would Katy fit into the drama of Sara and Mike's life as a couple? How would they shift the focus in a way that allowed all three of them to be productive participants in what would surely be an ongoing family venture?

That challenge is the subject of this chapter.

How to Think Like a Family Whisperer

As Tracy would say, let's get at this straightaway. In our earlier books, we wrote, "Baby whispering means tuning in, observing, listening, and understanding from the child's perspective." Now we're widening the lens, asking you to look at the bigger picture. Take out *child* in that sentence, and replace it with *whole family,* and here's what you get:

> *Family whispering means tuning in, observing, listening, and understanding from the whole family's perspective.*

What, exactly, does that mean? We've already written three parenting books to help you tune in to your child. This is a book that also draws on the principles of baby whispering but to help you tune in to your family. It asks you to shift your perspective from "parent-think" to "family-think" and to remember one of the key "secrets" of family whispering:

The whole family matters, not just the child(ren).

Family-think doesn't necessarily contradict parent-think. It is an-other perspective, a more expansive one that encourages you to be family-focused instead of child-focused and to view yourself and your family as a unit. It's a way of bettering your "familying" skills, so that you can pull to-gether *with* your partner and children to create a safe place where kids *and* grown-ups feel as if they matter. You—the parents—are still in charge, and of course, you continue to care for your kids and guide them. But *everyone* is considered, and *everyone*—to the best of his or her age and ability—pitches in to make the family work.

What does family-think look like in action? Sara Green, whom you met at the beginning of this chapter, instinctively knew how to apply it when her baby was born. Although she was instantly smitten by that sweet creature in her arms and was attentive to every gurgle and coo (parent-think), she also knew that everyone's welfare mattered, not just the new baby's (family-think). Three years later, when Sara gave birth to a sec-ond child, Ben, she was aware that the whole family would shift again, this time to accommodate him. As the years flew by, Sara and Mike tuned in to each of their children and knew their respective strengths and vulnerabili-ties as individuals (parent-think), but they were also able to see milestones and unexpected changes through the whole-family prism. Each time some-thing happened to one of them—Sara went back to work, Katy entered her tweens, Ben had trouble with a best friend, Mike lost his job—they were mindful that one person's change affected all of them (family-think).

Or let's go back in time with a family that started growing in the early 1980s. Nancy Sargent and Stephen Klein, both doctors specializ-ing in community health, are living on an Indian reservation near a small town in the Southwest. Their children, Ellie and David, are roughly four and two, and Nancy is pregnant with twins. For the past several years, the parents have shared childcare and a job at the local clinic, a decision they made with everyone's needs in mind (family-think). Since med school, Nancy and Stephen have known that they valued family above all. Both wanted to be involved in their children's life. They also wanted to be part of a community and to travel. They believed in exposing children to differ-ent cultures, which factored into their decision to take the job and live on the reservation.

When the twins, Seth and Rachel, arrive, they ask various members of their extended families to fly out from the East Coast and pitch in (family-think). "We had lots of family support," Nancy will later recall. "But then everyone left. Even with one of us always at home, I knew we *had* to find a baby-sitter."

The need is everyone's problem, not just Nancy's (family-think). To solve it, she enlists Ellie, telling her oldest child that they need to hang a sign in the post office. Would Ellie help make one? The "flier" Ellie creates is a crayoned drawing of six little heads, the Sargent-Kleins through her eyes. At the bottom, Nancy adds a row of tear-off fringes with their phone number. A family-think want ad!

And it works. They find a wonderful Native American woman who stays with them until they move back East—another decision made by weighing their collective needs (family-think). Although they love living on the reservation—a unique community of Anglos and Native Americans—Nancy and Stephen want the children to go to better schools (parent-think). In addition, their own parents are getting older, and it feels important to live closer by, both to support them and for the children to know their grandparents (family-think). They purposely choose a town with a strong sense of community, where they can join a house of worship and find other families with similar values of activism and good work (family-think).

Why Shifting Focus Is Tricky

Make no mistake, we know it's not easy to apply family-think to your daily comings and goings. In conversations about this book, we had to keep reminding people that our questions were about the family, not their child or the way they parented. And if we were to be completely honest, it was even tricky for us. Every now and then, in our own conversations, we slipped into parent-think, too. Why is it so hard?

PC Familying

In our third book, we introduced the idea of "PC Parenting," having patience and consciousness. The same principles apply to familying. Adults need to slow down and to cultivate mindfulness; children need to be shown how. Don't despair; most of us need help in this department. But we also get better with practice.

Patience. Having a family means drama every day. Issues don't necessarily resolve quickly or predictably. You need to hang on for the long haul. Patience helps us get through the day and stay calm during a rough transition or an unexpected change. It reminds us that at times, any one of us might forget, falter, or fail.

Consciousness. Applying your full awareness to whatever you do allows you to understand how you and others see the world and to know what makes each of you comfortable in it. Consciousness—mindfulness—is about seeing the bigger whole and using that sensitivity to think ahead, plan, and analyze afterward. It is being alert to "learnable" moments, not just teaching moments.

- We're used to thinking of ourselves as individuals.
- We've become overly child-centered.
- We ask little of our children.

Below, we take a closer look at these three issues and explain why we need to shift to family-think.

We're used to thinking of ourselves as individuals. Especially in the U.S., our long-standing tradition of individualism teaches us that if we set goals, we can complete them. When things are hard, we are supposed to "pull up those boot straps." We can do anything if we set our individual mind to a task. We tend to apply that philosophy to everything we take on, including child-rearing. We believe that we can affect another person—child or adult—solely by what we say and do. And who can blame us? Shelves full of how-to books promise to put us "in control," as if it's just a matter of getting it "right" or applying the "best" program. As if there *was* a best way. As if the future lay totally in our own hands. Life, and certainly families, don't work that way.

> *Why we need to shift to family-think: In every social exchange, we influence* one another. *No one acts alone.*

We do not act *on* our partners or children. We affect them, and they also affect us. Every day, we interact with one another and, sometimes, collide. Each conversation is a two-way street, a "co-creation" that changes both parties. For example, when your son comes home from school complaining about a kid in his class, it triggers a reaction in you. It may remind you of your own childhood. It may be disappointing; you want him to be able to stand up for himself. You might scoop him up in your arms and comfort him. Or you might say, "Oh, come on, Billy. That's just what boys your age do." Either way, how you act and react will influence what he says and does next. In each of these everyday exchanges, the two of you are co-creating a *relationship*, an entity that is formed by what you *each* put into it. It is a unique product "of" the two of you.

If we think of our family merely as a group of individuals, we miss an essential truth: A family is a collection of relationships that—ideally—prepare us for life and help us grow. We may think we're acting as solo players, but in reality, everything we do is a joint project, a "co-action." Each person in your family brings out something different in you, and vice versa.

From the day we're born, all of our thoughts, opinions, and behaviors are shaped in our interactions with others. Because we are so accustomed to seeing ourselves as "bounded beings," whose bodies and minds are separate from other bounded beings, it's hard to embrace the idea that even our consciousness is co-created in relationships.

In families, this give-and-take shapes us and determines our everyday existence. Countless conversations, exchanges in *and* outside the family, affect what goes on between you and your partner (if you have one), between you and your child, and, if you have more than one child, between siblings. Every one of these conversations is a joint venture, not something you make happen on your own. To think that we alone can control an outcome limits our understanding and our ability to connect. Worse still, it makes us feel alone.

We've become overly child-centered. When Tracy emigrated from England in the late 1990s, she sensed that children were in charge. When a mother told her she was "following the baby" instead of establishing a structured routine, Tracy would exclaim, "But he's a *baby*, darlin'! *You* need to be teaching *him*." And the hovering . . . oh, the hovering! One mother told Tracy that she didn't intend to put her baby down for the first three months ("just like they do in Bali"), to which Tracy replied, "But luv, we're not in friggin' Bali."

As those babies grew into toddlers, their parents seemed desperate to shield them from sadness, mistakes, or failure. Mothers in Tracy's Mommy and Me groups would sit behind their toddlers during a rousing rendition of "The Itsy Bitsy Spider." It didn't matter whether the children were actually singing—most don't at that age—or just sitting there motionless; every one of those mothers would applaud and shout, "Good job!"

What we dubbed the "Happiness Epidemic" a decade ago has morphed into full-blown *over*parenting. At one end of the child-focused parenting continuum are solicitous helicopter moms, and at the other are so-called tiger moms. They seem different, but with either extreme, the spotlight is on kids, not family. As a result, we are living in what one *New York Times* reporter called "the most chafingly child-focused era in modern history."

To be fair, parents' anxiety about children's safety, fragile egos, and success has been fueled, in part, by the flood of merchandise and programs that promise to improve and protect children. Other parents unwittingly act as pitchmen ("You're not going to enroll Caroline in Madame

Fowler's ballet class this summer?"). Journalist Nancy Gibbs, writing about a "backlash" to "intensive parenting," described the "insanity" in a 2009 *Time* cover story:

> *We bought macrobiotic cupcakes and hypoallergenic socks, hired tutors to correct a 5-year-old's "pencil-holding deficiency," hooked up broadband connections in the treehouse but took down the swing set after the second skinned knee. We hovered over every school, playground and practice field—"helicopter parents," teachers christened us, a phenomenon that spread to parents of all ages, races and religions. . . . We became so obsessed with our kids' success that parenting turned into a form of product development.*

Granted, extreme child-centeredness is most prevalent in middle- and upper-class homes where parents have the disposable income to provide lessons, sports experiences, family trips, and tutoring. However, in our interviews, we found that low-income parents also feel the pressure. "I feel bad because I can't give them the things their friends have," one mother told us, referring to expensive sneakers and electronic gadgets. A few weeks before Christmas, she put up her car as collateral for a loan. The holiday gifts made her eight children momentarily happy, but the family would suffer when the loan company later threatened to repossess her car.

When children occupy your entire field of vision and monopolize your time and energy, it's almost impossible to sustain a family perspective. The adults are exhausted, as journalist Judith Warner documents in her book *Perfect Madness*. The women she interviewed were victims of "a new set of life-draining pressures." The couple relationship suffers. The kids think that the world revolves around them and at the same time feel inordinate pressure to perform. Siblings fight over "things." Worst of all, the family—like a child left in an orphanage—begins to wither.

No, not in every home, but in many. Some parents—certainly many of Tracy's clients—have "right-sized" their children's place and see them as part of the bigger whole. Others sense that something's off, but they're so caught up in the frenzy they don't realize where the road is taking them.

"I feel sorry for my American friends and relatives," says Greg Perlman, who relocated to Europe a few years ago with his wife, Amy, and their daughter, Sadie, now eleven. "When I come home to visit, I see the constant escalation of what kids get, how much the parents go all out for birthday parties, what kinds of toys are considered necessities, and their endless safety concerns. Some of them don't realize how the pressure is ramping up, but we notice a huge difference since we left. It's almost like an arms race."

Why we need to shift to family-think: Kids need a sense of **family** *more than they need the spotlight.*

After decades of jumping onto the self-esteem bandwagon, educators and psychologists have concluded that looking out for number one doesn't make for healthy relationships or a good life. Being part of a loving family does. Of course, parents must care for and guide children; the adults *should* be in charge, protecting and monitoring, always striving to know their children and to keep them safe. But that's not the same as positioning your children at the center of the universe. Quite the contrary. If we're constantly micromanaging children's every movement—tending, helping, hovering, suggesting, scheduling, reminding, interacting, demanding, not to mention praising them for sitting still—how can they learn to be part of a bigger something? If we don't give them real roles in the family, how and when do they learn the skills they need to become independent? How can they learn to share and cooperate?

If you want your children to become competent and confident adults, don't just parent them. "Family" them, too. They need to feel as if they matter not merely as individuals but as "stakeholders," participants who have a vested interest in the success of a bigger entity. Being a member of a family and contributing to the common good are basic training for life. It teaches children *and* adults to see themselves as connected beings who have something valuable to give.

Oh, and by the way, it's critical to teach your kids these skills now, not when they're packing for college . . . which brings us to a third reason family-focused strategies are hard for so many parents today.

We ask little of our children. Often, we don't realize that they *can* help

> ## Food for Thought:
> ## The Failure of Self-Esteem
>
> "The self-esteem movement in particular, and the feel-good ethic in general, had the untoward consequence of producing low self-esteem on a massive scale," writes psychologist Martin Seligman in *Authentic Happiness.* "By cushioning feeling bad, it has made it harder for our children to feel good and to experience flow. By circumventing feelings of failure, it made it more difficult for our children to feel mastery. By blunting warranted sadness and anxiety, it created children at high risk for unwarranted depression. By encouraging cheap success, it produced a generation of very expensive failures."

in meaningful ways. It wasn't always this way. For centuries, children were seen as workers, contributors to the family. They were regarded as little adults, miniature and perhaps less mature but nonetheless capable. The more children a family had, the greater the family's productivity and income.

Children once worked long hours on farms, at street jobs, in factories. When interviewed in 1929, a mother explained why she gave her children factory work at home. "Everybody does it," she said. "Other people's children help—why not ours?" Asked why her children left school early to work, another mother was "perplexed" at anyone questioning what she perceived as an "absolutely natural proceeding," adding, "He's of an age to work, why shouldn't he?"

Then childhood got a makeover. In the course of fifty years, children went from "useful to useless," as one sociologist put it, from contributing to the family to being "economically worthless" and, eventually, "emotionally priceless." Parents were making more money, families became smaller, and mass marketing was coming into its own. By the 1930s, most children younger than fourteen were in school. Parents—mothers, really—took over many jobs children had once been expected to do. "Chores" were still assigned to them, not to help Mom but to build character. A 1934 article in *Parents* magazine warned readers to "take care not to overburden the child with responsibility . . . lest the weight of it should crush him instead of develop a greater strength."

Sadly, children today have become more "priceless," more exalted. And there's little talk about character. Some parents fight the tide, making children actually earn privileges, but in many homes, a free ride is as "absolutely natural" as child labor was a century ago. In an ongoing study of middle-class families with working parents, researchers report that the largest share of children's time after school and before bed—40 percent— is spent in leisure activities compared with 25 percent of fathers' time and less than 20 percent of mothers' time. The rest of the evening is devoted (in this order) to communication, homework, and personal care, such as bathing and dressing. Chores, the researchers conclude, are "not on children's radar screens." Ironically, many women complain that men don't do a fair share at home. But it doesn't occur to them to ask their children to contribute.

Why we need to shift to family-think: Everyone in the family plays a role in making sure that the family has what it needs to thrive.

The family is the building block of humanity. In order to strengthen society and to make the world a kinder, gentler place, all of us—children and adults—need to put time and energy into making our families work. The family is a "laboratory" for life and good citizenship. It's where you learn to be part of something, and to become someone on whom others can rely. Adults model these critical skills, and, with guidance, kids develop them as the result of good "familying." Working hard, giving to others, and hanging in—living through frustration and failure—build character. As we explain in chapter 3, you show up, and that makes you grow up.

If you're not convinced that we need to take the focus off kids and shine a spotlight on the family, consider what researchers found when they questioned young adults who reported being "overindulged" as kids. They were given too many material things (such as clothes and toys) and too little in the way of chores and rules, and they had parents who were "overloving" and provided them with "too much entertainment." In essence, they were denied the opportunity to develop a sense of responsibility. Nearly a third of these pampered kids were "deficient in interpersonal skills" as young adults. Smaller but still significant numbers had problems with overeating and overspending. And when they became parents they were more likely to overindulge themselves and their children.

The prognosis is not much better for adults who do it all while the children do nothing. The mothers in Judith Warner's book were tired, anxious, and guilty, and "it didn't seem to dawn on anyone that there could be another way."

But there is another way: Focus on the family. Think of it as a co-op, an enterprise in which everyone respects, acknowledges, and gives to one another. Everyone has a stake in how the family operates, everyone matters, everyone makes choices, and everyone pitches in. Shifting the focus away from kids makes them *want* to contribute, because they know that they're needed, and they know that they, too, have a stake in making the family better, stronger, and more solid. In turn, this benefits them as individuals, increasing their confidence and competence.

By being family-focused, you will still be amazed by your kids, just not blinded by them.

Practicing Family-Think at Home

It's not easy to sustain family-think. For one thing, we're all swimming in child-centered waters. Equally important, family life is complex, a perpetual juggling of everyone's time and energy. Life is often so hectic, and there's so much pressure on adults and children, that it's hard to concentrate on anything further than the next appointment, the pickup schedule, and what's for dinner tonight, not to mention keeping your focus on the whole family. We can't promise that the road will be straight or smooth. But we can help you take the first step, which is to *see* differently.

Start by describing your family as a whole. What adjectives or short phrases came to mind? Here are some of the answers we've heard in response to "What's your family like?"

A mother in New York (married, one son): "Adventuresome, open, caring. Involved. Talkative, quirky, dedicated, different."

A father in Chicago (divorced, son and daughter): "Splintered; I don't get to see the kids that often. Complicated, loving, distant, strivers, lots of emphasis on being successful."

A mother in California (single, one daughter): "Loving, hectic, athletic. We are like a fortress against the world."

A partnered lesbian from Massachusetts, recalling her family of origin (six siblings): "Dysfunctional, blue-collar Irish, crowded, competitive, totally dominated by my father, angry."

A father in Florida (married, two boys): "Tight-knit. The kids are best friends who hang out and take good care of each other. We're sensitive to one another. Have fun together—not manufactured fun."

These are only sketchy portraits. They don't tell us all that much about the particular individuals in each family, their relationships, or what they have to deal with (their context)—factors we look at in the next chapter. Still, rattling off a string of adjectives is a good way to start thinking about your family as a unit.

Being objective about your own family can be daunting. But the first Family Notebook exercise on page 21, "What's Your Family Like?" will help you focus on what's important (your values), what you like to do as a family (venues), and your challenges (vulnerabilities).

Admittedly, it gets a bit tricky to answer in terms of your whole family. For example, let's say everyone plays a sport, and you all engage in a lot of sports talk. You go to games, watch sports on TV, and go on sports outings as a family. Maybe Mom or Dad coaches. It would make sense, then, to list sports as a venue. Perhaps sportsmanship would also be included among your family's values. On the other hand, you could be a family that shows up at a Little League game week after week to support the one child who loves baseball and made the team. In that case, one of your family's values is to support one another's interests, but you might not think of the ballfield as a family venue. There's no wrong way to do this exercise. Whatever you write, you'll come out with a clearer idea of how you operate as a family.

If possible, have fun with this exercise by involving your partner, if you have one, and your children. Get the ball rolling by sharing your own observations out loud to other members of the family, in a lighthearted way. "Ever notice how we never get out of the house on time?" or "I realize that we start preparing for Halloween way before anyone else." Then ask, "What do you think that says about us as a family?" Jot down what everyone says, and don't be surprised if each of you comes to a different conclusion.

If you have trouble coming to a consensus, don't worry. In chapter 2, we help you look at the "Three Factors"—elements that combine and interact to make your family what it is.

FYN What's Your Family Like?

Once or twice a day for the next week, look at your own family objectively and notice its complexity and contours. Try to view your life together as you would a group of strangers, and describe what you see. Write down at least ten adjectives or phrases that capture what your family is like by zeroing in on your *values* (what you believe in), *venues* (favorite activities and places), and *vulnerabilities* (your challenges as a family).

For each category, we've given you some open-ended sentences **in bold** and suggestions [in brackets] just to get you started. Don't limit yourself; use words and phrases that fit *your* gang:

- *Values.* What's your family ethic? What do you stand for?
  "In our family it's important to . . ." [have a spiritual life? be a leader? compete? do good deeds? make money? be thrifty? look good? eat well? follow rules? live off the land?]
- *Venues.* What activities do you like to do as a family? What kinds of places make you happy and hold the best memories? Where do you go to recharge?
  "Our family loves to . . ." [be outdoors? play sports? go to movies? travel? go to the beach? play instruments? participate in community service? build things? read? travel? hang out at home together? volunteer? cook meals together?]
- *Vulnerabilities.* What is your family's Achilles' heel?
  "A weakness of our family is that . . ." [one person controls what everyone else does? it's every man for himself? we don't see enough of each other? we never talk about how we feel? we smother each other? we fight? we tolerate abusive behavior? we have few friends or relatives nearby? we have trouble making decisions? we are rigid? we overschedule ourselves?]

Notes on Family-Think

TWO

WHAT YOUR FAMILY IS
The Three Factors

*Abandon the urge to simplify everything, to look for formulas and
easy answers . . . begin to think multi-dimensionally . . . not to be
dismayed by the multitude of causes and consequences that are inherent
in each experience . . . to appreciate the fact that life is complex.*

—M. Scott Peck

Jane Wentworth, a competent, outgoing, energetic, and resourceful entertainment lawyer, gained a precious sidekick when Caitlin, an Angel baby,
arrived.* When Jane went back to work, she often brought Caitlin with
her. She was "good as gold," Jane often said to her husband, Bart. "I can
take her anywhere." And for three solid years, she did—to the office, to
the gym, to lunch dates with her friends.

Jane was pregnant again when Caitlin started preschool. Perfect tim-
ing. Then along came Noah. Unlike his older sister, Noah was a Touchy
baby who cried a lot and was ultrasensitive to noise. Not such a good fit
for Jane.

If you read our previous books, you might remember the discussion of "fit"—the notion that certain temperamental traits in individuals make for a better or worse match. It's a concept normally applied to
the parent-child relationship. A psychologist delving into the reasons for

---

*In our earlier books, to help parents tune in to their babies, Tracy identified five
temperamental "types": the very easy *Angel,* the right-on-time *Textbook,* the sensitive
Touchy, the energetic and active *Spirited,* and the do-it-my-way *Grumpy.* Children are
often a combination of types. Tracy also warned about pigeonholing kids as they get older.
Although you can see vestiges of earlier temperament, environment continues to shape
who they are.

a child's misbehavior might cite bad fit as a possible cause—Mom is a high-energy person, and her son is sensitive. As Tracy used to say, they're like "chalk and cheese." But if we apply family-think, we see that fit is also a family affair.

Having a second child puts a great deal of stress on any family, and bad fit adds additional and ongoing pressure, especially when the first child is an Angel baby. Jane was a no-nonsense mother, a woman who was accustomed to managing her life with efficiency and organization, the way she ran her law practice. Caitlin fit right in, but Noah didn't jive with Mom's idea of a "good" baby.

In truth, he wasn't. Tracy always said that some babies are easier to love at first sight than others. Noah was one of the others. Factor in Jane's temperament and expectations, and you've got a combination that can make even a second-time mother feel insecure about her ability to parent. Such a scenario might lead to a cascade of problems that don't stop in early childhood. How often do you hear a mother refer to her middle-schooler or teen as "my difficult one," explaining that he's been a "handful" since birth?

But temperament isn't destiny. More important, the future of any relationship isn't just dependent on mother and child. Other members of the family and what else is happening around them also play into fit.

Jane and Bart, married ten years by then, had a solid partnership and a commitment to family. He, a successful graphic designer, was a sympathetic and helpful partner and very much a hands-on dad. When Noah was born, he came home early from his studio, both because he wanted to get to know his baby boy and because, as he put it, "my family needed me."

Caitlin's sunny temperament also helped. In addition, she loved her preschool (her first "context" outside the family) and had many positive experiences there, all of which seemed to inspire her to act like "a little Mommy." This, in turn, deepened her connection to her parents. Feeling secure and grown-up, she continued to dote on Noah. She quickly became the person most likely to make Noah smile.

Also fortunate for the Wentworths, Jane's mother and sister lived nearby, and both offered to help. Friends dropped by with casseroles and offered to do errands. Other mothers reminisced about their own crabby babies, who were now in high school and doing quite well, thank you.

This outpouring of support made it easier for Jane to nap and, just as important, not to take Noah's temperament as a personal affront. Instead, she gritted her teeth, invoked her father's favorite saying ("This, too, shall pass"), and slowly opened her heart.

Not so incidentally, the family also had the resources to hire help and to see specialists when their pediatrician suspected that part of Noah's crankiness might be reflux. The initial "crisis" lasted a few months, but time and the right kind of advice from professionals helped the family get through.

Ten years later, Noah is still on the shy side. He blossomed into a serious "brainiac" whom teachers adore and classmates sometimes tease. His older sister is still solidly in his corner. Over the years, especially during tough transitions, Jane has had to remind herself, with Bart's help, that Noah is not Caitlin, who still takes most things in stride. Jane has come to appreciate that her son has different gifts—he can already beat everyone in the family at chess—and a different orientation to life. As long as Mom and Dad give him the space he needs to get used to each new situation, he is usually OK.

But What If . . . ?

Family life is an unfolding drama, dynamic and always in flux. The Wentworths' play might have had a starkly different ending if the actors, their interactions, or the setting had been different. Any one of those three elements might have made it more difficult, if not impossible, for the family to weather the storm of Noah's early years and continue to keep on track.

Let's say the individuals—the players—had been different. What if Jane was someone who resisted other people's help or, worse, was prone to depression? Noah's arrival might have plunged her into despair, regardless of how Bart and other family members reacted. She might have resented Noah and felt unable to bond with him. And if Noah had been a Spirited child, Jane might have met force with force. She might have ignored his temperament or tried to "make" him more like his older sister. Any of the above would have compromised their relationship, which, in turn, would have affected the whole family.

And let's not forget that this story is not just about Jane and Noah.

Two other members of the immediate family played important roles. What if, instead of being supportive of Jane, Bart had felt sorry for himself because his wife was always tired, frustrated, or angry? What if Caitlin had been a Grumpy toddler who stopped talking when her baby brother came along or had tantrums in an attempt to regain her mother's attention?

But actors alone do not determine the outcome. Their relationships—the interaction between them, how they speak and act toward each other—also affected this drama. What if Jane and Bart were on shaky ground as a couple? What if both were too immersed in furthering their respective careers to notice that their relationship was suffering? What if they spent increasingly longer periods of time away from home? That might have fractured their connections, to each other and to their daughter, even before Noah came along.

Finally, consider the family's context—the various arenas and settings in which they exist. Imagine that instead of being privileged, this had been a family who had trouble putting food on the table, had no relatives nearby, no support network, and few resources? What if they didn't know enough to seek professional help? What if they couldn't afford it?

To be sure, those are extreme what-ifs. Given any one of those possibilities, in fact, Jane and Bart might have not stayed together long enough to have a second child! But we tell this story about fit to stress the complexity of family life and the need for what we call "3-F glasses."

How the Three Factors Interact

If you think of family life as an ongoing drama, the Three Factors are always in play: the *individuals* (the actors/family members), their *relationships* (how they interact), and the *context* (the stage, or various environments and settings in which the story unfolds). The reason we need to be aware of these elements is to understand their collective impact. Realizing how the Three Factors affect your family on a daily basis enables you to react differently in the moment and to make a difference. (On page 28, we provide an at-a-glance view.)

In the Wentworth family, Noah's arrival and, simultaneously, Caitlin's going off to preschool changed everything that was happening "onstage" and took the drama in a new direction. Change always does. At this very moment, your own family might be reeling from a different set of new circumstances to which everyone has to adjust: a parent's job change, a death, a tornado decimating the family home. Peering through your 3-F glasses reminds you to look at where the upheaval started and, at the same time, to know that all Three Factors are always in play.

And it's not just the big stuff. We can see the everyday business of family life better through 3-F glasses, too. Harry, now in fourth grade, blows up at his little brother, Oliver, because Harry's work load at school has changed. Mom's out of sorts because the boys are fighting more. This broader perspective—family-think—allows you to see the complexity of family life and can help you understand why your family acts, reacts, and adapts—or fails to adapt.

The Three Factors, **working together,** *make your family what it is.*

Let's look at each of the Three Factors in greater detail.

- *The individuals.* Each of you brings to the family drama a particular history, temperament, mind, and body, as well as previous roles you've each played. And those elements, in turn, affect the lines you recite, how you deliver them, and how you act and react toward the other actors. Together, you are the "parts"—the **I**s that make up the whole—your **We**. Your family would not be what it is without each of its members.

  Individual family members have a considerable impact on the family as a whole. Common sense tells us that if family members are loving and compassionate, emotionally and physically healthy people who have good coping and relationships skills, the whole family is more likely to function well. But through your 3-F glasses, it's clear that individual family members' traits are only part of your family's story.

- *The relationships.* As we pointed out earlier, a relationship is the sum of two people, a unique entity that is "of" the two individuals. We cannot look at our family members only as individuals. We shape them, and vice versa. A loving adult partner can warm the heart of a Scrooge. A strong parent-child bond can help a child deal with

At a Glance: Your Family through 3-F Glasses

Families are as different as snowflakes, so it's impossible to portray a "typical" family. We can, however, help you see what makes your family what it is. Dog-ear this page, and refer to it whenever you need to take a breath, step back, and put on your 3-F glasses, which will help you see your whole family.

The Individuals
What each family member brings to the table

Temperament
How does each person relate to others, view the world, act and react, adapt to change?

History
What has past experience taught or given each one? How do race, nationality, ethnicity, religion, and/or spiritual practices play a part in each member's personal belief system?

Needs
Needs ebb and flow, depending on each person's situation—health issues, interests, hobbies. What resources does each person require in terms of time, energy, attention, and money?

The Relationships
How family members interact and support one another

The Couple
As partners, how do they communicate, make decisions, negotiate roles, spend time together, care for the children, deal with problems? If parents live in separate households, do they co-parent?

Parent-Child
Is there mutual respect and appreciation? Does the adult accept who the child is and dole out both love and limits?

Siblings
Do they love and support one another? Compete? Protect?

Other Relationships
If grandparents, aunts, and uncles play a role in day-to-day family life (e.g., childcare, financial help), how do those relationships affect the immediate family? Are there close nonrelatives who are "like family" or employed by the family (a nanny or *au pair*)? What are the benefits/disadvantages of these people who don't live with the family?

The Context
The territory everyone shares, directly or indirectly

The Household
Does the family's living space promote growth, encourage sharing, and allow for privacy?

School
Do the children feel supported, comfortable, accepted?

Work
Do parents work long hours? Late shifts? Do long commutes interfere with family time? Do negative relations with coworkers affect moods at home?

Extended Family
The extended family is also part of a family's context. Are members of your clan in sync with your family's values? Do they support your family's choices?

Personal Networks
Do other social connections—via parents' and children's peers, obligations (colleagues, classmates), or choice (fellow hobbyists)—enhance home life or pull members away from the family?

Neighborhood
Is it safe and easy to connect with neighbors? Is the community diverse, or is it made up mainly of one class or ethnic group? Does your family fit in? What resources does it provide—a community center, houses of worship, parks, playgrounds?

The Historical Moment
How does this point in time affect views and expectations about marriage, parenting, and families? What elements of the culture constrain or support your family?

whatever life throws her way.* Likewise, if you marry or remarry someone who has children, you "inherit" a new set of kids and another extended family. You bring your "self" to these relationships, but each of them will also bring out different, sometimes new parts of that self. We are whom we connect with, especially our intimates.

Every family consists of multiple relationships: the adults' relationship (assuming there are two parents), adult-child relationships, sibling relationships, and extended family ties. All continually develop and unfold. These relationships are also *inter*dependent; each affects, and can change, the other. A serious sibling battle can stress even a solid marriage. A rocky adult relationship causes problems in the children's lives and in extended family relationships.

Relationships are everything. When you feel "held"—supported—in a relationship, you like being part of that unit and are willing to extend your individual self. You feel connected, invested in the bigger whole. Not surprisingly, having good relationships is also linked to each individual family member's health, happiness, productivity, and success.

- *The context.* You and your loved ones do not exist in a vacuum. All families are "embedded" in a context—actually, a set of contexts—the various stages and arenas in which you play out your individual and collective roles. Your household is your family's immediate context, the one over which you have the most control (more about this in chapter 6). Each of you also goes out into a variety of other contexts, in real life and online. You play certain parts (worker, athlete, student) in these various settings, meet other people, and are influenced by their ideas and experiences. Consider, for example, how your children's school and your work environment can affect the family drama. Too much homework or long work hours can chip away at family time, compromise individual well-being, or drive a wedge into some or all of your relationships. Physical contexts—neighborhood, community, country—affect how much safety and privacy you can expect, what kinds of opportunities you have to play and to pray, what you can buy, and, as studies suggest, how you "family."

---

*Reminder: Switch the pronoun if you have a son.

Your family is also affected by larger and less obvious contexts, such as history and culture—what's happening in the world (the economy, new laws, wars), what's "trending" and how people think at this particular point in time. It's hard to believe, for instance, that parents in the 1930s were warned not to give their children too much attention. These larger contexts define what's "good" and "bad" and what it means to be a man, a woman, a child, a couple, a family, even what it means to have a relationship. Especially in the current media-saturated era, when images and ideas seep into our households 24/7, it is impossible to separate ourselves from this bigger surround, any more than fish in an aquarium can exist outside their tank.

At the same time, context is affected by the other two factors. For example, 2011 was a year in which the majority of Americans rated their current financial context as "poor" or "fair." Nearly half said they had encountered financial problems within the previous twelve months. In some households where there were concerns about money or job loss, the impact of context was considerable. Parents were more likely to be depressed (an individual outcome). They were less able to connect with their children, weakening their relationships. And when their children were tested a year later, they also showed signs of individual wear and tear. They were less likely to share, volunteer, cooperate, or respect others' needs. Not surprisingly, they were also less likely to do well in school or to develop healthy relationships themselves.

In the families described above, financial woes affected both their relationships and the individuals' ability to function. However, the same study showed that context can also be buffered. In other families surveyed, no one became depressed over finances. Parent-child relationships didn't suffer. The Is kept chugging along. Something protected them from a context that overwhelmed other families. We suspect that in those less susceptible families, the individual members had good coping skills to begin with and strong relationships that acted like life preservers and kept them afloat.

Different Contexts/Different Problems

Sociologist Annette Lareau, who spent more than decade shadowing middle-class, working-class, and poor families, found a "cultural divide between the middle class and everyone else." That didn't mean that middle-class families necessarily were "better."

- *Middle-class children were immersed in adult-run activities.* Parents treated them as equals, constantly talked, reasoned, explained, discussed ideas. This gave the kids a sense of entitlement, as well as an edge in school. Their language and social skills would serve them well later in life, too. However, parents and children were stressed and exhausted. The kids constantly negotiated with their parents; siblings fought more than those in less privileged households. They spent time with extended families only on special occasions.

- *Working-class and poor parents were concerned mainly with providing the basics—comfort, food, shelter—not enriching their kids or goading them to achieve.* Here Lareau found a strong sense of "family" and time spent together. Siblings were close; extended family was often around. There were clear boundaries between the adults and the children. Parents had no trouble giving orders; children rarely argued.

- *Class mattered more than race.* Although all black families had to deal with racism, middle-class black children were more like middle-class whites than blacks in the lower-income brackets.

How to Get Better at Family-Think? Practice!

The secret to sustaining this wide-angle view of your family life is awareness. Go about your everyday family "business" with consciousness, and keep those 3-F glasses handy. With practice, family-think will become more natural. It will eventually become easier to see the complexity and to remember that:

> *Your unfolding family drama is always influenced by who's involved (the individuals), how they speak to and behave toward one another (their relationships), and the setting in which it all takes place (the context).*

The strategies below are designed to help you practice by observing other families—fictional and real—and by talking to people who have given a lot of thought to "familying." Think of yourself as a holistic doctor, who knows that to determine patients' overall health, you have to factor in what's happening in their bodies and minds, who's in their life, where they go, and what they have to put up with every day.

Watch TV wearing 3-F glasses. Applying family-think to stories of real or fictionalized families will help sharpen your perception about how the Three Factors interact. Since television is such a universal medium and requires no reading ability, it's something the whole family can discuss. Check out TV families, a staple of sitcoms since the fifties. Although the goal of these programs is to entertain and attract viewers—and to poke fun—television has always told us a lot about how relationships and family roles are viewed and what kinds of problems parents and children face. We've come a long way from the sanitized *Father Knows Best* era in which the adults were portrayed as smart and in charge and kids like Dennis the Menace set the bar for "bad." In contrast, popular shows today (airing at this writing), such as *Modern Family, The Middle,* and *Parenthood,* take on autism, teen sex, bullying, financial woes, alcoholism, gay parenting, eating disorders, depression, infidelity—in short, real issues that affect us.

Pay close attention to the shows you and your children watch together and separately. The media itself is a powerful aspect of context. You may not realize that behavior of fictional characters gives us ideas, good and bad, about how to act and what it means to be a parent or to be in a relationship. Think about it. Maybe you tried out that tip you saw on *Dr. Phil* or experimented with a different approach to divvying up household chores or resolving an argument with your spouse because of a scene in *Parenthood.*

What kinds of ideas does your child (or your partner, for that matter) get from what he or she watches? Greg Perlman, whom you met in chapter 1, isn't super-strict about limiting eleven-year-old Sadie's TV time, among other reasons because of their context. They now live in Paris. Watching her favorite American shows dubbed in French helps Sadie learn the language, which, in turn, makes it easier for her to live in a very different culture. She's also a responsible, agreeable kid most of the time. She doesn't argue when Dad insists that she do homework and chores first. Still, Greg knows that certain shows dramatically affect Sadie's behavior.

"You can almost set your watch to it. After shows like *Hannah Montana, Zack and Cody,* and *That's So Raven,* she's almost bound to act rude and spoiled and to do something that requires discipline. The shows have the same template, portraying cartoonish adults who can't get out of their own way and kids whose real fun is to make fools of the adults."

Mediate antifamily messages by watching *with* your children. Dissect various story lines, and have discussions about objectionable content. Begin to make your children aware of the Three Factors, too. "We always watch *Modern Family* together," says Sara Green, whose children are now sixteen and eleven. "The people love and respect one another. And they're funny and dysfunctional in ways we can all relate to. We talk about their personalities and the kinds of relationships they have. If we had an extra kid, we could almost *be* the Dunphys!"

Find a "family mentor." Each of the authors of this book has benefited from the wisdom of someone with a longer-term perspective on life and family. For Tracy, it was her Nan, who always taught her that being part of a family was her most important role. In Melinda's case, it is her Aunt Ruth, age ninety-two at this writing, a woman who, like her mother before her (Melinda's paternal grandmother), holds forth like a queenly matriarch, peppering her conversation with wise truisms about the family: "People don't change; they just become more of who they are as they age." "For family, you sacrifice." As Ruth aged, even though her short-term memory began to fade, she could still remember her childhood and Melinda's childhood. Those stories and the dusty photo albums she had stowed away in a closet were precious reminders of the family's historical past.

It is wonderful to experience this kind of sharing with a parent or grandparent, and some do. More often, the honor (which it is) goes to a less emotionally charged relation, such as an aunt or uncle. These "forgotten kin" as psychologist Robert Milardo calls them in his book of the same name, can be great

---

Modern Family: Something for Everyone

If you've never seen the show, it's the story of three related families. In one household lives the father, Jay Pritchett; his (much younger) wife, the sexy, hot-blooded Latina, Gloria Delgado; her sensible fourteen-year-old son, Manny; and (in the 2013 season) Jay and Gloria's new baby. In another lives Jay's son, Mitchell, with his life partner, Cameron Tucker, and their adopted Vietnamese daughter, Lily. And in the third household are Jay's daughter, Claire, with her husband, Phil Dunphy, and their three kids, Haley, the popular kid; Alex, the smart one; and Luke, the quirky little brother. It's a humorous tangle of personalities and relationships, showcasing issues such as freedom, responsibility, chore wars, fidelity, honesty, jealousy, mothers and mothers-in-law, all through the lens of family. Characters say or do one thing and then turn directly to the camera, admitting how they really feel. Judging from the show's ratings and awards and the fact that more than 7 million Facebook fans "like" the show, viewers are looking for clues about their own families. And perhaps, as Christopher Lloyd, one of the show's creators, recently suggested to a reporter, they also "wish that their family communicated a lot more directly, the way our guys do."

family mentors. "In the sharing of personal experiences—and especially stories about parents as young children, adolescents, and young adults," Milardo observes, "aunts and uncles help their nieces and nephews gain a better perspective on family members." If your parents don't have siblings, perhaps it can be an old family friend.

Family mentors are often older though not necessarily related by blood—someone who has lived longer than you and has a different sense of urgency about life and a broader perspective. This is why so many people are drawn to Zelda Fields, born in 1911. She's no one famous, but she attracts quite a following wherever she goes. Healthy and active at 102, she still walks three miles a day and only recently quit playing tennis. To keep her memory sharp, she recites poems and quotes she's memorized, words of wisdom that speak to her own experience. Zelda has a way of cutting through the complexity. You listen; you believe that she knows what she's talking about. When her daughter's husband had a stroke, for example, she was relieved after their first phone conversation: "He said to me, 'Well, at least I didn't lose my speech,' which tells me that he's already found something good about his stroke. No matter what happens to you in life, you have to look for the silver lining." Coming from Zelda, it's not a cliché.

Choose a family mentor whose own family you admire and who seems to make conscious, well-thought-out choices rather than simply do what everyone else is doing. It could be another parent, a teacher, even someone younger than you. Pick a person you trust and who trusts you enough to speak honestly and is willing to tell stories about his or her own family. Ask about the everyday and the rough spots. Every family has both.

Play Nan's game to sharpen your powers of observation about real families. When Tracy was a little girl, she and Nan would go on an outing of some sort—a walk, a shopping trip. Let's say they crossed paths with a fancy lady in a red dress. Nan would ask questions such as "Where do you think she's from?" "Where do you think she's going?" "Why is she dressed that way?" "Do you think she has a husband at home? Children?" "Do you think she *wants* to do what she's doing now?" Nan would urge Tracy to look for clues—expressions on the woman's face, her body language, the people she talked with, the place, what her clothing or her purchases said about her. It helped Tracy learn to think about people's choices and their different paths in life. It's a good way to start looking at families, too, especially if you pay attention to the Three Factors.

Imagine that you're in a diner. At the next table sits a pregnant blonde with an adorable tow-headed toddler squirming on her lap. *What's her story?* you wonder. She's in a tailored suit, wears gold earrings, and has a scarf around her neck. You suspect that she is successful—her context probably affords her lots of "stuff." *A bit overdressed for a diner.* You also wonder about her relationship to the child. Is she a working mother who picked up her daughter from day care and is now waiting for her husband and older children to show up? Then again, she could be a single mother, the child's aunt, or a friend.

The woman does her best to keep the little girl from what any two-year-old considers a good time: clanging the silverware and then throwing it on the floor, spilling the salt, pulling out multiple napkins. The woman looks a little embarrassed. *Must be the mother!* Will she take the child's antics in stride or punish her, maybe slap the girl's hand? That answer depends on both personalities—hers and the child's—and what usually goes on between them and the kind of day she's had at the office. She pulls a picture book out of her bag to distract the toddler. As she reads, she stops at the end of each sentence, allowing the little girl to fill in the right word.

At the next table sits a boy with short dark hair. His head is down, his legs swing wildly, rhythmically—annoyingly—banging the metal frame of his chair. He looks up to see if the woman is watching. Is he just curious? Or does he belong to her, too—a nephew, a much older child from a previous marriage, a friend's son or her own? Did she banish him from the table, or is he just trying to seem more grown-up by sitting alone? Does he have ADHD? Does he feel upstaged by his little (perhaps unexpected) sister? Is he trying to get his mom's attention?

Even when the woman looks sternly in the boy's direction and mouths "Get over here now" through clenched teeth, it doesn't answer all your questions. But by flexing your family-think muscle, you'll get better at noticing how the Three Factors play out, and it will make it easier for you to shift to family-think.

FYN Look at Your Own Family Through 3-F Glasses.

In chapter 1, we suggested that you come up with your family's values, venues, and vulnerabilities. Now, for a more expansive view, consider how the Three Factors interact in your family drama. Think of a specific time—perhaps right before dinner or Sunday breakfast—when everyone is together. Consider what factors play into the actions and reactions.

- *The individuals.* List the members of your family—the **I**s who make up your **We**. List anyone who lives with you or plays a role in helping your family run—for example, a grandmother who supplies childcare when you go to work, an ex with whom you co-parent, a stepchild who comes on weekends. Then, using the questions in the "at-a-glance" chart (page 28) to guide you, jot down a few words or phrases that describe your own and other family members' temperament, history, and needs. What do you think each of you brings to the family drama? What role do you each play? (Note: This exercise is from *your* personal perspective. Know that what *you* think of other family members has more to do with who you are than with who they "really" are. In other words, identity is in the eye of the beholder. They see themselves and you differently from the way you see them and yourself. Keep this in mind if you later compare notes with your partner!)
- *The relationships.* How do the various relationships in and outside your home—couple, parent-child, siblings, extended family, personal networks—affect your family? Which relationships feel best? Feel most challenging? Are any of these relationships problematic?
- *The context.* In what kinds of environments, including your residence, is your family embedded? How does what's going on in the world now—the "historical moment"—affect your family? What about the culture? How do media messages and images play a part in your everyday life?
- At times, one of the Three Factors might seem to occupy center stage. It could be that one family member (a child is ill, Mom is fired) or that one of the relationships is in flux (siblings change grades, parent disagree about a big decision). Or perhaps the context looms large (your company merges, school hours change), affecting the whole family. What's happening in your family's life *now*? Does one of the Three Factors seem more prominent or influential in your family? Can you think of another time when another factor was front and center?

Notes on the Three Factors

THREE

INDIVIDUALS: GROW UP AND SHOW UP

Getting REAL

I am what I am because of who we all are.

—Definition of *Ubuntu*

A person with Ubuntu is open and available to others, affirming of others, does not feel threatened that others are able and good, based from a proper self-assurance that comes from knowing that he or she belongs in a greater whole and is diminished when others are humiliated or diminished, when others are tortured or oppressed.

—Archbishop Desmond Tutu

The Hightower family—Corbyn, Larry, and their three kids—are living the American dream, nestled comfortably in a tony suburb, store catalogs arriving daily to entice them to spend. Corbyn pulls down a hefty income as an independent sales rep for an organic-products company, and Larry, an IT guy, stays home with the two younger ones who haven't yet started school.

Cut to a few years later—2008. The bottom falls out of the economy, and Corbyn's income is reduced by 90 percent. At first, the Hightowers only think about downsizing. Their savings gets them through the first year. But eventually, Corbyn writes (in a blog that will later morph into a memoir), "we began sifting through anything we could sell on eBay. We had the big daddy of all garage sales. It took us a couple months to accept that the following nonessentials had to go: spring water bottle delivery, gym membership, health insurance, purchasing books, our CSA box, cable TV, and internet connectivity."

Although they also move to "a rickety, rambling old house . . . a stone's throw from the train tracks and the homeless shelter," ultimately the day comes when the savings account is empty, and they can no longer afford rent. Finally, "half joking," Corbyn suggests that they not only sell their silver Honda SUV but they live without any car. "The joke gained seriousness," Corbyn later recalls, "when we reasoned that it might actually work. It might feel good. It might feel like the right thing to do."

In California, they don't have to worry about winter. Everything they need is within a four-mile radius. They present the idea to the children, ages ten, three, and two, as "an adventure."

"I think we both felt such intense relief with the decision that the children picked up on our positive feelings," says Corbyn. "The first time we took a long bike ride as a family, postcar, my tween said, 'This is BLISSFUL! I can't believe this is my life.'"

There's nothing wonderful about poverty, or food stamps, or Dumpster-diving to supplement what the Hightowers grow in their driveway-turned-garden. Nor is it romantic to get caught in a rainstorm on foot with a tween and two toddlers in tow or to find yourselves stranded after the last bus departs. However, this isn't just a story about a family suddenly becoming "have-nots."

If you look at the Hightowers' situation through 3-F glasses, it's a story about the members of a family pulling together to survive a very difficult and challenging context. Corbyn, age forty-one, admits that "the most dramatic changes we have made were those that were forced upon us."

How Do You Develop—and Inspire—the Right Stuff?

Indeed, when the individuals in a family have the right stuff—personal qualities that inspire cooperation and commitment—*as a unit,* they can handle just about anything. They "grow up and show up."

That's not simply a clever catchphrase. By "grow up," we mean that both generations become increasingly mature and competent. But that's just half of it. You also have to "show up"—support, participate, and give as much as you get. You don't leave it to the other guy. Your family counts on you. And it's in your best interest, too, because having a strong, resilient family also makes your own life better.

"Grow up and show up" is a reinforcing loop.

As you grow up, you are able to contribute more to the greater good—you show up. As you show up, you gain confidence and competence, which makes you more mature—you continue to grow up. It doesn't matter whether you're five or fifty, the same principles are at work.

You relish your *inter*dependence—the African philosophy of *ubuntu* (as described in the chapter opening quote)—not just your independence. In the process, you become a better person.

Getting REAL

So what's the secret to developing that we're-in-this-together feeling? Getting REAL. REAL reminds us of four qualities—**R**esponsibility, **E**mpathy, **A**uthenticity, and **L**eading with love—that make us better people in general and better at relationships, while inspiring us to contribute to the greater good.

REAL gives family members a practical, emotional, and spiritual compass that guides how they act and react to whatever life throws their way. Although they might not have been doing it consciously at the time, in dealing with their financial situation, the Hightowers got REAL.

Corbyn is rightfully proud of her own sense of *responsibility*. "It satisfies me that I can make that effort, that things aren't easy for us but we soldier on, that we're not soft and self-pitying."

The Hightowers are the only family that arrives at Costco by bike—at least once in a downpour. " '*It's just rain,*' we say to each other. '*We're tough, aren't we?*' the kids say." The Hightower children—no doubt taking a cue from their parents—never complain about carrying packages long distances or riding in the bike trailer with heavy groceries on their laps. They show up, and that helps them grow up.

The Hightowers engage fully with one another; they listen; they care. They exhibit *empathy*. They always try to put themselves in one another's shoes. "We are incredibly skilled," Corbyn says of herself and Larry, "at avoiding conflict through respectful, compassionate, and tolerant treatment of each other."

They are honest with their children—a key aspect of *authenticity*. And because of this, the kids have no reason to doubt that their new situation is going to be "an adventure." Corbyn and Larry are who they are; they

How REAL Satisfies Our Basic Needs

We have four essential needs:	Each need is best met when we strive toward:	And this is how it works:
TO BE PART OF:	**R**esponsibility	Pitching in when you're needed gives you a role in something bigger than yourself.
TO BE SEEN:	**E**mpathy	It's hard to feel invisible when you connect with your loved ones and know you matter to them.
TO BE SAFE:	**A**uthenticity	A sense of security comes from trusting that others say what they mean and accept you for who you are.
TO BE NURTURED:	**L**eading with **L**ove	Love, kindness, and warmth—delivered and received—help you grow and withstand change.

don't candy-coat their situation. If the kids see them argue, they make sure the children "witness the resolution" as well.

The Hightowers try to put forth good feelings and positive emotions, rather than negativity. In short, they *lead with love,* put their "better self" out there. Larry, for example, was forced to take a minimum-wage job. "He almost never complains about his work," Corbyn observes, "just says, 'Today was hard,' if I ask. He leaves it at that."

Getting REAL is not an end point. It's a practice, a mind-set that individual family members might naturally possess or have to develop. Adults model REAL; children gradually learn it. Over time, both get better at it. All the parts work together. A person who feels valued is more likely to pitch in when help is needed, more likely to lead with love.

Remember, too, that your family—every family—is subject to change. When one of you, a particular relationship, or your context changes as it did in the Hightowers' case, to weather the storm, you all have to adapt. Especially at those times, responsibility, empathy, authenticity, and leading with love are more important than ever. Whether it's an everyday issue, an unpleasant encounter, a mild problem, or something more cataclysmic, when family members get REAL, they somehow manage to make the best of the worst. They are resilient, and they're willing to slog it out.

Getting REAL with *Your* Family

So how do you get REAL? Below, we dissect the four letters, and for each of the qualities, we look at:

- *The Payoff.* We explain why responsibility, empathy, authenticity, and leading with love will strengthen your family.
- *The Predicament.* In the thick of family life, it's sometimes hard to sustain each of these qualities and put forth our better selves. Sometimes, too, living in our particular culture—the larger context—presents its own challenges.
- *The Practice.* The goal is to cultivate these qualities in yourself and, at the same time, demonstrate them in your interactions with family members. Therefore, in this section, we encourage you to *know where you stand* (gauge how much practice you need) and *be a power of example* (model the behavior). The checklists and quizzes will help you with the first part. Your "scores," though unscientific, will give you a sense of your capacity for responsibility, empathy, authenticity, and leading with love.

Only when you accept what **is** *can you do what needs to be done and be a power of example.*

Practicing the four aspects of REAL takes willingness, honesty, and effort on your part. Especially at first, it might be lonely; you might even feel resentful: *Why am I the only [responsible, empathetic, authentic] one? Why am I the only one who leads with love?* Let it go, and keep practicing.

By all means, if you have a partner, share these ideas with him or her. Even better, read this chapter together. But remember, these are individual qualities; you can't make someone else embrace them. The goal here is not to teach other family members to get REAL but to lead by example. *Show them how much better life is when you do.*

If you work on cultivating these qualities in yourself, there's a good chance that your partner and children will, too. It might take time, but you *can* train your mind and heart to react and act differently. Your own personal growth and the health of your family are at stake.

Responsibility

The Payoff

We use the word *responsibility* as shorthand for responsibleness, a clunky word at best. Responsibility is the willingness to pull your weight, to work toward long-term goals, to do the right thing. A responsible person is invested and involved and can be counted on to show up. And showing up, even when it's hard, builds character. Arguably, responsibility is the basis of being a good citizen.

"Conscientiousness"—a synonym—is one of the so-called Big Five personality traits, which are linked with all sort of benefits in life. Conscientious individuals do better at school, at work, and in their relationships. Of all the Big Five (the others are extroversion, agreeableness, openness, and emotional stability), conscientiousness is also most strongly associated with long-term marital satisfaction.

Responsibility means more than keeping the hamster cage clean or putting the garbage out. It's also about *thinking* and *seeing* what needs to be done. That includes the little things—noticing that the plants are drooping or that there's no toilet paper in the bathroom. A responsible person says, "I just drank the last of the milk," and goes to the store—or if too young to get there on his or her own, at least lets a grown-up know. It's about asking, "Can I help you?" without being asked. It's about doing, and not always getting a reward for it.

Responsibility propels us to develop the kinds of skills we need to handle the minutiae of everyday living and the grit to get through the tough stuff. We hang in, because we know we should. We learn that we can practice, persevere, and get better, that we can take risks, suffer disappointment, even fail. The effort and commitment matter more than the outcome. As Stella McCartney, daughter of Sir Paul of Beatles fame, explained to the *New York Times* reporter who wondered if she'd ever con-

sidered asking her famously successful and wealthy father for a loan when
she started out as a fashion designer, "We don't do things like that in my
family. We work." Good job, Sir Paul.

The Predicament

Left to chance or whims, the burdens of everyday life are not divvied up
evenly in most households. One partner does more than the other, and as
we pointed out in chapter 1, the children do almost nothing. After sex and
money, housework is the most common battleground in couples' relationships. No surprise there.

You've got that right, you might be thinking. *I can't get them to put
their dirty laundry in the bin, no less think about what has to be done to run
this household.* You're not alone. In almost every family we interviewed,
one partner is exasperated by the other's "shirking" and both are embarrassed by how little their kids do, albeit in different degrees and versions.
Someone is always trying to "get" someone else to do something, and the
household becomes a battlefield. The biggest war is between the parents,
but that's only part of the predicament. Children growing up in such a
household will then perpetuate the problem, which is why the last several
generations of families have been beset by "chore wars," a huge and unre-
mitting problem to which we devote all of chapter 8.

The Practice

Know where you stand.

Before we can help you deescalate the chore wars in your household, you
have to look at your attitude toward responsibility. Do you feel as if you
"do enough" or that you "do most of it"? The "it" is different in every
household—earning a paycheck, housework, bill-paying, childcare, yard
work, keeping track, packing lunches, or whatever other "jobs" are required
to keep your family running.

Whether you believe that you do most of it or do enough and don't
think you can or should do more, have you asked yourself whether you've
chosen this role or assumed it by default? To help you answer that question,
complete either Checklist A, "Why I Do Most of It," or Checklist B, "Why
I Don't Do More." Be honest with yourself, and pick the checklist that calls
out to you.

Read the section below that corresponds to the checklist you an-

Checklist A: Why I Do Most of It

Keep your partner and/or children in mind, and check all statements that ring true.

- ☐ 1. It's faster to do it myself.
- ☐ 2. I don't want to start a fight by asking.
- ☐ 3. I do it better.
- ☐ 4. I don't want the other person to feel frustrated or fail.
- ☐ 5. It's excruciating to watch how the other person does it.
- ☐ 6. He/she is purposely incompetent or doesn't want to learn how.
- ☐ 7. I grew up in a home where I was expected to do housework.
- ☐ 8. I feel sorry for my partner/child(ren) after a long day at work/school/activities.
- ☐ 9. I don't want my family members to resent me, so I don't ask.
- ☐ 10. I measure others' performance by my own abilities and standards.

Checklist B: Why I Don't Do More

Although some items also could be applicable to your children, keep your partner in mind, and check all statements that ring true.

- ☐ 1. I'm too busy.
- ☐ 2. My partner does it better.
- ☐ 3. I was brought up in a home where I wasn't expected to assume household responsibilities.
- ☐ 4. My partner does it before I get a chance to do it.
- ☐ 5. I resent being asked.
- ☐ 6. I earn the bigger (or only) paycheck.
- ☐ 7. I am micromanaged and/or criticized for doing things wrong.
- ☐ 8. I just don't want to.
- ☐ 9. If I do more, I'm afraid my partner will expect more.
- ☐ 10. I intend to; then I forget.

swered. When you've learned what your challenge is, read the other section, too, to understand your partner's perspective.

Checklist A. If you checked five or more of the "Why I Do Most of It" statements, responsibility is not a trait you necessarily need to cultivate. Your challenge is to hold back, rethink your role, and allow others to pitch in.

Also look at the statements themselves. Do you take on family responsibilities because it's in your nature or because you've been brought up to think you have to do it all and be in control? Is it hard for you to allow other family members to participate for other reasons—pity, fear, defensiveness? Or is it expedience—you do it faster and better? Whatever the reasons, consider the "price" you pay for being *over*responsible. You might become (or already are) resentful. Worse, you're depriving your family members of the chance to show up.

Be a power of example.

- Create an environment where your partner and children can be and want to be responsible. If you bitch about the burden of doing it all, are you really ready to encourage responsibility? Are you harping on your partner without asking the kids to pitch in? Take a hard look at what your *over*responsible self has unwittingly created. If you want to inspire other family members to be stakeholders, you must *allow* responsibility to be shared.
- Listen to other family members' suggestions. Let them participate in *their* way, not according to your own standards. When you find yourself getting impatient or frustrated, ask yourself, "How important *is* it?" And instead of micromanaging, look within yourself to see *why* it's so important to you that things be done your way.
- Slow down. Often, the person who does it all is caught up in a drive to get things done. The baby-whispering acronym SLOW—Stop, Listen, Observe, and then figure out What's up—was designed to help parents tune in to their infants. But the strategy works wonders when it comes to the whole family, too, because it stops you from rushing in.
- Let family members know you need them. Adults *or* children are more likely to contribute to the greater good when they believe they bring value to the family. "We can't do this family without you" is far different from "I'm sick and tired of doing it all myself." The first statement is grounded in family-think; the second makes it personal.

Checklist B. If you chose the "Why I Don't Do More" checklist, chances are you've been accused—or secretly feel—that you're doing less than you should. How many of the odd-numbered statements did you check? They suggest that something in you—your personality, how you were brought up, your current circumstances (such as a demanding job)—stands in your way. The even-numbered statements suggest that your sense of responsibility is, at least in part, a reaction to your partner's requests or expectations. Look carefully at both. Especially if you feel put-upon by your partner, your own resentment might be getting in the way of committing yourself fully to your family.

Be a power of example.

- Stay focused on what it means to be part of a family. Everyday life is filled with difficult decisions and tasks that, truthfully, no one wants to do. If these burdens fall unfairly on one person's shoulders, the whole family suffers. If you support the idea that everyone in the family should contribute, you have to pitch in, even when you don't feel like it!
- Remember that being responsible is a choice. It's a choice you make for your own benefit, for the sake of your relationship, and for the good of your family. He said/she said battles notwithstanding, ultimately, you know whether you're showing up—and probably why. Even if you're on the receiving end of a tirade, you can always choose how you react.
- Just do it. In other arenas of your life, such as work or in the community, you are probably responsible. You do things simply because they need to get done. You help with hard or unpleasant tasks. And if you're a runner or any other kind of athlete, you have learned to push past your fatigue or do a series of boring, repetitive exercises to build up your muscles. Apply the same standards and drive to family life.

Empathy

The Payoff

Simply put, empathy is the ability to put yourself in someone else's shoes. Empathy is related to love, in that we (theoretically and ideally) have the deepest empathy for the ones we love the most. But if you've ever been at the scene of an accident or a natural disaster or watched a tear jerker, you know you can also feel empathy for a stranger.

Empathy is part instinct, part learning. We couldn't have survived as a species without it. Humans are helpless at birth and become self-sufficient much later than other animals; they need older humans to care for them. Your baby's first cries were designed to solicit empathy. And when you responded, he slowly began to learn that his behavior had an effect on others.

Empathy is the foundation on which connection is built. It's a complex interplay of observation, thinking, memory, knowledge, and reasoning, all of which combine to give you, as one scientific definition puts it, "insight into the thoughts and feelings of others." In best-case scenarios, therefore, empathy allows us to gauge where the other person is, making it easier to dial down arguments and resolve disagreements. In a family, empathy has a huge payoff. It enables individuals to become more patient and understanding. If you are empathetic, you're less likely to overreact or take it personally when a family member says or does something you didn't expect or don't like. You're more willing to cooperate when you "get" where the other person is "coming from."

The Predicament

It's not enough to leave empathy to chance. Empathy must be taught to children and practiced by the whole family. Sometimes, we're too busy to really tune in; other times, we just don't have it to give. Say your partner comes home from the office, looking worried and exhausted, and you've had a hellish day yourself. The empathetic response would be to take a breath and a step back. Instead of berating her for forgetting the cheese you'd asked her to buy, you say, "No problem, I'll work around it." But responses like that take restraint and consciousness and practice.

The culture of intensive parenting and social striving doesn't help. If it's all about who's going to end up with the most toys, it's no wonder that your children's victories sometimes feel like your victories and that their defeats crush you, too. Or that your partner's behavior at social gatherings sometimes colors how you feel about yourself. When so much is on the line, instead of feeling empathy, we feel anxious. And instead of doling out empathy, we offer sympathy or pity, which is not the same thing.

When we overidentify and *feel* the other person's pain, rather than just bearing witness to it, we can't be truly empathetic, because our own discomfort or anxiety limits us. Even more important, it robs people when you feel *for* them. Disappointment, mistakes, loss, and failure hurt, but they're part of life. Shielding a family member only makes the next bump harder to handle.

The Practice

Know where you stand. Some of us are naturally more empathetic than others. In part, it's a matter of what we're born with. Impatient and driven personalities often score low on empathy. Scientists also link certain sets of genes to empathy, although they stress that biology alone is not responsible. It's also a matter of what life throws at us. How you are raised, what you were taught, and your relationship history can determine whether that set of genes will become activated. You can get a rough sense of your EQ, or empathy quotient, by taking the "Empathy: Where Do You Stand?" test on the opposite page.

Empathy: Where Do You Stand?

Empathy expert Simon Baron Cohen devised a widely used sixty-item test for subjects' empathy quotient, or EQ. A third of the statements are fillers and have nothing to do with empathy. A third suggest that you are empathetic if you "agree" or "slightly agree." But if you "agree" or "slightly agree" with the remaining third, it lowers your EQ. The test is available online at http://www.guardian.co.uk /life/table/0,,937442,00.html. But this adaptation will give you a sense of what kinds of behaviors suggest empathy and which don't. In which column do more of your answers fall?

Empathy or . . .

- ☐ I can easily tell if someone else wants to enter a conversation.
- ☐ I really enjoy caring for other people.
- ☐ I can pick up quickly if someone says one thing but means another.
- ☐ I find it easy to put myself in somebody else's shoes.
- ☐ I am good at predicting how someone will feel.
- ☐ I am quick to spot when someone in a group is feeling awkward or uncomfortable.
- ☐ I don't tend to find social situations confusing.
- ☐ Other people tell me I am good at understanding how they are feeling and what they are thinking.
- ☐ I can easily tell if someone else is interested or bored with what I am saying.
- ☐ When I talk to people, I tend to talk about their experiences rather than my own.
- ☐ It upsets me to see an animal in pain.
- ☐ I get upset if I see people suffering on news programs.
- ☐ Friends usually talk to me about their problems, as they say that I am very understanding.
- ☐ I can sense if I am intruding, even if the other person doesn't tell me.
- ☐ I can rapidly and intuitively tune in to how someone else feels.
- ☐ I can easily work out what another person might want to talk about.
- ☐ I don't consciously work out the rules of social situations.
- ☐ I am good at predicting what other people will do.
- ☐ I tend to get emotionally involved with a friend's problems.
- ☐ I can usually appreciate the other person's viewpoint, even if I don't agree with it.

. . . Not So Much

- ☐ I find it difficult to explain to others things that I understand easily when they don't understand it the first time.
- ☐ I find it hard to know what to do in a social situation.
- ☐ People often tell me that I went too far in driving my point home in a discussion.
- ☐ It doesn't bother me too much if I am late meeting a friend.
- ☐ I often find it difficult to judge whether something is rude or polite.
- ☐ In a conversation, I tend to focus on my own thoughts rather than on what my listener might be thinking.
- ☐ When I was a child, I enjoyed cutting up worms to see what would happen.
- ☐ It is hard for me to see why some things upset people so much.
- ☐ If I say something that someone else is offended by, I think that's their problem, not mine.
- ☐ If anyone asked me if I liked their haircut, I would reply truthfully, even if I didn't like it.
- ☐ I can't always see why someone should have felt offended by a remark.
- ☐ I am very blunt, which some people take to be rudeness, even though this is unintentional.
- ☐ I am able to make decisions without being influenced by people's feelings.
- ☐ People sometimes tell me that I have gone too far with teasing.
- ☐ Other people often say that I am insensitive, though I don't always see why.
- ☐ If I see a stranger in a group, I think that it is up to them to make an effort to join in.
- ☐ I usually stay emotionally detached when watching a film.

Regardless of your score, empathy comes and goes. We are better able to respond empathetically at certain times and with certain people. Know your own hot buttons. Many of us have trouble being empathetic, for example, with a screaming toddler, a surly teenager, warring siblings, or a partner who is constantly late. Empathy is particularly hard to muster when your attention is elsewhere or when you're depressed or anxious—your own emotions get in the way. If you're not comfortable in certain social situations or if you're highly organized and like things your way, that will affect your capacity for empathy, too.

We all suffer from occasional lapses. But taking stock at least allows you to recognize whether you're just having a bad day, whether the situation evokes feelings from your past, or whether you need to work at becoming more empathetic in general. Pay attention to your reactions when others experience strong emotions. For example, your son is in tears because he didn't make the orchestra. Your reaction will depend on your emotional state at that moment and everything you've learned and experienced in the past. Perhaps *you* think it's unfair, too; he practiced and struggled with the hard parts. Shouldn't he be rewarded? Perhaps you *over*identify. You took piano lessons as a kid. Your primitive responses will kick in, but so will your conscious mind and emotions. Pay more attention to the here and now. The good news is that we can practice and get better at empathy.

Be a power of example.

- Work on making empathy your default reaction. That doesn't mean allowing a partner or child to hurt you or another family member. It doesn't mean relaxing your standards of respect. And it certainly doesn't mean feeling sorry for the person. An empathetic response puts the tape on pause. It allows you to rewind, reel the other person in, and reconnect. It dials down the drama.

  For example, at the Greens' house, Katy, now twelve, is starring in her own movie, *Middle School Meltdown*. It seems as if she has only two moods these days, weepy or snippy, at which point she rolls her eyes and lets fly a blast of surly tween back talk. Her mother, Sara, has two choices. She could launch immediately into an angry, you-can't-talk-to-me-like-that speech, which is sure to escalate the situation, because Katy will be forced to defend herself and push back, as tweens seem to do. Or Mom can make empathy her default reaction: Take a deep breath, and consider the bigger picture. She must ask herself if she really wants to impose her rules on Katy at this moment or if it might be better to slow down long enough to imagine herself in Katy's shoes.

"Whenever I take a minute before I react," Sara says, "I realize how rejected, hurt, and disappointed she is feeling about friends whom she thought she could trust. These are real problems in her world, even if I want to dismiss them as unimportant." Sara makes it clear that Katy can't take her angst out on other family members, but she gives her daughter a graceful exit: "I'm sorry you're so upset. Anyone would be angry and upset. But I don't deserve to be yelled at. So why don't you do something to calm yourself down, and we can talk later." Being empathetic and acknowledging Katy's private preteen hell leaves a "space" for her daughter to step into.

• Stay in your own boat. Good empathy implies a separation between self and other, between your agenda and the other's destiny. When couples take one of psychologist David Schnarch's workshops, the intimacy guru suggests that instead of imagining themselves in the same boat, they need to visualize traveling in separate boats going down the same river. Think of your family as a similarly interdependent unit, a small flotilla of boats on a shared journey.

Your partner's and your children's lives are not yours to live.

You might rationalize, "I'm just trying to [help, guide, direct]." But "doing for" is not the same as "being with." Tune in, listen without judgment, and try to see the situation from the other's perspective. That lays the groundwork for a solid relationship built on respect and mutual caring. Also, when you validate another's feelings and then help him sort through the emotions, make different choices, or try another way, it's a win-win. You have stayed in your own boat. And the other person realizes that even though he might have capsized this time, you were there for him. That makes it more likely that he will keep trying.

Your Child's Journey toward Empathy: 0 to 10

Use the following information to set realistic expectations. Know what your child *might* be capable of and find creative ways to nurture his or her capacity for empathy.

Babies and Toddlers (0–2)	Preschoolers (3–4)	Elementary Schoolers (5–10)
• *Where they might be.* Within twenty-four hours after birth, babies make eye contact and show a preference for human faces, which help them elicit empathy from care-givers. Rudimentary signs of empathy emerge sometime after eighteen months, when they start to recognize distress in others and form attachments to toys and "blankies" or other security objects. They can feel pride and embarrassment but don't have much inner control.	• *Where they might be.* They have fewer emotional outbursts, increasing control and tolerance of frustration. They can wait for a cookie, understand right and wrong, and play on their own. They have a rudimentary sense of self, but their self-image, such as it is, is based on what others think of them. They understand more than they can express. They want to please but, at the same time, have no idea that others have a different perspective. That kicks in around age four for most children.	• *Where they are.* From ages five to six or seven, they can recognize others' perspectives but can't quite put themselves in another person's shoes. Between eight and ten, they recognize the difference between just doing something (a behavior) and meaning to do it (with intent). By ten or eleven, most can recognize and consider others' viewpoints, but that doesn't mean they always want to be kind or helpful. Their self-esteem increasingly comes from how they perform; they are aware of different abilities in themselves and others. They are capable of problem solving and finding alternative approaches, but they need to be taught these skills.
• *What you can do.* Meet their needs to build trust in their environment, and show them that it's a safe place. Talk to them, sing and dance. Explain what they're seeing, even if you don't think they understand yet. Don't yell at or shame them. Don't overpraise. Start talking about emotions and how others feel. Show them what emotions look like by pointing out happy or sad faces in books and other media.	• *What you can do.* Continue the kind of parenting noted in the first column. Repeatedly remind them to be polite. Don't respond when they're not or when they whine. Ignore tantrums. Use their vivid imaginations to role-play. Incorporate stories about others in the fantasy; on a "train ride,"	• *What you can do.* Ask more of them. The better they feel about themselves by learning new skills and having a stake in the family, the more likely they will feel generous toward others. Have a zero-tolerance policy about interrupting others, being disrespectful, and common courtesy. Work on organizational skills if

talk about how the other "passengers" feel. Play games that require patience and waiting. If your child hits another child, explain how it makes the other child feel. Use books and TV programs to talk about caring ("See how the big sister helped her little brother?"). Even young children can understand the notion that helping others makes both people feel good. "Catch" them being empathetic, even if they don't realize they are: "I was so tired when we came home from the supermarket. I bet you knew that, and that's why you helped me bring all those packages in. Didn't it feel good to know that you made it easier for me?"

they're lax. Compliment them only when they deserve it. Respect their fears, which now are based on what's happening in their lives when you're not with them. Identify and mirror emotions in everyday exchanges ("You must have been proud when Mrs. Foster asked you to carry the flag"; "I can understand that you're disappointed because Robby didn't invite you to his house this afternoon"). Deliberately work on impulse control and the need for immediate gratification. Try to just listen; don't offer a fix or a consolation prize for every disappointment or loss. Share more about your own day, instead of only concentrating on what happened to them. Remind them to ask about your day and to ask others about theirs. ("How was your trip to Paris, Grandma?") Bring empathy into your everyday conversations. If an older child voluntarily helps a younger sibling who's struggling to sound out a word, acknowledge it: "That was really nice of you, Tyler, because you saw that Elijah was having trouble, and you helped him." Also, expose them to situations in the community where they can be of service—collecting money for UNICEF, participating with you at a local food drive, donating or baking for a charity event.

- Model and discuss empathetic deeds. Children don't develop empathy until around age four (see pages 52–53), but simple acts leave an impression. Take notice when someone is sad. Stick up for the underdog, in real life or in the media. When a TV character or someone in the news displays empathy, discuss it. Talk about how you told Mrs. Smith down the block that she's looking better since her operation. Mention that you took an extra minute out of your busy day to thank someone whose services you might rarely acknowledge or gave a hand to someone who needed it. When you hear about a relative or a community member's death, suggest that your family work together on a condolence card. It's amazing how these tiny moments not only make another person feel seen and cared about, but they also change the empathy giver. It's another of those self-reinforcing loops.

In time and as opportunities present themselves, you will all become more empathetic.

Authenticity

The Payoff

One of Tracy's favorite bits of advice was "Say what you mean, and mean what you say." She wasn't just talking about sticking to your word, although that's a part of authenticity. You also must speak *your* truth to others and live by *your* values, no matter what others do or say. It takes courage, practice, and honesty. Authenticity is not something that can be achieved perfectly or all the time. But it's certainly something to strive for in your family.

Authenticity is linked to better relationships, to feeling good about life. Authentic people tend to have high positive emotions and low negative emotions. A team of researchers in England concluded that authenticity is "one of the strongest predictors of overall well-being." People who rank higher on the "Authenticity Scale" also do well on the Big Five personality traits. They tend to be more extroverted, agreeable, conscientious, open, and emotionally stable. In other studies, authenticity is linked to "psychological well-being," which is derived from feeling independent and accepting who you are, being able to cope, experiencing personal growth, having a sense of purpose in life, and enjoying positive relationships with others.

This doesn't mean, of course, that authenticity *causes* those positive, life-bettering traits. No one knows whether authenticity leads to well-being or well-being gives you the courage to be truer to yourself and others. It just might be both. Either way, it's clear that authenticity is an important piece of the happiness equation, especially when it comes to your family.

When family scholars identify family strengths, open and honest communication is, not surprisingly, on every list. As one researcher put it, "[Authenticity is] more than not lying; it is an absence of manipulation." The parents present themselves as real people, who sometimes feel out of sorts and make mistakes. The adults talk to each other with respect and to their children in a tone that's appropriate and as if the children understand. And when parents are wrong or act badly, they apologize. They create an environment in which it's safe to be who you are.

The Predicament

It's not easy to be authentic or to sustain it. As adults, we carry with us our own set of rules that we learned in our families and from the culture. *Never let 'em see you sweat. Don't air your dirty laundry in public. No one likes a crybaby. Don't wear your heart on your sleeve.* Eager to fit in, we tend to pay more attention to our outsides—whether we're doing the "right" kind of work and wearing what we think "they" will like. And by not being who we really are, we teach our children to do the same.

Perhaps you grew up in a family in which needs were rarely acknowledged. You got in trouble for saying out loud what you felt or saw. You might now find yourself believing that your feelings don't matter or that speaking out isn't polite. The truth could hurt another person's feelings, make someone jealous, or start a fight. Even in interactions with your most beloved confidants, you risk hearing "the committee" in your head, a cabal of private demons who whisper and warn, *Don't say a word. You should be ashamed of yourself! They won't love you or accept you. You'll be rejected, abandoned.*

What happened to us as children is not the only reason we spend time and energy trying not to rock the boat. Living in a more-is-better consumer culture such as ours, it's easy to confuse wants with needs. We're bombarded 24/7 by messages that make us feel we need it all. It's hard to resist the siren call of the latest fashions, gadgets, media, and equipment, along with the activities, lessons, self-improvement plans, memberships, subscriptions. And let's not forget to factor in the hidden costs in stress and exhaustion from the endless planning, scheduling and canceling, car-pooling and schlepping.

The one with the most toys in the end *isn't* better off. In the avalanche of research about what makes people happy, money matters *least*. According to one study, it's just the opposite: Pursuing material goals contributes to depression, insecurity, and problems with intimacy. Thus, part of authentic living is asking ourselves, *Is this what I really want for my family, or am I buying into someone else's ideas of what families must do?*

The Practice

Know where you stand.

Start by taking the authenticity quiz on page 57, and then continue reading here. Your answers to specific items suggest where you stand on three key aspects of authenticity.

Items 2, 7, 10, and 12 measure "self-alienation." If you put 1, 2, or 3 next to these statements, you are, more or less, in touch with yourself. But if you gave yourself a 5, 6, or 7, you lean more toward self-alienation. That means your conscious awareness and actual experience don't always jive. Trauma victims tend to be self-alienated, as do children who don't have much hope. They stop tuning in to their own needs. Most self-alienated individuals also rank high on stress and anxiety.

Items 1, 8, 9, and 11 reflect whether your public self matches your private self. No one walks around with his or her deepest secrets on display, and no one says what's on his or her mind all the time. But if you identified strongly with those statements (scoring them 5, 6, or 7), your emotions, thoughts, values, and beliefs are in sync with what you say and how you act and react most of the time.

Items 3, 4, 5, and 6 measure the degree to which you are influenced by others and whether you accept their beliefs as your own. We all go with the majority and give in at times. And sometimes we don't speak up in order to avoid confrontation. However, if you identified strongly with these statements (scored 5, 6, or 7), you might want to work on bending less to the will or opinions of others. Typically, people who constantly acquiesce and, most important, *feel* as if they're being inauthentic tend also to report lower self-esteem and more depression.

It also helps to look at what kind of baggage you carry with you from childhood. Shame, guilt, fear, and self-doubt are enemies of authenticity.

For example, Gilda Benson's father, who had failed repeatedly in numerous business ventures, took his anger out on Gilda and her mother. "She was like his doormat, and he constantly belittled and embarrassed me," Gilda recalls of her childhood. "I grew up feeling that no one would ever want to know or love the real me."

Gilda unwittingly carried those negative feelings into her first marriage. Guilt-ridden and ashamed to do anything for herself, whenever Gilda bought a new outfit, she'd immediately remove the tags and hide the shopping bags so Stan wouldn't see them. For years, she fashioned herself into the woman she thought *he* wanted. Only his needs mattered. She let him make the rules, right down to how to wear her hair. She'd throw lavish dinner parties for his clients, and afterward, he'd sit on the couch while she cleaned up.

"When Stan walked out on me, it was a crushing blow, but it shocked me into reality. My life was a lie." With the help of a therapist, Gilda began

---

How Authentic Are You?

The items below were adapted from the Authenticity Scale used by researchers.* In this form, it's not a "scientific" measurement, but it can help you understand how authenticity might play out in your daily life. For each statement, give yourself a score between 1 (does not describe me at all) and 7 (describes me very well), and then read what your answers mean on page 56.

____ 1. I think it is better to be yourself than to be popular.
____ 2. I don't know how I really feel inside.
____ 3. I am strongly influenced by the opinions of others.
____ 4. I usually do what other people tell me to do.
____ 5. I always feel I need to do what others expect me to do.
____ 6. Other people influence me greatly.
____ 7. I feel as if I don't know myself very well.
____ 8. I always stand by what I believe in.
____ 9. I am true to myself in most situations.
____10. I feel out of touch with the "real me."
____11. I live in accordance with my values and beliefs.
____12. I feel alienated from myself.

* This scale was published in "The Authentic Personality: A Theoretical and Empirical Conceptualization and the Development of the Authenticity Scale," Alex M. Wood et al., *Journal of Counseling Psychology*, 55:7, 2008. © 2008 by the American Psychological Association.

to understand that she didn't have to carry her "enemies" into her second marriage. Now the single mother of a seven-year-old, she still struggles at times with her childhood demons, but she is better at not listening to them.

Be a power of example.

- Pay attention to truth-telling moments in your everyday interactions. In *Lying*, social observer Sam Harris maintains that telling the truth is like holding "a mirror up to one's life—because a commitment to telling the truth requires that one pay attention to what the truth is in every moment."

  Every day, we're faced with circumstances, challenges, and decisions that pull us up short. When we respond authentically, we take a giant, life-enhancing, but not always comfortable, step.

  A friend whom you *think* you know makes a racist comment that you find offensive. Do you say something? Do you admit that you have a different opinion?

  An unpleasant thought presents itself in your consciousness: *Hmm . . . I've been passing out every night. Could I be drinking too much?* Do you answer truthfully?

  Your son's tantrums are getting worse. Do you connect that behavior to his teacher suggesting that you have him tested for ADHD?

  You always have a choice: to hide your head in the sand or deal with situations head-on. You can automatically do what you're expected to do or ask yourself, *What really matters to me? Are the decisions I'm making authentic?* Such questions aren't for cowards, but they make for a better life and a stronger family.

- Practice deep listening, which inspires authenticity in others. Authenticity is not just about your own truth-telling. It's about allowing others to tell theirs, too, to be who they are. It means listening, even when you don't like what the other person has to say, even if it's uncomfortable. "Concentrated listening," as Buddhist teacher David Xi-Ken Astor also calls it, requires you to be fully present and allows us to bond. Listening, he says, is a "blessing we give to others." Research bears out the spiritual: People tend to be more authentic when their "self" is accepted by others. This makes perfect sense. By accepting mates and children, we send them an unspoken message:

It's OK to be you. I will listen without judging. I won't deny you your feelings. I am a safe person to share with.

The foundation of baby whispering is respect and acceptance. Tracy always recommended that her clients draw a "circle of respect" around each of their family members, to remind themselves that they are separate beings. You can't change family members. You have to meet them where they are. If not, you unwittingly compromise the relationship and limit that person's growth.

• Make choices that allow you to live authentically as a family. What you value and believe in should be in sync with how you spend time, energy, and especially money. The middle-class parents Annette Lareau interviewed (see box, page 31) took for granted that they were *supposed* to shower their children with endless opportunities for enrichment, disregarding whether it was at their own expense. They tended to make "automatic and unconscious" choices. The remedy? Use family resources mindfully and in keeping with your values.

Let's be clear here. There's nothing inherently wrong with spending money you earn to nurture talents or to make your life more enjoyable or easier. But signing a kid up to take lessons he's not ready for is *inauthentic*. Buying stuff to keep up appearances is *inauthentic*. Spending what you don't have is *inauthentic*, not to mention stressful and potentially dangerous to the family's well-being. The secret is vigilance and consciousness. Think about what you can afford and what will allow you to live authentically (see "Bringing Up Money" on pages 172–175).

Also, find ways to enrich your family through connection, not consumerism. "The hardest

Authentic Family-Focused Comebacks

It takes courage to buck the culture. Especially if you live in a community where consumption is taken for granted, arm yourself with comebacks. Here are a few suggestions. Think of other incidents where you have felt pressured by another parent, and decide now how you might respond next time.

"No, we're not getting Jonas a cell phone when he turns ten."

"Sally, you don't need new sneakers just because all the kids are wearing a different kind."

"I'm sorry, Coach. Sean can't play this weekend, because we planned a trip to celebrate his great-grandparents' 70th anniversary."

"I'm sure that your Daisy loves being on the elite soccer team, but we feel we just don't have enough family time with Madison as it is."

"Instead of sending Carl to the Saturday art program at the Y, he'll be spending that time at his grandfather's house, where he can learn from an old pro."

"We've decided not to join the tennis club this summer. We want to spend more time involved in neighborhood projects, like the community gardens. Being exposed to so many different kinds of people that way is good for all of us."

things," Corbyn Hightower admits, "are when we have to casually tell the kids that 'we can't go there' or 'we can't do that,' when it seems like such a small request, some simple want that shouldn't go unmet." But not accepting reality and spending money the Hightowers don't have would not only be inauthentic, it would have a far worse impact on the family. Instead, they find ways to be together and make their own fun, which is far better, as it turns out, than going to family-friendly restaurants or the mall.

Lead with Love

The Payoff

We can't oversell love and all the good that comes with it and from it. Researchers link love and affection with better mental and physical health and stronger families. To lead with love is to make caring and support your first response. You love without strings. You love even when you're disappointed in others' behavior, even when they make you angry. You may need time to regroup and reenergize yourself, but you still lead with love. And you eventually forgive and ask to be forgiven, because you realize that it goes both ways.

Leading with love also means that unless you learn otherwise, you take family members at their word. You trust them, because you know them. You believe their actions are not motivated by selfishness or greed or wanting to do you in. In short, they're innocent until proven guilty. After all, if we are willing to give complete strangers the benefit of the doubt in a courtroom, why not do the same at home?

To suggest that you lead with love doesn't mean that you'll never argue or that you will always want the same thing. It doesn't mean stuffing your feelings or glossing over them (which would be inauthentic). But it does take restraint to keep yourself from making a thoughtless or unkind comment.

It's better for *you* to lead with love, too. You might get angry—you're human, after all. But people who can restrain themselves from hurling aggressive insults or becoming abusive feel better about themselves and are better at making and keeping their connections than those who repeatedly lose it. The biggest payoff is family solidarity, a sense that we're in this together.

The Predicament

Leading with love is strongly linked to empathy, kindness, openness, and a host of other positive traits, but it's also a matter of self-control. In the heat of the moment, you have to acknowledge and manage your emotions and, at the same time, use your conscious mind *before* you react. We are not all similarly endowed. Some are naturally more impulsive than others. It's harder for them to monitor what they say or do.

It's easy to lead with love when, for example, your toddler comes running into your arms and declares, "Mommy, I love you soooooo much!" It's easy to lead with love when you're out with your eight-year-old, and he automatically holds the door for a patron who's exiting the restaurant at the same time. And it's easy to be warm and kind to your partner when he comes home early to surprise you with a bottle of champagne for no reason or notices that the screen door needs painting and does it, unasked, just to be helpful.

But what about the other times, when your toddler is having a meltdown or is glued to you all day? Or when your middle-school child is out of sorts because her brother has a play date and now wants you to play Monopoly with her? Or when your partner comes home in a mood? And even when you put your most loving self forward, your family members might be so wrapped up in their own emotions that they might not notice. At those moments, it's hard to manage your emotions and keep leading with love, because it seems to be getting you nowhere.

It's also challenging to lead with love when *you* have had a bad day— say, a series of disappointments at work, a particularly difficult assignment that required a lot of mental energy, interactions with an aging parent who refuses to get the help he needs. At such times, you experience what psychologist Roy Baumeister calls "ego depletion"—you just don't have it in you to lead with love. Your energy is at its lowest ebb, making it harder to regulate your thoughts, feelings, and actions. Watching subjects in a study agonize over choosing a radish over a warm cookie, for example, Baumeister concluded that "willpower . . . seemed to be like a muscle that could be fatigued through use." His theory helps us understand why family life is so often a test of self-control.

Consider this typical scene. Farley, age nine, starts a new school, a life change that requires him to meet strangers, deal with their differences, learn new routines, and take on the more challenging work of fourth grade—all of which drains his reserves of self-control. By the time he comes home, he's depleted—grumpy, reluctant to listen, and full of excuses about his homework. According to Baumeister's theory, it's not stress that's causing Farley to unravel and to slam the door of the bathroom when he's asked to wash up for dinner. It's that he has only minimal energy *at that moment*. Leading with love will take considerable effort on his mother Regina's part because this kind of situation depletes her reserves, too. However, Regina is the grown-up. Although it's a challenge, she has to take steps to increase the likelihood that she will lead with love. Luckily, there are several.

The Practice

Know where you stand.

Your capacity to lead with love can be easily depleted, but it also can be built up. As with other aspects of REAL, we don't all start at the same point. Take the test on page 63 to see how you compare with others when it comes to self-control, which helps you manage your emotions and makes it more likely that you will be able to lead with love.

The fact is, stuff happens in families: Your partner will forget to take out the recycling. Your child will want to watch TV instead of getting dressed. Your teenager will thrust a permission slip at you, even though you've told her time and again that she shouldn't wait until the last minute. In each case, it might be a challenge to lead with love.

Rest assured, though, no one can *always* lead with love. But it's something you can get better at. Awareness and practice can help you engage in the kind of self-talk that encourages you to reach for a kind response.

Be a power of example.

- *Think before you speak or act.* Pause for a moment, remember what your partner or child means to you, and ask yourself:

  ### *What do I need to do now to better this relationship?*

  Keep that question in mind as you read on; we will come back to this idea. It will remind you to consider what *you* can do *in that moment* to deepen your connection rather than drive the two of you apart. Yelling or stomping out of the room might temporarily feel

Measuring Self-Control

This quiz is based on a much-used self-control scale, developed by a team of social scientists in 2004.* This version will give you a sense of the kinds of items social scientists consider when measuring self-control and how you compare with others who have taken the test.

How much do the following statements reflect how you *typically* are? In the score column, give yourself a 1, 2, 3, 4, or 5, with 1 indicating *not at all* and 5 *very much*:

	SCORE	REAL SCORE
1. I am good at resisting temptation.	_____	_____
2. I have a hard time breaking bad habits.	_____	_____
3. I am lazy.	_____	_____
4. I say inappropriate things.	_____	_____
5. I do certain things that are bad for me, if they are fun.	_____	_____
6. I refuse things that are bad for me.	_____	_____
7. I wish I had more self-discipline.	_____	_____
8. People would say that I have iron self-discipline.	_____	_____
9. Pleasure and fun sometimes keep me from getting work done.	_____	_____
10. I have trouble concentrating.	_____	_____
11. I am able to work effectively toward long-term goals.	_____	_____
12. Sometimes I can't stop myself from doing something, even if I know it is wrong.	_____	_____
13. I often act without thinking through all the alternatives.	_____	_____

For items 1, 6, 8, and 11, copy your scores as you wrote them into the "real score" column.
For items 2, 3, 4, 5, 7, 9, 10, 12, and 13, reverse your scores (5 = 1; 4 = 2; 3 = 3; 2 = 4; 1 = 4) before putting them into the "real score" column.
Add up your "real score." According to psychologist June Tangney, one of the authors of this test, the average score for "a diverse sample of college students" is around 39. However, "high" self-control in a college student might be different from that of an adult in her forties. About 68 percent of people score between 31 and 48. Scores below 31 indicate lower self-control than average. Scores above 48 indicate high levels of self-control.

* The test was developed by June P. Tangney, Roy F. Baumeister, and Angie Luzio Boone and originally published in the *Journal of Personality* 72:2, April 2004, as "High Self-Control Predicts Good Adjustment, Less Pathology, Better Grades, and Interpersonal Success." © Blackwell Publishing, 2004.

good, but restraining those impulses, pausing to come up with a compassionate reaction, is the secret to individual well-being and to sustaining healthy relationships.

• *Know when your own reserves are low, and replenish them.* Just as airlines tell adults traveling with children to put on their own oxygen masks first before assisting others, that advice also applies to family relationships. If you can't "breathe," it's hard to concentrate on anything or anyone else. Because we have limited reserves of energy, we deplete ourselves when we take care of others, concentrate on work, solve problems, and, at the same time, have to restrain ourselves from overreacting.

   You can't prevent ego depletion. On a daily basis, most of us have an abundance of responsibilities. But you can learn the signs. Overblown feelings or inappropriate reactions should send up a red flag. Inconsideration, crankiness, and nitpicking are among the more subtle signals that your reserves are low. Hunger and fatigue are likely culprits. Likewise, if you have a headache or neck ache, a bad back, or a sour stomach, or if work is stressful or you've had too little downtime or too much screen time, it might be harder to lead with your best, most loving self.

   Heed these signs, and follow suggestions you would give someone else who felt depleted. Sleep when you're tired, exercise to get your blood pumping, eat in ways that feed your body and soul. Restrain from the things that drain you, such as too much screen time, sugar, and other substances that do you no good. Taking care of your physical being will benefit your mind and your spiritual self. Also seeking social support outside your family. Dinner or a game of tennis with a friend will help replenish your reserves.

• *Embrace whatever form of spirituality helps you feel connected to something bigger.* It's no accident that "spirituality" and "religion" come up not only in studies of secure families but also in studies of health, depression, and loneliness. To be spiritual is to feel connected to something bigger and to have a moral compass. In many families, spirituality comes from worship—92 percent of Americans believe in God. Some attend a house of worship regularly or occasionally or celebrate a particular religion's rites of passage and holidays. Others have no connection to an organized spiritual practice. Still, they take time to pause and to give thanks. They create some kind of sacred space in which everyone slows down and tunes out the everyday.

Your children might roll their eyes when you pause before a meal to say grace. They might fidget during a candle-lighting ceremony, or balk at wearing their Sunday best. They might someday reject these practices. But in the meantime, creating a sacred space and discussing what's right and wrong at least exposes them to a way of being that helps them learn to lead with love.

Perfect Family or REAL Family

What's the difference?

A perfect family is about . . .

POSING AND PERCEPTION

Those who strive for perfection are usually more concerned with satisfying an external ideal—the culture's, their parents', their friends', their own childhood fantasy—of what a family "should" be. Energy is put into looking good to outsiders, and family members are expected to fall in line.

A REAL family is about . . .

ACTION AND SATISFACTION

Of course, there's no such thing as a perfect family! When family members are REAL—responsible, empathetic, authentic, and lead with love—they work with what they have. They accept that family life can be hard, unpredictable, and messy, and requires effort. REAL families honor individual needs, know their strengths and weaknesses, and work together to strengthen the family.

If you feel overwhelmed by the information in this chapter, just let these ideas niggle around in your brain. Little by little, getting REAL will become an easier and more automatic choice. You'll feel the difference in yourself. Ideally, you have a partner or other supportive adults in your life who are also striving to be responsible, empathetic, and authentic and to lead with love. But even if only *you* get REAL, it will make a difference. Other family members will catch on. Eventually, you will become a

REAL family but not a "perfect" one (see the box on page 65 for the difference between the two). Each of you will cope better. Your relationships will get stronger. And as a family, you will be better prepared for whatever life—your context—throws at you.

It probably won't happen overnight. In the meantime, take baby steps. As Vincent van Gogh observed, "Great things are done by a series of small things brought together."

FYN What's REAL about Your Family?

Each family, a unique mix of the Three Factors, is different from all others. Even the best-run, happiest, most loving families are not REAL in the same way. We come to the table with personal agendas and unique conditions and challenges, not to mention past programming and long-held beliefs, and all of it is stirred into the family pot. In what ways do the letters of REAL play out in your family?

- Do both you and your partner have a sense of responsibility? Do you ask anything of your children?
- Is empathy modeled and taught? Are you more empathetic toward a particular family member? Do you confuse empathy with pity?
- Do you speak to your partner and children authentically? Consider your words and your tone. Do you say what you mean and mean what you say? Does your family live an authentic life?
- Do you consciously try to put your best self forward on a daily basis? Do you model self-control? Does your family have a spiritual center? Do you practice compassion, forgiveness, and acceptance?

Notes on Getting REAL

FOUR

RELATIONSHIPS: YOUR FIRST PRIORITY

The Connection Questions

Live without pretending,
Love without depending,
Listen without defending,
Speak without offending,
Give without ending,
Build without rending.

—Nina Roberta Baker

Looking back at the breathtaking photographs of the scene, forty-three-year-old Elizabeth Weil can't believe she "wanted to flee." But there she was, 11,000 feet above sea level, with her in-laws, her husband, and their two daughters, camping in a "dust pile at Chickenfoot Lake." Having grown up in a cushy Boston suburb, this wasn't her idea of a great family vacation. But she knew that marriage involved compromise. This trip was her way of supporting her outdoorsy, nature-loving husband, the son of Berkeley lefties.

Ironically, her tortured tryst with the great outdoors in Northern California coincided with the completion of her book, *No Cheating, No Dying*, a memoir about her yearlong quest with her husband to improve their already "good" marriage. When the idea first began to present itself in Liz's brain, she reasoned that she had always "applied" herself. She was, like her mother, an inveterate doer. Why not put the same kind of effort and energy into her relationship? With a little coaxing to get Dan on board, the two of them worked on self-help exercises, bared their souls in marital workshops, and saw a medley of therapists. Uncomfortable and conflict-inducing as the experience sometimes was, she hoped the process would enable her to "look under the hood of our marriage, see how it worked."

The examination, she would later write, led to the conclusion that "commitment is two-pronged, requiring dedication and constraint." Luckily, she exercised both that day on Chickenfoot Lake. Although she retreated to the tent for most of the afternoon, playing War with her six-year-old, caring little for the scenery and less for the mosquitoes, she managed to soldier through the day. "Dehydrated and filthy, I thought this was the height of marriage ridiculousness." And yet she kept that to herself.

To her surprise, though, Dan pulled her aside later that evening. "I know this isn't your first-choice vacation spot," he said, looking into her eyes. "But it means the world that you would do this for me." The moment stunned her.

Do this for him. Holy cow. I felt my face relax. I didn't have to want to be there, and we didn't even need to discuss it in one of those stilted, active listening styles we learned in marriage class—start with the positive, mirror each other's emotions, find a compromise. I could just do this uncomfortable thing for my handsome and sunburned husband because it meant the world to him. That was it. That was enough.

Was it the year of reading and researching or the various relationship boot camps? Or was it a developmental leap, her forties kicking in with newfound maturity? Was it that Dan joined her in the quest to make their marriage better? Or perhaps all of the above? Whatever it was that caused Liz to gain a new insight about her marriage, she miraculously turned some sort of cosmic corner.

Few of us have the time or inclination to embark voluntarily on a journey like Liz Weil's, dedicating a solid year to marital betterment, but her story underscores a truism about the state of our unions and also about why harmonious families put relationships first:

Family life goes better when you're good at relationships. And if you prioritize, practice, and tell yourself the truth, you get better at being in relationships.

Why Prioritize Connection?

Relationships are everything. It pays to get good at them.

Although the Three Factors work together and each contributes to the mix of what family is, relationships form the bedrock on which your family and all of humanity stand. Our modern-day selves are descendants of the first humans who realized it was a good idea to band together. They made it through the millennia by using their combined strength and know-how to stave off woolly mastodons and pool whatever they found, killed, or made. More than any other factor, their relationships ensured that the tribe would endure and its distant offspring—us—would someday walk the earth.

OK. So it's a little more complicated today. Our consciousness and our vistas are far beyond those of our ancestors and still unfolding. But the same social programming propels us to seek relationships. Now, as then, we need others to survive and thrive. People who are good at relationships find family life most satisfying.

To say that relationships are everything is to echo a boatload of research that keeps coming to the same conclusion: Close connections have a measurable *physical* impact on our brains and bodies. Healthy relationships are linked to general well-being, happiness, greater productivity, and success. They can help adults heal old wounds, set the stage for children's future relationships, and—most important—help family members deal with whatever life throws at them. With loving people in your corner, you have a ready source of support and opportunities to grow.

Of all relationships, family ties matter most. They are the longest-lasting and most intimate connections. You share everyday life, responsibilities, physical space, and special occasions with one another. Whether you're coping with the demands of your day or fielding the unexpected, it is easier with a loved one squeezing your hand.

Being Good at Relationships

If you're good at relationships, it's a pretty safe bet that you . . .

1. Know who *you* are.
2. Are willing to stretch yourself.
3. Try, though don't always succeed, to access your "better" self.
4. Have a sense of humor.
5. Can handle your own emotions (they're the only ones you *can* control).
6. Practice REAL: you are responsible, empathetic, and authentic and lead with love.
7. Accept the other, and resist the urge to tweak.
8. Know where you end and the other begins (boundaries).
9. Can identify what you get from each person and, therefore, know who can best satisfy your various needs.
10. Remain curious about the other person.

The pressure and risks are greatest in the family, too. Today, our primary relationships—partner, children, parents, siblings—are supposed to provide us with what entire villages once did. But when family ties are secure, they can be a source of solace and personal satisfaction. You feel loved and loving; you feel competent and grateful. It doesn't mean you'll never have conflicts or days in which you want to run and hide from everyone. Having good relationships makes it more likely that at those difficult moments, you'll be able to take a deep breath and reach inside to access your better ("sage" self, as we describe it in chapter 9) self. On your good days, you'll remind yourself that you're not there to cajole, control, or change but to learn, to hold on to yourself, and, at the same time, to have "good enough" family relationships, which gives you, to use Liz Weil's words, "the strength and bravery required to face the world."*

The Challenges of All Relationships

It might seem odd to lump all relationships together as we do in this chapter. How can you compare the dynamics between two adults with what goes on between an adult and a child or between two children? And as we point out in the next chapter, even adult relationships aren't comparable. The "rules" of being an adult child or an uncle are different from those of being a partner or sister-in-law.

However, when you look at relationships through 3-F glasses, it becomes clear that relationships also have a great deal in common. For all the differences between different kinds of relationships, there are also basic principles that ring true about *all* your family ties.

Every relationship is a two-way street. How a relationship develops in part depends on what *you* put into it and how you react to what the other person offers. The old saying is true with adults and children: You get as good as you give. If Liz Weil had begun to carp and criticize that afternoon on Chickenfoot Lake, she would have undoubtedly gotten a very different response from her husband. *We go to your parents' all the time. Why can't you can't spend a few days camping with mine? How can you be so*

---

*In psychiatry, as Weil points out, a "good-enough mother . . . loves her child well enough for him to grow into an emotionally healthy adult." Weil uses the term *good-enough marriage* in her book to stress that "the goal is mental health, defined as the fortitude and flexibility to live one's own life—not happiness."

selfish? That kind of negative give-and-take would not only have worsened Liz and Dan's partnership, but their discord, in turn, would have "contaminated" their daughters and his parents and turned the outing into a very different context for all of them.

Every relationship brings out a different you. No two relationships, regardless of type, are the same. As we pointed out in chapter 1, every relationship is a "co-creation," a unique entity that is a mix of each person's personality, expectations, past programming (their individuality), and what each one needs in "the now" (their context). No relationship gives you everything, but each offers a special set of gifts and challenges. How you act, what you say, what you are willing to give, and even who you are also change from one relationship to another. You not only assume a different role (say, spouse versus parent), but you also trot out different aspects of your self. A poem recited at many weddings nowadays captures this fluidity: "I love you not only for what you are but for what I am when I am with you."

Every interaction with another person feeds or starves the relationship. In the best relationships, both people feel loved and supported for who they are. And each consciously makes choices that benefit their union. Liz Weil's restraint bettered their partnership, as did her husband's empathy—his recognition of how hard it was for her to be on a camping trip. Naturally, with children adults have to take the lead, but kids learn to give what they get from their parents. In a good relationship of any type, the two talk and act respectfully toward each other, which nourishes their connection. They are kind to each other; they listen, pay attention, and support each other. Each adult or child "partner" feels he matters to the other—is important, valued, depended on, and appreciated. The two say nice things to each other. And when they don't, they try to get back on track as quickly as possible.

Relationships are a moving target. They shift in small increments every day as the two parties age, interact with others, and deal with life. In all

---

Reminder: Get REAL in Your Relationships

To stay connected, strive toward:

Responsibility. Act like a grown-up. Know your own "stuff," and use self-control to express negative feelings in a constructive manner. If you feel overwhelmed, ask for a time-out.

Empathy. Step into the other's shoes. A perspective unlike yours is not wrong. Try to understand why the other thinks differently. If you don't know, ask.

Authenticity. Be yourself; speak your truth. Otherwise, instead of feeling *in* your relationship, you'll feel engulfed by it or want to run from it.

Leading with love. Put your best self forward, and expect the best from the other. There are no guarantees, but leading with the positive increases your chances of getting a positive response.

of our parenting books, we wrote, "Just when you think you've got it, everything changes." In the course of a day, a year, or a decade, a given relationship, with a child or an adult, unfolds in ways we can't imagine. You can't cease this perpetual motion; it's the stuff of everyday life. But in every exchange, you can make a conscious choice every day to accommodate these changes and thereby "feed" the relationship.

Your behavior is the only aspect of any relationship over which you have control. Your part is half the equation. You can't—and shouldn't try to—manipulate or manage the other person. And yet what you do and say can change the dance between you. That's why we spent a whole chapter on "getting REAL." Possessing those qualities and monitoring your own behavior help you lead with your best, most honest self and inspire others to lead with theirs (see box on previous page).

Taking Stock

You probably already know a lot about what you could do to better your relationships. On a random day in 2012, in fact, we asked Facebook users, "What's the most important thing you've learned about handling relationships—with a child or an adult?" Turn the page; their answers bear a striking resemblance to research findings about what it takes to have a high-quality relationship. But don't their suggestions sound familiar? Couldn't you contribute a few pointers yourself?

The tricky thing about relationship advice, wherever it comes from, is using it. In every relationship, you've got three elements: you, the other person, and the relationship that the two of you create. It's a tangle of emotions, personalities, and needs. A set of guidelines is great, but whether you can actually implement relationship tips depends on your awareness in the moment and whether you can slow yourself down long enough to take an action that will be good for the relationship.

As we explain in detail on pages 87–95, we teach you how to make good choices by using the "Tell Yourself the Truth" mantra, which can be applied not only in your relationships but in any family dilemma. But we start here with the "connection questions," which will make you more aware of:

who you become *in each relationship,*
what the other person brings to the table, and
what you bring out in each other.

Relationship Advice from the Trenches

Tracy often used the Baby Whisperer forums to gather information "from the trenches." The following is from Facebook users who were asked to identify "the most important thing you've learned about handling relationships—with a child or an adult."

Compassion.

Don't expect it to be perfect.

Don't sweat the small stuff. Most of it *is* small stuff.

Compromise.

Empathy for the other person's struggles.

People you can count on, patience, and looking at the big picture.

Sense of humor.

If you have a child, do you wake up each morning and decide whether to continue being a parent, or does the commitment preclude such an absurd question? To a significant degree, relationships are defined by commitment.

Don't lose yourself.

Commitment, compromise, support, positiveness (is that even a word?), and if you don't have something nice to say, don't say anything at all.

No unsolicited advice.

Giving unconditional love is really hard.

Care—relationships require you to care.

Best thing I've learned about everyone's close relationships: A relationship *only* has to make sense to the people in it, not to me or anyone else. Whatever works for them . . . works. Period.

It doesn't matter whether you're dealing with a child or an adult. These questions will help you see where you click and where you miss. It's the kind of information you need in order to tell yourself the truth and make conscious choices. The questions are naturally addressed to you, because you're the only one you can control!

Before you read further, though, we suggest you take a few minutes to do the following exercise, which encourages you to think about who you want to keep in mind while reviewing the ten connection questions.

FYN Who's on Your Relationship Inventory?

Make a list of your closest family members, including your partner (if you have one), children, an ex if you co-parent, parents if they're a part of your everyday life. After you read through the explanations and examples for each of the ten connection questions, come back to the questions themselves, and apply them individually to each of your family members. Leave space in this section of your notebook. You might want to come back later to take a second look or perhaps to add names of others who play a part in your family drama—sisters, brothers, aunts, uncles, grandparents, nieces, nephews, close friends, and nonrelated individuals who affect your family life. Although family ties are the subject of this book and figure most prominently in the story of your life, the connection questions also could be applied to any of your relationships—your boss, a baby-sitter or housekeeper, a close friend.

The Ten Connection Questions

1. Do you factor your "self" and your own issues into the relationship equation? Knowing yourself is a critical aspect of relationship building. With each connection, different aspects of your I emerge. With your child, you might give free rein to your nurturing, fun-loving self. In a rocky adult relationship, your jealous, angry self might emerge. A sibling might elicit a competitive or protective self, sometimes both. And a loving and wise old aunt might bring out a younger, curious, more dependent self.

But you're never a finished product. As our various family relationships develop, studies show that we refashion our beliefs about the other person and about the relationship. And sometimes, "the virtues become the vices," as one psychologist put it. You feel smothered by the same guy who was so attentive when you first met. The woman who initially impressed you with her logical mind you now view as a neat freak, and her standards make you feel inadequate. The son who delighted you with his antics as a toddler now exasperates you with his adolescent pranks. So if you see yourself getting snippy, defensive, or distant in a relationship, and you'd like to restore a sense of well-being, ask yourself what new attitudes or feelings are cropping up lately. You might have to look in the mirror.

Running down the "What's Going on with Me?" checklist on the following page can help you zero in on you. What do your answers tell you? Do you have to take better care of yourself? Are you spreading yourself

What's Going on with Me?

If you're out of sorts and sniping at everyone, ask yourself:

- ☐ Am I responsible for too much?
- ☐ Have I made too many commitments?
- ☐ Am I trying to change something outside of my control?
- ☐ Am I expecting others to make me whole or happy?
- ☐ Am I physically well?
- ☐ Have I suffered a trauma that I'm not acknowledging?

too thin? If you're physically, mentally, or emotionally below par, it's going to be more difficult to see any situation from the other's perspective. However, if you are willing, flexible, and mindful, you will become more "relationship-worthy." And that alone will make you feel good about yourself, which will also better your connections.

2. Do you watch your opening lines and then listen to the other person's response? As Grandma always said, you catch more flies with honey. How you initiate a conversation influences how your partner or child responds. When you're kind and respectful, you're likely to get back the same from them. Here are two lists of possible opening lines:

List 1	*List 2*
I can help.	I told you so.
I can show you if you like.	You did it again.
I know how you feel.	I'm right/you're wrong.
I love you.	It's your fault.
I'm with you.	I can't listen to this.
I'll get it for you.	You drive me crazy.
I hear you.	You are too [fill in the blank].
I feel like . . .	You should . . .
Sorry if I interrupted you.	You never/always . . .
I need to calm myself down.	I'm outta here.
I forgive you.	Who do you think you are?

You don't have to be a rocket scientist to figure out which list is more likely to short-circuit conversation and which one leads to more positive engagement. Good communication is at the heart of every solid connection. It's best to lead with kindness and a genuine desire to meet the other person. It opens the door.

Practice good opening lines. On a sheet of paper, write the heading "Good Conversation Starters," and copy the phrases on List 1. Add others that feel right to you. Paste it on your mirror or in the kitchen, a place where you're bound to see it every day. All the better if other family members also notice it.

When the other person responds, be sure to actually listen. One popular method in marriage workshops, "active listening," involves one partner parroting what the other says.

Your child says, "I really don't want to visit Grandma today," and you say, "I hear that you don't want to visit Grandma." Your partner says, "Every time you yell at me about household chores, I feel like I'm ten again and you're my mother," and you say, "I hear that when I yell at you, you feel like you're ten again and that I am your mother."

Active listening is a rather stilted way of having a conversation, but it helps sensitize both parties to each other's perspective. It also slows down the action and brings more awareness to the moment. And the more consciousness and commitment you bring to conversations, the greater the likelihood that they won't spin out of control.

3. Do you look for the sweet spot? There's a place in every relationship where your expectations of each other are just right—the "sweet spot." If the bar is set too low, we don't grow. We stay only in our comfort zone, avoiding risks that, though scary, are also usually life-enhancing. If the bar is too high, we ask too much of ourselves or the other person.

In a *New York Times* article summarizing the research about expectations, journalist Alina Tugend came up with a commonsense formula: "It seems as if it is best to have low expectations of things out of our control, realistic expectations of things we can control to some degree, and high expectations of ourselves."

Expectations about our relationships also fall into those three categories. When your expectations are in line with reality—right-sized—it strengthens a relationship. The smaller the "ideal/real gap," the difference between what you hope for and what actually is, the better you feel about life. When it comes to relationships, if you accept who the other person is, and know what you can realistically expect, you are less likely to waste energy trying to turn her into something she is not and might never be.

Empathy can help you find the sweet spot. When you expect or demand something of a family member, try to imagine being on the other end. Listen to what you normally say to that person, how you say it, and what kind of unspoken messages you send. How would you feel on the other end—pressured and stressed? Would the words or the delivery make you want to forge ahead or stop trying? Putting yourself in the other's

Finding the Sweet Spot: What's Reasonable?

Expecting children to accept responsibility appropriate for their age.

Expressing your needs to your partner or parent.

Reasoning/compromising with an older child or another adult.

Explaining rules to a child rather than assuming he or she knows them (or gets it the first time).

Accepting that the other person thinks differently from you.

Expecting your partner and your children to be interested in who you are.

Knowing that one person can't be everything to you.

Realizing that sometimes people disappoint; sometimes things go wrong.

Having a Plan B when things don't go as you expected.

Agreeing to "disagree" at times. Even long-married "master" couples never resolve 69 percent of their conflicts.

shoes can inspire you to take a different tone, dial back your expectations, and find a more comfortable middle ground.

As one gregarious woman, married to a loner, pointed out, "I've learned what he can tolerate, and it doesn't help to push him. Do we have friends over and go out as much as I'd like? No, but we don't isolate as much as he'd like, either."

4. Are you as curious about your loved ones as you are about people you hardly know? With your partner, the drive to ask each other questions sometimes diminishes over time. With children (and our own parents), we often assume, instead of asking. As kids begin to flirt with adolescence, if we haven't been curious all along, they become reluctant to answer our questions, so it's best to start early. And with your parents, knowing them is even trickier. You have a lifetime of baggage between you, memories of a time when they were in charge and you had to listen. In order to step out of these old roles, you need to see them as *people,* not just as Mom or Dad.

To find out about your loved ones, just ask. Posing questions during the course of a routine day and listening to a child's or an adult's response is a way of saying, "I'm interested in you and in who you're becoming." It keeps the door open. That's why many marital workshops remind partners to share not just their big dreams, triumphs, and disappointments but also the minutiae of their day. Besides teaching communication skills, many of these seminars feature partner exercises similar to the old "Marriage Game" in which the contestants score points when they know random bits of information, like each others favorite song.

Also, curiosity itself is a life-enhancing trait. Curious people have more fun and they make better pals. In effect, asking questions is a way of feeding relationships, because it makes others know that you're interested in who they are.

Find out what he likes and dislikes, what she cares about, how he likes to spend his free time. What foods does she love, what kind of music or nature sounds soothe or energize him, what flowers make her feel special, what sights would he like to see, what kinds of caresses make her feel loved and protected, what's on his bucket list? Do you know what flavor ice cream she craves, whether he likes crisp or flannel sheets? Do you know what's happening at work or school or in a project that has nothing to do with you? Have you ever asked his favorite or worst childhood memory? Did he play outside a lot as a kid? Does she have any health issues or concerns? Do you know what he'd like to do if money were no object? If you have aging parents, do you really know who they are and how they feel, or are you busy now, trying to get them to live or act in a way that *you* think is best? It's better to ask than to assume. (For ideas about topics of conversation, see the "Index of Possibilities.")

The process is not merely an endless fact-finding mission. It's a way of saying, "I accept you as you are now. I applaud our differences and want to learn from you." It also helps you gauge the best way to connect and get through to each person. Do you know, for example, who in your family is most likely to open up in conversation? Who feels more comfortable talking while doing or learning something together? Who writes notes or stories that reveal information?

An Index of Possibilities

There's no end to the things you can learn about another person—adult or child. The topics and questions below cover a lot of biographical territory. With children, adapt according to their age. With everyone, the more you traverse all these hills and valleys, the more you will know about "O"—the other. It's a never-ending journey.

GENERAL DOMAIN	COULD APPLY TO	SAMPLE QUESTIONS
Attitudes/Beliefs *What are O's perspectives and attitudes?* *What does O believe in, find important?*	Children, family, relationships (current and past), money, work, love, sex, pets, health, the environment, social responsibility, leisure time, religion/spirituality, social life.	Do you like spending time with other families? Where would you put work on your list of priorities? What made you want to become a mother/father? *(continued on next page)*

General domain	Could apply to	Sample questions
Experiences *What moments stand out in O's life story?*	Firsts, best/worst, most surprising, most life-changing, most frightening, most embarrassing relationship, job, moment.	How old were you, and who taught you to [ride a bike, cook, read, etc.]? What memory of your childhood best defines your family? What is your greatest accomplishment so far?
Environment *What kind of space makes O feel most comfortable? What part does O have in making that space what it is?*	Houses/places/community preferred; relationship to physical space (clean/dirty, neat/messy); involvement in creation or protection of home (role in decoration or renovation); types of locales preferred (rural/urban, manicured/rustic).	In what ways do different types of environments affect you? What's your ideal living space look like—size, how it's decorated, location? Do you like to spend time in nature?
Family *What about O's background and history seeps into your present together?*	Childhood memories, relationships with parents and siblings, the importance of extended family, ideas/beliefs/attitudes exposed to as a child.	What's the most important thing you learned from your sister? Did your parents argue a lot? In your family, were children expected to participate in adult conversation?
Interests *What captivates O's attention?* *What does O like to do, learn about, participate in?*	Preferences, participation, relationship to and knowledge about sports, music, films, books, food, restaurants, social media, culture.	If you suddenly had an extra hour every day, what would you spend it doing? What parts of the newspaper do you like to read first? What's something you've always dreamed of doing?
Relationships *Who else is in O's life?*	Importance of and relationship with relatives, friends, college chums, army buddies, boss, coworkers, teachers, clergy, and others who cross O's path.	What makes him your "best friend"? If we moved, whose presence would you miss the most? What's the difference between your online relationships and your real-life ones?
Triumphs/Struggles *What challenges has O had to face—or want to face?*	Health, career, physical feats or trials, discrimination, acts of God.	Do you think you do enough for yourself to stay healthy? If you knew you could get strong enough to do a triathalon, would you be willing to take the time out to train?

5. Do you limit your knowledge of the other to your own perceptions and experiences? Watch your loved one in other contexts, with other people and in situations outside the household. One woman we interviewed, married to a judge, loved to watch "Her Honor" performing "improv," because a different, less familiar part of her emerged. You might feel the same way watching your partner at a cocktail party or observing your child help a neighbor.

Warning: Seeing a loved one in a new light also can be jarring ("How come he's not like that with *me*?"). Don't take it personally. Instead, take in the new information, and use it to better *your* relationship with that person. For example, Bettina barely recognized her seemingly "absentminded" daughter, Mary Lou, in her karate class. The little girl had focus, self-control, and confidence and willingly practiced on her own at home. "I had to ask myself, why is she so different with her sensei? I realized that at home I wasn't giving her credit for what she could do; I was only worried about what she wasn't doing." She began to talk to her daughter in a much more direct and authentic way, and their relationship gradually improved.

Relatives, friends, and acquaintances who are observant, level-headed, and honest can be an invaluable source of information, *if you're willing to listen.* A psychologist friend told Marie Daniels that she was worried about Marie's seven-year-old son, Christopher: "He was hanging over the balcony, and when I said to him, 'Watch out, I wouldn't want you to fall,' he answered, 'I don't care.'"

Marie didn't immediately take seriously her friend's concerns ("You know how shrinks are—they read into everything"). But when Christopher's teacher also commented about his negativity at school, Marie realized that she had been too preoccupied in her own drama to see her son clearly. She and her husband had recently separated. Obviously, their split had taken a greater toll on Christopher than she had realized. "It killed me to think that he was sad," she admitted, but she realized that she had to use her friend's insight to help him adjust to their new family arrangement. Dealing with Christopher's feelings—and her own—allowed her to strengthen their connection and keep him from spinning away from her.

Turning to others for information is especially important as your kids approach the tweens and teens. A 2004 study found that parents who turned to neighbors, parents of peers, siblings, or relatives were, "on the whole, more knowledgeable of their adolescents' whereabouts, associates, and activities."

Sometimes, the best intel about someone comes from the person himself. "Amy's parents never argued in front of her as a child," says Greg Perlman of his wife, "so she assumed that parents don't argue. My parents didn't hesitate to have a disagreement in front of me or to show their emotions. In the early years of our marriage, when I expressed negative feelings, she always thought I was upset with her, but I was just angry at the situation." In Amy's head, any emotions were "bad" or "scary."

Because Amy listened and was willing to consider someone else's perception—in this case, her husband's—she finally got that it wasn't about her. Greg airs feelings easily and often; it is who he is. Now when Greg holds forth about an annoying parent at Sadie's school or any other unpleasant encounter in his day, Amy is less likely to take his rants personally.

6. Do you take advantage of "oboe" moments, everyday interactions that feed the relationship? Conversation and shared moments fuel connection. Sometimes parents scrimp and save for a family vacation, imagining it as a time for everyone to be together and reconnect. That's one plan—vacations can be good for a family, if you can afford them. But vacations are not enough to continually refuel family relationships. You have to infuse *daily life* with mutually enjoyable everyday moments in which you consciously connect. Dad and son cook dinner. Mother is the soccer coach for her son's team.

Also, find ways to spice up the endless daily schlepping by making the journey itself a valued part of the event. The Sargent-Kleins dubbed these times "oboe moments," a term they coined when David was no longer practicing or looking forward to lessons. "We knew he was over it, but we didn't push him to quit, because when we drove him there, that's when he'd open up to us. We didn't want the oboe moments to end!"

Unfortunately, adults are often better at taking advantage of oboe moments with their children than with each other and have to work harder to make them happen. Lanie and Bill Allen, parents of four, consciously carve out "mini pockets of time" from their busy days. There's no expectation of having a heartfelt talk or working out a problem. The goal is to be together and reenergize the connection, and everything else emanates from that. "We latch onto simple things," says Bill. "We stay up a little later, have a beer on the front porch, and talk about the day. We'll go to the store together. Last night, we went for a run. You get out of a relationship what you put into it."

7. Do you review and revise? Because relationships are always in flux, we have to continually gather good intel, especially when a family member surprises us. For example, your partner is grumpier than usual. He yells at you for forgetting to have the car washed. He talks about quitting his teaching job and going back to the motorcycle shop where he worked ten years ago. Don't just dismiss it as "crazy talk." Instead, wonder what else is going on and what's happening in his life. Ask him about it. Whatever it is will affect you and the rest of the family.

Or perhaps your nine-year-old has suddenly become secretive, spending more time in her room. She seems moody and says no to everything. Is she dealing with an issue from the past, a new challenge in her present, a concern about her future? Did something happen to her recently? Have you ever been here before? Might something *you* did have contributed to what's going on? Is there anything outside your relationship that has affected her? Has the pressure ratcheted up at school or in one of her other activities?

Sometimes these shifts are the result of a developmental change. Your son wants to ride his bike to town without you. Inside your head, a voice shouts, "No!" The idea scares you. You long for that sweet little boy who once loved to curl up in your lap. But there you are, confronted by a middle-school boy who can multiply fractions and already beats you in tennis and chess. Accepting who he is now will better your relationship. Decide whether and how far you let him ride based on how responsible he's been in the past and what he's now capable of doing, not your fear or longing.

As we stress in chapter 9, trying *not* to notice change gets you nowhere and, worse, can lead to more serious problems. Let's say your dad has been forgetting things lately. Tune in; watch what's happening; listen carefully. Perhaps he just has a lot on his mind these days, or perhaps he needs help. You may not have expected to shift seats at the generational table quite so soon, but what is *is*. If you recognize change and are willing to accept what comes with it, it is always better for your relationship—and for your family.

8. Do you more often turn toward than away from? One afternoon, when her son came to her proudly showing off a picture he had drawn, Callie was trying desperately to catch up on her email. She barely looked away from her laptop and said in a flat, almost robotic voice, "Oh, that's great, Juan." But Juan knew better. "You didn't even look at it, Mom!" he shouted, and stormed out of the room.

You've been there; we all have. In the hubbub of everyday life, we inadvertently fail to "show up" for the people we love. You barely manage to eke out a hello when your partner comes home from work. You're distracted by the toddler on your lap who's spilling salt all over the counter and the five-year-old next to him who's working on his "This is me" collage, which is due tomorrow. Your mother phones, and you're filling out invoices. You act as if you're listening until you hear, "Hello, are you still there?" coming out of the receiver. And of course, you're not.

We all do several things at once; it's how we get through the day—or so we think. A Stanford University study found that "people who are regularly bombarded with several streams of electronic information do not pay attention, control their memory or switch from one job to another as well as those who prefer to complete one task at a time." Even more important, this "turning away," as renowned researcher John Gottman calls it, doesn't bode well for the health of a relationship.

But what can you do instead? In the moment, when one of your significant others—child or adult—makes a bid for your attention, literally turn your head toward him. And if your children barely look up when you or your partner enter—a reality in many homes—call them on it. Make them turn off the TV or power down the iPad or the Game Boy. Even homework can wait.

The payoff is huge. That momentary connection in which you listen and respond might take just a few seconds or a whole minute, but it makes all the difference in your relationships. Gottman found that four out of five couples who are still married six years after their wedding have an 86 percent "turning toward" rate—that is, most of the time, when their partner asks for a moment of their attention, they look up, make eye contact, and listen. With children especially—but with adults, too—paying attention and being responsive tell them you care. And if you weigh the two options—clearing out your in-box versus letting a loved one know that she matters—it's no contest.

Be proactive; try to cut down on potential interruptions, too. The Green family, among other close-knit clans, has rules around their devices. No sending or checking messages once you walk through the door. No calls in the car unless you're alone (and then only on a headset, of course). No answering the house phone during meals. Even if one of them slips up occasionally, the family at least has its priorities straight.

9. Do you know who gives you what? Every relationship has benefits and burdens. None gives you everything. You learn something different; you reap different rewards. Your relationship with your eight-year-old child, for example, might keep you young and make you notice the world in a different way. In addition, she might have incredible talents that thrill you, such as a beautiful singing voice, or perhaps she's extremely compassionate and her presence soothes you. Still, she would *not* be the person to lean on if you were worried about a health issue or to confide in if your marriage was in trouble.

Likewise, even if your ex-partner is a great listener most of the time, he may not be the "right" adult to turn to when it comes to certain issues. Imagine that your teenage son says something hurtful, and it isn't the first time. His father would be the logical person to talk to—he loves the boy, too. But whether you seek your ex's advice should also depend on what you've gotten from him in the past. If he is unfailingly supportive and empathetic, a real rock in these kinds of situations, it makes sense to engage him in discussion. But if he *over*identifies with your son's behavior— maybe it reminds him of himself as a boy—he might take your criticism personally. Even worse, if in the past he has dismissed your feelings, accused you of being "too sensitive" or "melodramatic" or "controlling," talking to him about your concerns would be, as Tracy loved to say, "like shopping for oranges in the hardware store."

FYN What's Given and Gotten?

Look at each of your significant relationships in depth to see what you get and what you give. Especially if you're having any kind of conflict, your answers might help you see what needs to change.

- *Identity.* Who do I become with her? Who does she become with me? What kinds of traits, values, desires, and attitudes does this relationship bring out in me? What does it bring out in her? What do we "co-create"?

- *Self-reflection.* What does seeing myself in his eyes make me feel? What kind of mirror am I for him?

- *Learning.* What information/knowledge/skills does this relationship give me? What do I give her?

- *Novelty.* Does he lead me to new experiences? In this relationship, do I try to be my most curious, expansive self?

- *Emotional sustenance.* Do I feel supported? Do I give my support? Am I heard? Do I listen?

10. Do you ask yourself, in the midst of a potentially tense talk, "How do I want this discussion to end?" This question is the Big Kahuna of everyday exchanges in the family. The key to positive engagement is to put your best self forward. Every moment that you reach inside yourself for a responsible, empathetic, authentic, and loving response—a REAL response—you increase the likelihood of bettering the relationship. It's not easy, especially when an angry barb is hurled in your direction. Verbal attacks activate the same part of your brain that processes physical assaults. When you say, "That really hurt me," you're not exaggerating. Also, being on the end of a caustic comment sets in motion a chain reaction. You feel vulnerable, which makes you anxious. You then become clingy or controlling, or you look for the door. But by being mindful even at these difficult moments—asking yourself, *Where do I want this to end?*—you can stop or at least slow the downward spiral.

It becomes easier with practice. The more you can remind yourself that your goal is to strengthen the relationship, the more you will be able to act in ways that do. For example, your partner calls you at the office to tell you he cleaned the gerbil cage, a job that usually falls in your lap. He tells you he knows how much you hate doing it. Do you take what he says at face value and assume the best? Or do you wonder about an ulterior motive? He must have done something else he knows you won't like, or he's buttering you up to ask for something in return. Do you assume you're right? Do you get annoyed because he's looking for a compliment? A not-very-loving response flies through your mind: *I never brag about cleaning the damn cage. What does he want, a medal?* Have you been here before and blurted out such uncharitable thoughts?

How you engage will depend, in part, on what kind of day you've had, the nature of your relationship until now, and the degree to which your expectations are in sync with reality. But:

No matter what bears down on that moment, you always have a choice.

You can fight, or you can get off the phone with a friendly "See you in a bit." That simple act of grace can give you time to pause and ask yourself, *How do I want this to end?* Chances are, you will then see the bigger picture. Cage cleaning is one fewer thing on your nightly to-do list. What's the big deal if he bragged about it? The important part is that he *heard* you. He also gave you a gift: extra time. When you walk through the door, instead of attacking, you lovingly throw your arms around him and say, "Thanks, honey, that was so sweet!" He beams with pride, and you both bathe in the good feelings of this particular reunion. This is not about backing down or swallowing your feelings. It's about taking the high road and making choices that, ultimately, not only better the relationship but make you feel better about yourself.

Telling Yourself the Truth

As we said at the outset of this chapter, relationships are everything. You do best in a relationship—any relationship—when you right-size your expectations and when you commit to hanging in instead of heading for the door. It helps to review the connection questions from time to time, but the real secret of relationship success is to tell yourself the truth.

> ### At-a-Glance: The Tell Yourself the Truth (TYTT) Mantra
>
> *Look around you.* Gather evidence. *Tell yourself the truth.* Admit what *is.* *Take an action.* Do or say something that is true to yourself and to your values and that betters the relationship and/or the situation. If it doesn't work, go back to the first step, start again—and this time do something else!

Here's how it works. You're tooling through life on automatic pilot, and you're brought up short by a decision, a question, or an action—your own or another family member's—that forces you to say to yourself, *Whoa! This is not what I expected. This is not right. This is not comfortable. I have to think about what this means.* Such *Whoa!* moments can take you by surprise—a telephone call with bad news, a statement or action by a loved one that brings up strong feelings in you. They can also happen when an idea or feeling that's been lingering on the edges of your consciousness is suddenly impossible to ignore. They can happen when you have to reckon with a family member's change or demand. You might be able to tamp down your feelings or shut out the other person (for a while). Or your emotions might overcome you. You might explode or punish—order your child to her room, give your partner the silent treatment, slam the phone on a parent or sibling. None of these alternatives is likely to better the relationship.

When *Whoa!* moments happen, the better choice is to distance yourself from the action for a few moments so that you can evaluate your own reaction and consciously decide how to handle what's facing you. However, you only can choose how you want to respond *if* you tell yourself the truth.

The Tell Yourself the Truth (TYTT) mantra has three steps.

1. *Look around you.* Put yourself outside of the action as a neutral observer. What, exactly, is happening? What do you see? What do you hear? What led up to this moment? Gather evidence about each of you, so that you can act on what *is*. What were you each doing right before this interaction? Are other family members involved, if only indirectly? If a decision is looming large in your thoughts, is it really a matter of life or death—or does it just feel that way?

2. *Tell yourself the truth.* Admit what *is*. Has a new element been introduced that you haven't factored in—a developmental change, other people, other influences, the context? Is the situation really new, or does this moment have a we've-been-here-before feeling? Might you have seen it coming if you let yourself? Could you have planned better? Don't focus on what you feel as much as why you feel it. Are you telling yourself everything—your motivation, what you've contributed to the situation, what it really means to you, and whether you have any control over it?

3. *Take an action.* Do something. It might mean starting or ending, changing direction or doing it differently, getting more involved or letting go. The goal is to figure out how to best cope with this particular reality and to make a conscious choice. Do or say something that is true to yourself and respects what you can give in the moment, but put the *relationship* first. If you make a wrong move or a bad decision, you can always make another choice later, but at least now you're getting past "stuck," which is a bad and isolating place to be.

This might sound like a superhuman undertaking. But in the heat of the moment, the TYTT mantra inspires what Nobel Prize–winning psychologist Daniel Kahneman calls "slow thinking." Our brains have two systems that guide our actions and reactions. The system responsible for "fast thinking," Kahneman explains, "operates automatically and quickly, with little or no effort and no sense of voluntary control." In contrast, "System 2" is the part of our brain that accesses our wiser self. It involves taking deliberate actions, making choices, and concentrating.

Although the TYTT mantra has never been put to a scientific test, its effectiveness is confirmed by the work of psychologist James Pennebaker, a researcher who studies how people process and deal with "negative events," everything from minor scuffles to serious trauma. Stress takes a terrible toll on our bodies, our immune systems, and our satisfaction with life in general. Pennebaker found that stepping back is a more effective strategy for dealing with stress than mindlessly repeating the story or, worse, wallowing around in the feelings ("immersion"). When you relive bad times, it's easy to get stuck in a cycle of rumination. You go over and over the unpleasantness, feeling the same old feelings, which doesn't help you learn anything about yourself or the other person. But if you step back and use your energy and consciousness to figure out *why*, it ultimately helps you get *through* it. Pennebaker uses a writing exercise to help people gain distance from the event and then try to see it more clearly as a neutral observer. The same principles are at work with the TYTT mantra.

It isn't always easy to catch ourselves in the moment and change course. Even people who have been in therapy or have taken parenting or marital enrichment courses have a hard time calming down during a fight. Whether you feel like you're on the receiving end or are about to lash out yourself, it's *not* a good time to engage. Be savvy and brave enough to call a time-out.

Tell the other person—adult or child—that you need time to compose yourself, but make it clear that you're not running away. You just want to give yourself a chance to cool down and gather your thoughts. Before you even attempt to run through the TYTT mantra, go to Plan D, distraction. Pick up a book, or watch something funny on TV. If you make a phone call to a supportive friend, use the time as a reality check, not to vent or get your buddy to take your side. When you've calmed down, start Step 1.

It's best, of course, to tell yourself the truth before a serious *Whoa!* moment occurs. It's far easier to look at and review your relationships when you don't feel backed up against the wall and when tempers aren't flying. If you practice telling yourself the truth on a regular basis and in everyday interactions, it will strengthen your better self, and it will become easier to make conscious choices that feed the relationship even when things get out of hand.

Harriet and Gretchen: A Relationship in Trouble

At a holiday party, the adults are gathered in the living room, talking, drinking, eating. A few toddlers are underfoot, but most of the older kids are playing in the basement. On the couch sits Harriet with her nine-year-old daughter, who won't leave her side. It's clear from the look on her face that Harriet is a little embarrassed. She wants Gretchen to be like the other kids, not stand out so much. She believes her daughter's antisocial behavior reflects badly on both of them.

She also identifies with Gretchen. Harriet was an unpopular kid in junior and senior high, a band geek and a science nerd when neither was considered cool. She was the last to get picked for teams, the last to get her period. In tenth grade, her so-called best friend was repeatedly mean to her. Looking at Harriet today, you'd have trouble picturing her in thick glasses and sensible shoes and skirts that never sat right on her skinny body. She now wears contacts, sculpts her body in Pilates, and is a much-heralded scientist at a biotech firm. It's hard to imagine her as unpopular. She has a circle of good friends and a very happy life as a single mother, but that shunned teenage self is still part of her identity. In the dark of night, she often ruminates, *God! Please don't let Gretchen suffer the way I did.*

Now, sitting next to Gretchen at the party, Harriet tries to cajole the reluctant nine-year-old, using a phony, saccharine, singsong, inauthentic voice: "Honey, don't you want to join the other kids? You know how you love to play Ping-Pong. I think there's a table down there."

Her daughter shakes her head and grabs her arm. "I want *you* to come."

"Gretchen, stop it. You're too big for this," Harriet says through clenched teeth. She pries Gretchen's fingers, gets up, and says, "I can't. I have to go to the bathroom." Gretchen starts to follow. To distract her, Harriet hands her an empty wineglass. "Be a good girl, and while I'm gone, get me a refill, OK?"

Harriet's not a bad mother. But her expectations are clearly out of whack. Gretchen has never been an outgoing child. At this moment, Harriet is tense, worried, and overidentified with her daughter. She does not *intend* to hurt Gretchen. All the same, she's trying to turn Gretchen into someone she's not. Not surprisingly, Harriet's mother did the same thing to her. Whenever Harriet came home crying over the indignities she suffered at school, her mother told her not to be such a crybaby. Harriet is not aware of her past at this moment. All she knows is that she's worried, uncomfortable, and angry—and worst of all, she fears she has no solution. None of this bodes well for her relationship with Gretchen.

Using TYTT to Get Unstuck

When Harriet is alone that night, an entire tape of *Whoa!* moments replays in her head: *Gretchen's behavior is getting worse. What if she gets teased? Maybe I should consider therapy or drugs. I've been drinking more lately. I feel like life is spinning out of control. I'm becoming my mother.* Harriet is stuck. Her behavior is the very definition of insanity: She keeps doing what she's always done and keeps getting what she's always gotten—anxiety. Meanwhile, none of it is changing Gretchen, and all of it is damaging their relationship.

Harriet is mired in her disappointment and embarrassment. That prevents her from seeing Gretchen clearly and adjusting her expectations. She may not realize it, but instead of bettering the situation, she's using her energy to control Gretchen. She is overinvested and engages with her daughter in negative ways—not accepting the child she has, at times even pushing her away.

Suppose we rewind the camera and replay this scene in slow motion, so that Harriet can see what's really happening. Only by stepping back and distancing herself from the problem will Harriet be able to bring her full awareness to the situation. If she puts herself outside the action, instead of panicking or continually wishing Gretchen was different, she will see who Gretchen is and what's happening to their relationship. Even better, she might then be brave enough to do something that will strengthen the bond with her daughter.

To get unstuck, Harriet needs to look around at what's happening when she and Gretchen interact, to tell herself the truth, and then to take an action. In this case, that means figuring out how to do it better next time. That's the trickiest part. But by seeing her relationship with Gretchen for what it really is, she is more likely to realize that she has options, choices that will strengthen rather than strain their connection. Imagine that we can listen in as Harriet works through the steps of TYTT.

What Harriet saw when she put herself back at the scene of the holiday party and looked around. "We are at the party. Gretchen didn't want to come in the first place, but I didn't want to bother with a sitter, and she's too young to be left alone. I made a mistake in bringing her. She doesn't know any of the kids here. She's miserable, and she's making me miserable. I have also been under a lot of stress at work, since they hired that new director, and that has made me grumpier than usual." Harriet has to look at that reality and ask herself a series of questions that will help her see the situation more clearly:

What does this tell me about Gretchen?

What does this tell me about me?

Did I try to manipulate?

Was I being responsible, authentic, and empathetic? Did I lead with love?

Am I factoring in any recent changes in my life or hers?

What Harriet realized when she told herself the truth. "Gretchen has *always* been slow to warm up to new social situations. She was the toddler who didn't get off my lap in play group, the preschooler who was the last to let her mommy leave the room. It is unreasonable for me to expect her, at nine, now to be a social butterfly. At the party, Gretchen was just being herself, and I kept pushing her away. The truth is, I'm at the end of my tether—so many problems at work. I wanted to be at that party on my own, without having to worry about Gretchen fitting in or entertaining herself. That makes me feel like a horrible person. Making matters worse, I am often totally fake with her. I talk down to her. I am embarrassed when she hangs on me. I am afraid of what the other parents will think of me. I am doing to her what my own mother did to me. I'm afraid Gretchen feels I don't love her. Maybe she even understands what's going on."

What Harriet can do better next time. First, she can acknowledge why Gretchen's behavior threatens her by asking herself:

How does this remind me of the past or my past?

Is this due to something happening in the present?

Does it make me anxious when I contemplate our future?

Instead of trying to change Gretchen, Harriet can offer constructive advice that allows her daughter to be herself. She might even talk about how hard it was for her as a child. Children love to hear their parents' stories; it helps them see Mom and Dad as real people. The *process* of parents and grandparents sharing family lore, notes psychologist Marshall P. Duke, helps children "grow stronger and healthier."

Now, knowing what she knows, Harriet will also prepare differently next time, making Gretchen part of the process. Instead of focusing on somehow making Gretchen behave differently, she can use her energy to recruit Gretchen as a partner in the planning: "We're going to Dale's christening tomorrow, and there will be a lot of people there. I'm looking forward to going—there will be cousins I haven't seen in a while. I know big parties are sometimes hard for you, so let's think of ways that might make it easier, so we can both have a good time."

If Gretchen says, "I don't want to go," Harriet has choices: Get a baby-sitter, or tell Gretchen that's not an option. If the latter, she might suggest that Gretchen bring a book or a game and help her make a contingency plan: "If the other kids are doing something you don't want to do, you can play by yourself."

Harriet can also lay down ground rules *before* they get to the christening. It's Gretchen's job to amuse herself, not Harriet's. It's not OK for her to whine or complain. If Gretchen is more comfortable talking to adults, that's fine, as long as she doesn't interrupt or dominate the conversation. If, at the party, Gretchen launches into the old dance, Harriet can at the very least change her own steps. She might say, in an *authentic* voice, "Gretchen, we talked about this. You can either listen quietly to my conversation with Christine or read your book."

Finding the sweet spot can be tricky in any type of relationship, and it's a common struggle for all parents. But it's also a way to alleviate the stress. Harriet must right-size her expectations. Her daughter, at nine, is a not-very-sociable child. With help, she can learn to navigate social gatherings better as she gets older, but there are no guarantees; unfamiliar situations might never be easy for her. Harriet needs to teach and guide and then step back. If things don't go as planned, she has to encourage Gretchen to get up, dust herself off, and try something different the next time. Harriet then has to keep reminding herself, *I cannot determine or foresee Gretchen's destiny.*

When you use TYTT to "deconstruct" a parent-child relationship, do it alone, as Harriet did, or, run through it with an adult partner. If your *Whoa!* moment happens *with* a partner, though, it might not be easy to do it together. But you can at least run through it on your own. For example, Marla gives special occasions a lot of thought. She loves to make surprise parties and to shop for the perfect gift. Larry, on the other hand, rarely remembers her birthday, and when he does, he's apt to say, "Honey, go out and buy yourself something wonderful. I'll pay for it." It drives Marla crazy. Feeling wounded and disappointed, she rants about Larry's "lack of attention" and "thoughtlessness." And they're off and running.

They might as well play a tape of these old arguments—only the details would be different. She rages, and he backs away, angry and confused. "I don't get it. Here I am, offering you anything you want," he counters, "and you get mad because I didn't bring something home for you. What am I, a mind reader?"

If Marla manages to restrain herself and, instead of launching into a tirade, pauses and tells herself the truth, it will change everything. Larry has always been "a lousy gift giver," and neither her hints nor her haranguing have made a difference in the ten years they've been together. She might *want* Larry to put in the kind of effort *she* puts in, but it's not going to happen. He is who he is. In any partnership, each person can contribute only what he or she is capable of giving. The two aren't clones of each other.

So how does Marla move on? She starts by accepting her husband, warts and all. In the mental ledger she keeps, she has a long list of what he *doesn't* do. Now she has to make a list of all that she's grateful for, such as his unending generosity and kindness or that he's usually solidly in her corner. She needs to understand that her expectations are influenced by her past. Growing up, her salesman father brought her gifts to compensate for his long absences from home. To her, "presents" have always symbolized "presence." To move on, she has to see her situation through grown-up eyes. If Marla then shares her new insights with Larry, choosing a time when they're both calm and also listening to *his* truth, it's bound to strengthen their connection.

When you do TYTT, remember that you're not looking for agreement; you're striving for awareness and for ways to improve the relationship. It isn't always pleasant to tell yourself the truth. You might become aware of your powerlessness in a particular situation. You might have to accept that although you are willing to put in time and thought, the issue isn't yours to solve or change. Still, it's what you have to work with. As the Buddhists say, don't argue with reality.

FYN Try a Test Run of TYTT.

Apply the "Tell Yourself the Truth" mantra to a recent incident in your household that involved a family member. Use the directions on page 88 to guide you through each step. Write down what you learned. You can probably now answer these questions:

- What does this tell me about the other person?
- What does this tell me about me?
- Did I try to manipulate?
- Was I being responsible, authentic, and empathetic? Did I lead with love?
- Did I factor in any recent changes in my life or his/hers?
- Did this incident in some way threaten me, remind me of my past, bring up a fear I have about the present, or make me anxious about the future?

Notes on Improving Relationships

FIVE

ADULT FAMILY TIES

By Choice and by Chance

Stop fighting with your family members, spouse, or friends. . . .
Enjoy each other. Stop looking at the other's faults. Start to appreciate
each other's qualities. Life is short. . . . When the person goes, you
can appreciate the quality of life that you had together, instead of
regretting that you wasted time, that you could have done better. That
will give you comfort. It will help you to overcome loss and sadness.

—GELEK RIMPOCHE, IN *TRICYCLE*

Picture the grown-ups at your last big family dinner (a holiday, a special occasion, or a milestone). Opposite you, maybe at the head, is your partner—the one relationship you actually choose. Around the table is an assortment of other adults, younger and older than you. Some have been around forever, assigned to you by chance—the parents who conceived or adopted you, the siblings who came before and after you. Others are part of an entire constellation of people you inherited when you picked a mate—his or her parents and siblings, your in-laws.

Your partner, if you have one, is your most important significant other, your co-director. If you have a good relationship, it bodes well for your whole family. Reading this book with him or her, for example, is like dieting at the same time or training for a marathon. Having a joint vision and a mutual commitment, and trying new strategies together, increases your likelihood of making changes that benefit all of you.

Viewed through the lens of family, though, your partner isn't the only influential adult character at your holiday table. Your parents, siblings, and in-laws are your *other* significant others. You might not think about them that way, because they're the peripheral players. But they are part of your past, and they shape your present. As grandparents, aunts, and uncles, they give your kids a more expansive picture of family and (in varying degrees) are a potential source of love and inspiration for all of you. When these bonds are strong and mutually supportive, all three generations benefit.

In this chapter, we deal with close adult family ties, by choice and by chance. Each of these relationships requires careful tending. We open with suggestions for keeping on track with your chosen one, as a couple and as parents.* In the latter part of the chapter, we offer strategies for nurturing (or repairing) your other significant others.

Your Partnership: Coordinating Your Is

The ideal couple, if one were to exist, would never argue over housework. They would always strike a perfect balance between taking care of their individual selves and supporting each other. They would happily last until death do they part.

Of course, no such couple exists!

Some come close—they are balanced most of the time. We think of them as "coordinated." Each party is mature and independent, has good coping and communication skills and a strong sense of identity—a solid I. At the same time, the two are also *inter*dependent. They love and respect each other and have similar values. They know it's important to stay in touch with each other, to stay interested, and to surprise each other at times. They make decisions together, with both their needs in mind. They sometimes argue, but they know how to handle conflict and rarely forget what brought them together in the first place. On par, they say more nice things to each other than not-so-nice.

They're a minority. Marriage researcher John Gottman dubbed only 17 percent of the couples he studied as "masters." They experience better "outcomes" in life, Gottman's and others' research suggests, than couples who can't maintain that delicate balance between I and **We**. As individuals, these master partners tend to live happy, fulfilling, emotionally stable, and socially enriched lives. They are typically in sync as parents, too, making it more likely that their children will also live happy, productive, and engaged lives.

---

*If you have an ex-partner in your life, many of these suggestions apply equally to your situation. If you're a single parent, read the couples sections anyway to review past relationships, arm yourself with information, and plan for the future, especially if you're contemplating remarriage.

No couple is coordinated all the time, and none is perfect. Even Gott-man's master couples fail to resolve 69 percent of their arguments. Why is it hard?

- We're human; one partner's needs invariably go against the other's.
- Living together is challenging, especially with kids, a well-documented source of stress. Having a family means taking on a ton of responsibility, being confronted daily by a multitude of choices, and having to make decisions together.
- Modern life is like Russian roulette. You never know. . . . At any moment, a change of circumstance can upset the balance (more on change in chapter 9).
- Most of us are at least a tiny bit scared of intimacy. Committing to another person is like closing your eyes, falling backward, and believing that your partner will actually catch you. To allow ourselves to trust completely feels like a risk. It taps into our "lizard" brain, the part that's as old as the first humans, the part that interprets primitive feelings, such as fear, as a threat. Although we've evolved since then, our automatic reaction to a threat is similar to our ancestors' when facing a tiger: fight or flee.

Even couples who stay together for decades have moments when one becomes skittish or strikes back. At those times, they are less coordinated, tipping either toward coexistence (being together but unconnected) or contentiousness (fighting).

In varying degrees of *coexistence,* one or both partners avoid intimacy. All's quiet on the home front, but the Is aren't connecting. They get along, are decent to each other, and take care of things that need to get done. But there's an underlying distance between them. Their boats (see page 51) may be on the same river but not necessarily heading in the same direction. Some couples in a state of coexistence focus more on the kids than on each other. Their decisions "kind of happen," as one couple put it. Or one partner mostly calls the shots, and the other is happy not to be in charge. From the outside, partners who linger at this pole might seem like a happy couple. But if you look more deeply, their relationship—the entity that the two of them have co-created—is languishing for lack of interest and enthusiasm.

In varying degrees of *contentiousness,* one or both partners become anxious about intimacy. The Is are at odds. They might hassle each other, snipe, make unkind remarks, all of which are symptoms of a troubled relationship. When one accuses, "You don't love me," the other withdraws or strikes back. Either way, the unspoken message is "Get outta my face!" Couples who linger at the contentious pole often have difficulties reaching a consensus or even agreeing to disagree. At the extreme, decision making is difficult; or, one might bully the other into compliance.

Neither coexistence nor contentiousness should serve as a steady diet. Of the two possibilities, constant sniping is obviously more damaging to a relationship and more harmful to children. But if you stay too long at one pole or the other, you risk getting stuck there. You disconnect and become distant, or you become polarized and petulant. Either way, your Is are not in sync, and you become increasingly less invested in supporting each other.

Righting the Balance

If you recognize your own couple dynamics in the above descriptions, it could mean that your marital scale has tipped a little—or a lot. Don't panic. It doesn't mean you have a bad or hopeless relationship. Almost all couples go through rough spots and dry periods, leaning in one direction or the other at times.

The challenge is to pay attention when you feel your relationship sliding toward either pole and to right the balance.

Coexistence. You'll know you're coexisting if you're humming along as a twosome but really doing mostly your own thing. You are more like roommates than romantic partners. Tipping in this direction is often so subtle and quiet it's sometimes hard to notice. Your I is taking what it needs, and there's not a lot of negativity, but you might feel lonely or disconnected. In the back of your mind, something doesn't feel quite right. Maybe you're tired of being the only one who [cooks, remembers to buy toilet paper, takes the kids to the doctor], but you don't want to upset the status quo. You might not listen all that intently when your partner talks. You might become increasingly disengaged. You make time for the kids and do activities on your own, but you don't seek out opportunities to be together.

Tracy observed that partners can drift toward coexistence within months after their first child arrives: "Mum is more tied to the house once the baby arrives, and Dad starts staying later at the office or going out more with his friends." Some women are initially happy with this arrangement, especially if family and friends take up the slack or they have paid help. But as time goes on, many begin to feel like this mother of a newborn and a four-year-old: "I'm not far from giving up and just doing it all myself, to be honest, because it's just easier, and then there's less conflict in our family and day-to-day lives." If she truly gives up, there's a good chance that she and her husband might get stuck in coexistence.

Contentiousness. It's a lot harder to ignore contentiousness. Even if you try to gloss over relationship issues, an event or an awareness eventually shakes you up. You experience a *Whoa!* moment that forces you to face that something needs to be acknowledged. It's time to tell yourself the truth.

Daria Wilkerson wasn't initially alarmed by the disappointment she felt when her husband, Conrad, failed to meet her expectations or by their arguments. It was her increasingly fragile state of mind that prompted her *Whoa!* moment. "I became quite depressed," she recalls. "I knew I really needed to make changes in my perception of things."

Daria, age thirty-six and the mother of three-year-old Isaac, has been married to Conrad for nearly ten years. Early on, she and Conrad locked horns over differences. She likes her home to be tidy; he can let dishes pile up in the sink. She makes decisions easily—if she tries on a piece of clothing she likes, she buys it immediately—whereas he'll go back to the store several times before making a purchase. "It used to drive me crazy," Daria admits.

"Whenever I asked Con to do something and he didn't do it or didn't remember to do it," Daria recalls, "my immediate reaction was to think he didn't care or that he was being disrespectful. My default reaction a lot of the time was anger." Their relationship began to slip toward the contentious pole.

Making matters worse, the family lives on a small island in the Mediterranean, far from Daria's native England. They have a handful of friends, but it's mostly just the three of them. He works outside the home; she holds down the home front. Neither of them gets much alone time. That's a lot of pressure on a marriage.

At first, Daria did what many women do: judge, complain, criticize, yell, harp, and—most futile of all—try to change the other person. The fantasy is that one day, she will get through to him. He'll do it her way, and they'll get along better. The reality is that when a partner's **I** is confronted in this way, arguments not only get worse, but they become chronic. He retreats, and she takes it personally.

Fortunately, Daria realized that the anger was not only poisoning her, it was also driving a wedge between them. There wasn't much she could do about the fact that Conrad was at work all day—he really *couldn't* be more available to care for Isaac and their home. But she *could* assess her own part in the drama and at least change her script. Willingness, reading self-help books, and talking to a good therapist helped ease Daria's depression. From this more positive vantage point, she then began to see Conrad's **I** in a different light. She discovered that she didn't have to attack him. Instead, she could step back and self-reflect. She now knows that Conrad doesn't intentionally ignore her.

"I still have to ask him several times, because that's Con. It's not in his consciousness. Eventually, he'll get around to it. I'm very much a do-it-now kind of person, but I can't expect him to be me. I need to make room for both of us. He needs time to mull things over, whether it's buying a pair of shoes or making a big decision. It is futile for me to get angry. That's the way he does things. And I just have to keep that in mind."

If Your Relationship Slips . . . and Stays There

Do you and your partner often drift toward coexistence or contentiousness? Do you stay there, or can you nudge yourselves back toward coordination? If not, you're probably waiting too long. Whenever you feel yourself slipping, *immediately* take steps to restore the balance. What to do depends, of course, on which pole you're headed toward.

If, as a rule, you lean more toward the coexisting pole, try to talk to each other about what's happening. Admit (if you feel this way) that you're afraid; your relationship seems to be slipping into complacency. There's no spark, no sense of togetherness. You're more like roommates. To make a change, admit to yourself and then to your partner that you feel lonely or disconnected. If you've hidden your concern or discontent for a while, you might need a showdown to shake up the status quo, an argument over something insignificant or a bigger issue that you've swept under the rug for too long that finally forces you to be authentic and discuss how each of

Couples: A Delicate Balance

Adult relationships are constantly in flux. It would be wonderful if all couples could be peacefully and happily balanced—coordinated—all the time, but that's not real life. Pay attention. Recognize the signs of tipping in one direction or the other, and take steps to right the balance when you do.

Coexisting	Coordinated	Contentious
At the Extreme. More I than We; a honeymoon-is-over aura taints the relationship. There's not much joy or passion between the couple. Decisions often made by default; much distancing; each pursues independent activities at the expense of the relationship; "fun" activities are for the kids.	**The ideal.** I and We are balanced; decisions made as a team; problems solved together; positive feelings outnumber negative feelings, at least 3 to 1. There's a lot of couple interaction and "memory-banking"; each party is good at seeing situations from the other's perspective.	**At the Extreme.** Is jockey for position and prominence—there's often a "winner" and a "loser"; a range of discord might span from everyday hassles to constant, bitter arguments. Either way, too much negativity eats away at the relationship; polarized and entrenched views make it hard to make decisions and solve problems. The worst environment for children.
What to do. Spend more one-on-one time; infuse the relationship with new ideas, new activities; teach each other and explore together; right-size the focus in your family—nurturing the partnership is as important as nurturing the children.	**What to do.** Cherish it. Be vigilant, and monitor changes in your selves and in your environment. Stay acquainted with each other; keep it fresh; remain interesting and interested.	**What to do.** Learn how to listen and talk to each other; find ways to be kinder and more respectful; question whether expectations for each other are unrealistic, which might cause disappointment and/or anger. If you've been here too long, you might need professional help.

you experiences the relationship. Being "in it" undoubtedly evokes different feelings for each of you.

Also look at your routine. Does it allow for couple time? If not, start figuring out ways of spending time with your partner. Remember what you were attracted to about him or her in the first place. Catch up; become more interested in each other's I. Surprise each other. Send the kids off to your parents for the weekend. Run or shop together, like Lanie and Bill (page 82).

If you're not spending time together or, worse, seem to be avoiding it, who are you with instead? There's nothing inherently wrong with having outside relationships and interests that don't involve your partner. But it's also important to continually infuse your partnership with new energy and ideas. For a relationship to grow, you need shared experiences—things you do and try *together*. If, instead, you put everything into the children or spend most of your time away from your partner—at work, in another social setting—or become involved in an emotional or actual affair, there's not much to draw from or build on.

Undertake a joint project. Try something neither of you has ever done before. Liz Weil, whose story we told in Chapter 4, found that training with her husband to swim across the icy waters of San Francisco Bay gave them a shared sense of adventure.

As she waited for Dan on their first day of practice, Liz writes, she "felt, for the first time in years, like I was on a date—a real date, with someone who might unnerve or surprise me, not out on a date night, the pale married person's substitute." Several months later, they made the swim from Alcatraz back to San Francisco. "We'd jumped into the Bay only seventy-five minutes earlier and traveled only the distance of a nice, modest walk. Yet we'd slipped out of our daily lives and taken a dip into the unknown. Together."

If you and your partner more frequently visit the contentious side, lower the volume, listen to each other, and see yourselves as advocates instead of adversaries. Learn how to talk respectfully. Consciously work on seeing situations through each other's eyes. And when things begin to spin out of control, stop the action and cool down until each of you can regain your composure.

For example, in the heat of an oft-recurring argument over yard work, one woman suggested that she and her husband "forget the last five minutes." Her partner agreed. They both managed to contain their angry feelings and resist having the last word or being "right." Later, they restarted the conversation with a new attitude, as if the negative discussion hadn't happened. It wasn't easy, but it was such a simple and loving idea—and it worked—that they've been using it ever since.

Cool-down strategies sidestep blame and short-circuit the kind of I said/you said arguments that tend to escalate. Liz Weil admits that she and Dan don't always have the kind of "skilled conversations" they learned in their marriage-betterment quest. "But ten minutes or an hour or a day after we'd start fighting, one of us would say something like 'C'mon, we need to do better than this,' and we'd work harder to abandon our entrenched posts and inhabit each other's views."

If you don't know where or how to start, enroll in a couples workshop where you can learn conflict-diffusing skills. If you've been here for a while, you also might need a referee, a professional who can help the two of you get back on track and will remind you that your skirmishes affect the whole family, not just your relationship.

Seeing a counselor for only six sessions did wonders for the Awads'. Salma was becoming increasingly resentful of her husband's work schedule after their second child was born—a critical time in many families, because responsibilities increase dramatically, more so in this case, because the baby had special needs. They sometimes fought and sometimes avoided each other. They had almost no couple time, and their connection weakened. Salma and Ari not only lacked communication skills, but they needed a new perspective on their relationship.

Months after we first met her, Salma wrote this email (abridged and lightly edited), sharing what she learned in therapy:

I think one of the best things I took away with me is the knowledge that everyone has a different truth, a different reality. Even a couple living the same experience together will have different views on the same shared experience. Another thing that really stayed with me is the idea of "sitting on the tree together." When we tell our partner what to do, it is like one partner is on a tree (in difficulty), and we are on the ground, shouting instructions through a megaphone. Which doesn't help, because what they actually need is for someone to climb on the tree and "rescue" them. But when we acknowledge the emotions and empathize with the other, then the problem-solving part of our brain engages. That's when we're sitting on the tree together. We give support instead of instructions.

Regardless of where you are in relation to the two poles, being conscious and conscientious will help. Visualize the space between you, and know that each of you fills it with different things. In Jack and Nina's

Marriage: The Journey

In the best marriages, partners try to maintain a good balance between supporting each other's **I** and maintaining a strong **We**. It takes love and work, as lawyer-author Jim Moret notes on his thirtieth anniversary:

How have we lasted for three decades? I adore her. Keri has always been supportive but, more importantly, she encouraged me to be my own person. Our marriage has been a partnership. We are friends, lovers and parents—together. But we also have our own jobs and our own friends. That conscious commitment to maintain our individuality has strengthened our bond as a couple.

The journey has not always been easy and it has not always gone the way either of us imagined it would. There was a time when our marriage itself was threatened. Midway through this journey we briefly separated. We both feared we might not last seventeen years, let alone thirty. But we came back together when it was toughest and persevered. In short, we fought for each other. I'm so grateful we did.*

* http://www.huffingtonpost.com/jim-moret/still-the -one-on-our-30th_b_1536867.html?ncid=wsc-huffpost -cards-image.

case, he complained that her constant instruction and advice made him feel inadequate. "But I was just trying to be helpful—or so I thought," says Nina. Their therapist gave Nina an assignment: "Instead of making comments when Jack talks, pay attention to *your* thoughts and reactions. Don't actually say anything, though; just listen."

A week later, Nina realized how often she wanted to micromanage her husband. She could see how it might make Jack feel. "But there's one problem," she added. "Now that *I'm* not talking, nothing's happening in the relationship. Jack isn't talking."

"You can't expect Jack to be you," the therapist responded. "He's going to put into your relationship what *he* puts in, not what you put in."

The therapist helped Nina realize that she wanted advice and support *from* Jack. But instead of asking directly, she kept offering it *to* him, hoping that he'd learn from her example. The therapist helped Jack understand that Nina didn't think he was incompetent. She just wanted to be seen. Jack softened as he, for the first time in years, saw a more vulnerable side of Nina. She needed him. He was finally able to let down his guard. And for both of them, holding on to the image of a "space between" helped them remember that their relationship was an entity that they both had to care for and protect—in their own ways.

If your relationship is languishing or under siege, talk about it, and do something immediately. At least strive to stay open and engaged, to honor your **I** and to nurture your **We**. The important thing to remember is that you *can* come back from the abyss.

FYN Some Questions about Your "Coupleship"

Refer to the chart on page 103 to see where you are now and what you can do to keep your relationship coordinated most of the time. Then take out your family notebook to answer a few questions about what's happening. If the scale has swung too far toward coexistence or contentiousness or your partnership has stayed too long in either direction, ask yourself:

- What's making me unhappy—not enough time together, irritation at my partner, no sex, no time for myself, lack of passion, lack of privacy, or something else? Is my unhappiness causing me to shut down or run away? Am I frightened?
- Am I locked into a particular role—always the nag, the boss, the victim? Am I a "distancer" who avoids the hard stuff or a "pursuer" who's constantly asking for reassurance of love and loyalty?
- Do I feel as if I'm struggling to hold on to my **I**? Is my partner overbearing? Or, am I playing the martyr?
- Have I lost interest in **Us** as a couple? How much am I willing to work toward balancing our relationship? (It might help to look at why you chose this partner in the first place and what keeps you here now.)
- Am I seeking out other relationships instead of my partner?
- How long do I think it's safe for me—for **Us**—to stay in this unbalanced state?

Bringing Children into Your Partnership

Children add both joy and stress to the marital (or cohabitation) equation. Having a child means that you not only have a responsibility to each other, but you have to play both partner and parent, two major life roles that can conflict. Even as the children become less dependent in terms of physical care, they compete for time, energy, and attention. At worst, they distract and deplete you, and your partnership flounders. At best, you and your partner are mindful of the stress and coordinated most of the time. Your relationship acts like a family anchor and bodes well for your children's development.

Better partners make better parents. It's not a simple formula—many factors collide. But studies consistently suggest that adults who are attuned to each other are also more likely to be sensitive to their children's needs. In turn, the kids are less likely to be at risk and tend to function better.

What's Best for the Kids?

In order to tease apart which matters more, the partners' relationship or their parenting skills, a 2004 study looked at more than 1,300 families and assigned them to five types.

In *consistently supportive* families (14%), the parents have a good relationship *and* good parenting skills. Mom is sensitive to the kids' needs; Dad is involved, too.

In *consistently risky* families (16%), the partners rank low in both.

Consistently moderate families (43%) fall somewhere in between those two extremes.

However, in some families, relationship quality and parenting skills don't jive. They are either *good parenting/ poor marriage* families (20%) or *poor parenting/good marriage* families (7%). Comparing the two, the study concluded that it's best for kids when the two "subsystems" are strong. But if one has to be weak, the parent-child relationship is more important than the husband-wife bond. Other research suggests that it's also a matter of degree. Although having a loving, thoughtful, sensitive mother and father can compensate for a lukewarm marriage, good parenting is far less protective in households where the adults constantly attack each other or, worse, use the children as pawns.

You don't have to be a scientist to conclude that it's better for children to live in a household where parents care about them and get along well with each other. The good news is that in 57 percent of families, there is at least "moderate" consistency between the two. The adults are good parents, *and* they have a solid relationship.

What helps you get there?

Get REAL. Have a sense of responsibility to your children and to your family. Be empathetic; always strive to understand the other's perspective, not judge it. Be authentic and honest with each other and the kids. Always try to lead with love. Because you're human, though, you'll never be 100 percent successful.

Take care of your own Is and, at the same time, protect your adult relationship. Of the top ten practices culled from decades of research on what goes into good parenting, love and affection naturally rank number one. Perhaps more surprising, stress management—handling what's thrown at you—comes in second, and relationship skills are third. The best parents we've met are proactive on all fronts.

Commit to caring for your children together. The best parents see themselves as co-parents. They are in it together. Both are capable of and willing to provide tangible help (drive a kid to piano lessons, buy new sneakers), practical information/guidance (show how to ride a bike or use the microwave), emotional solace (comfort after a big disappointment or when a child is scared), and spiritual guidance (talk about what's important and what they believe in). No one keeps track of the time contributed, only that the child is cared for by both parents and that neither one is bound by gender stereotypes.

The Art of Co-Parenting

By "co-parenting," we don't mean to imply that you think or act the same way. You are, after all, two different people, and your family life is all the richer because of it. It doesn't matter if one of you expresses love by hugging and the other by taking your child to a ball game. Both of you bestow different gifts on your children, and one's contribution doesn't have to match the other's.

For example, as Isaac Wilkerson grows up, he might learn expedience from his mother and careful deliberation from his father. Daria's and Conrad's individual personalities and the way they approach life are different, but they also have values and goals in common: to guide and protect their son, to strengthen their own relationship, and to nurture their family. As the old saying goes, there are many roads to Rome.

Co-parenting also takes practice and know-how. Stephen Klein, whom you met in chapter 1, points out that the three months after their first child was born, he didn't share parenting equally, because his wife,

---

Ten Keys to Successful Co-Parenting

The following, originally conceived as guidelines for parenting in separate households, are equally applicable to any family.* In fact, current research indicates that co-parenting, regardless of living arrangements, is a protective factor for children. It's good for the couple, too, because responsibility is shared equitably.

1. *Heal yourself.* Handle what happens to you; get help if you can't.
2. *Act maturely.* Access the best in yourself; think before you act.
3. *Listen to your children.* Get their input; don't simply push *your* agenda.
4. *Respect each other as parents.* Focus on what each of you gives the kids.
5. *Divide parenting time.* It doesn't have to be equal, but both parents need to spend time.
6. *Accept each other's differences.* Your way is not better than your partner's—it's different.
7. *Communicate about (and with) the children.* Share information; help each other stay current.
8. *Step outside traditional gender roles.* Mom can coach baseball; Dad can apply nail polish.
9. *Anticipate and accept change.* Be vigilant and flexible; don't argue with reality.
10. *Know that co-parenting is forever.* You will both be parents 'til death do you part.

* From *Families Apart: Ten Keys to Successful Coparenting,* © 1994, Melinda Blau. All rights reserved.

Nancy, was home on maternity leave. "I had to work full-time, so we were like a traditional couple. During that time, whenever I took care of Ellie, I had to ask Nancy what to do and had to defer to her. Time with little ones matters. Being with them and getting to know them makes a difference. Once Nancy and I started job sharing, I then spent whole days with Ellie. So I understood her rhythms and knew what she needed. I didn't have to ask."

Whether or not co-parents live together, the same rules apply. As Melinda once wrote of "families apart" in which parents live in separate households, "Divorce ends a marriage. But it does not end a family." Whether you co-parent with your current partner under one roof or with another adult or a coalition of exes and new partners who live elsewhere, it requires maturity, awareness, and skills. Even if you're a single parent by choice who never had a parenting partner, most of the "keys" in the box on page 109 also apply to you. The only difference is that you don't have to coordinate your efforts with another adult.

Your Other Significant Others: For Better or for Worse

Usually, when you speak of your significant other, you mean your main squeeze, the one you've chosen to travel down the river with, ideally, each in a separate boat. With your children in tow, you make up a small flotilla. But there's a larger fleet of *other* significant others on that and more distant rivers with whom your boats converge: your parents, siblings, and in-laws. Regardless of how often you see them or how close you are, they are part of you. They affect who you are, how you function, and how your family fares. They are the adult characters in your life story, whom Robert Frost meant when he wrote:

> *Home is the place where, when you have to go there,*
> *They have to take you in.*

Your other significant others can provide caring, sharing, and support. When they welcome the man or woman you choose, it's better for your partnership, better for your children. When you're reeling from a recent family crisis—someone is ill or has gone through a bad breakup—having an array of concerned others softens the blow. Then again, extended-family members can also be a source of ongoing tension. On both sides, these re-lationships can be plagued by jealousy, old resentments, clashes over values and child-rearing practices, different agendas, and slights, real or imag-ined.

And here's the rub: Whereas you don't have to continue working with an overbearing boss or play tennis with a sore loser, it's a lot harder—and potentially problematic—to walk away from a parent, a sibling, or an in-law. Even though you didn't choose these relatives, you're stuck with them, for better or for worse:

Your parents—for better. Your parents adore your children as only grandparents can. They share their life experience and pass down what they learned from *their* parents. Whether you have good or bad news, you share it first with them. They help care for the children, run errands, pitch in when money is tight. They listen when you have a problem. They wait until asked to offer advice. They want the best for you.

Your parents—for worse. Your idea of "the best" differs from theirs. You wish they'd keep their opinions to themselves. Because they lived and parented at a different time, their suggestions sometimes feel wrong. You bristle when they covertly criticize ("Shouldn't Robbie be eating in a high chair by now?"). You resent their spoiling the kids—keeping them up too late or feeding them foods you disapprove of. And their support comes with unspoken demands ("Do it my way," "Love me more because I do all this for you").

Our parents know how to push our buttons, as the old joke goes, because they installed them. No surprise that interactions with Mom and Dad also fling us back to childhood. A competent and accom-plished forty-year-old can feel like a fourteen-year-old in her parents' presence. It's not necessarily because her parents treat her like a child—some do, some don't. It's because both generations revert to their former roles.

Your in-laws—for better. Your partner's parents and siblings welcome you into their family. It's great having another set of wise elders and close contemporaries by marriage, especially because you start off with a clean slate: no baggage from childhood (at least, not *your* childhood). You gain insight into your partner because these other significant oth-ers on her "side" share stories and photos with you. Both generations of in-laws dote on your children. If one of your parents is deceased or out of the picture or if you don't get along with your own mother or father, a parent-in-law can be a welcome ally. A sib-in-law can become a cherished confidante.

Your in-laws—for worse. Problems with in-laws are not just the stuff of sitcoms and TV dramas. It takes time to get to know this bevy of strangers who infiltrate your family, and the experience runs the gamut from joyful to excruciating. After money and sex, in-laws are on the short list of why couples argue. A recent story line on *Parenthood* captured what often happens. Jasmine asks her suddenly laid-off mother to move in until the older woman finds a new job. Mom sacrificed for her when she was growing up; now Jasmine is happy to help her "get back on her feet." Crosby, her husband, feels as if he's being invaded.

Your siblings—for better. Close brothers and sisters pull together and are almost always there for each other. Of all family ties, sibling relationships are the most enduring. They are part of your childhood, and long after your parents are gone, you will have each other to compare notes and rehash history. Your siblings are also your children's aunts and uncles, carriers of family lore. They do for your kids what your favorite aunts and uncles once did for you. For example, a sister who works in fashion invites your tween to the city for a sophisticated "big girl" weekend. A brother buys your son the complete set of *Harry Potter* books and shows him the magic tricks he learned as a boy. Aunts and uncles also bring your children into their homes to play with their kids, the cousins, which widens and enriches your family circle.

Your siblings—for worse. Just because you grew up in the same household, you're not necessarily friends, nor is it a given that you have similar values and interests. Siblings judge and criticize each other. They freeze you in time. At forty-five, you're still "the baby" or "the bossy one." Leftover resentment crops up as parents age and siblings argue over what's needed, who's going to do it, and who's going to pay for it. Past animosities seep into the present around kids, too. You watch your brother "pretend-wrestling" with your son, and it reminds you of many times he pinned you down until you promised to be his slave. Seeing your sister whispering to your daughter, you remember the "No Entry" sign on the door to her childhood room and the sound of her giggling with a friend about her "stupid little sister."

When your adult siblings marry, you also have to deal with their partners, the sisters- and brothers-in-law on your side of the family. Some become instant comrades, others not so much. Either way, it doesn't matter whether you like them. Their boats are also part of the fleet.

Charting a Smooth Course

On any given day, the relationship you *actually* have with your parents, your in-laws, your siblings, and their spouses falls somewhere between better and worse. It depends, naturally, on who each of you is, your respective personalities, past experiences, how well you cope with stress and deal with relationships in general, and what's happening in each of your lives *on that day*. But it also depends on the choices you make. To be sure, dealing with the fleet of significant others that affect your family can be daunting at times. But you're more likely to steer in the right direction if you remember this key secret of adult relationships:

> *Instead of putting energy into trying to change the other person, work on bettering the relationship.*

Start by applying the connection questions in chapter 4, especially to relationships that fall at the "for worse" end of the spectrum. Tell yourself the truth. Are you doing everything you can to get to know this person? Are you jealous of him or her? Competition often goes with the territory. In order not to act on bad feelings, you have to consciously "re-view" your parents and siblings with adult eyes. Are you getting stuck in old hurts? Can you see who they are today and appreciate their struggles? With in-laws and other new members of the fleet, have you made snap judgments? Have you taken the time to find common ground?

Come with an open heart and mind. You build a relationship by sharing who you are and by extending your best self. Be kind, respectful, and empathetic. Just take small steps. Make a kind gesture—for example, clip an article she might enjoy. Give a small gift. Offer to help out (and mean it).Surprise the person with something that you know he likes. Acting from this better part of yourself will shift *your* attitude and perceptions, too. You will see or learn something that you hadn't seen or thought about before.

Focus on what you're getting, not what you want. A woman we'll call "Other Grandma" laments that her daughter-in-law has photos of *her* parents on the mantel but none of her or her husband. "We are definitely 'the other grandparents,'" she posts. "No pictures of us—just her family. She has her parents on a pedestal. I am constantly getting my feelings hurt and constantly biting my tongue. Fortunately, we get to see the grandkids a lot, as her parents moved away."

Other Grandma first needs to change her focus. She is already getting from her daughter-in-law what she wants most: access to and time with her grandchildren, which is far more important than being revered. Her grandchildren are getting to know her, and vice versa. That's a gift that she surely wants to keep. So instead of putting herself in competition with her daughter-in-law's parents, her energy would be better spent on getting to know the young woman.

Besides, if Other Grandma wants a spot on the mantel, complaining won't help. Building a relationship with her daughter-in-law might. The next time Other Grandma takes the grandchildren somewhere, she might take pictures, pick the best one, frame it, and give it to her daughter-in-law as a gift ("I wanted you to have this picture of us with the kids, because everyone looks so good").

Here's the catch: Other Grandma's motive has to be to better the relationship, not to manipulate the daughter-in-law. And she has to keep at it. Nice gestures add up and will at least set the relationship on a more positive course. And it just might earn Other Grandma a bit of real estate on that mantel, or at least in the house. It won't be easy, especially if one or both of them has been cold, withholding, or even nasty. But someone has to take the first step.

Don't confront. Let's say your brother-in-law is, in your opinion, loud and inappropriate. You could ask your sister to talk to him (which puts her in the middle). You could lecture him about being inconsiderate (which he will probably resent, especially from someone he barely knows). A better approach might be to *do* something that, in some small way, shows your brother-in-law that you are open to *him.* For example, talk to him about his hobby or music he likes. If you establish a connection with him, when you then ask him to please be more quiet when the children are sleeping—not because he's a bad guy but because you need his help ("It's a nightmare for me when they don't get enough sleep")—he's more likely to listen and cooperate.

In any relationship, it's best to come from your heart and stay with your I, your frame of reference, your experiences ("I feel embarrassed and angry when you make comments about how klutzy I am in front of my children," "I feel like I'm not part of this family when I'm the last person to hear about plans"). Remember, too, that even if you are honest and you listen carefully, it won't change the other person. But if you give it time and allow positive interactions to accumulate, you might change the relationship.

Act your age. You are no longer "Mamma's boy" or the "baby" of the family. You're an adult. If being in the presence of a parent or older sibling makes you feel like a child, know that it goes with the territory. It helps, though, to dress as if you're going to a business meeting, and bring your adult self to the table. You might have old wounds and grudges, but try to look at your parents and siblings *today.* As one grandmother, upset about her married children's behavior, put it, "I've made some mistakes, but that was thirty years ago, and I still feel like I'm paying for them. What about the good things I've done since then?"

Be open to surprises. When you make assumptions about other people, it leaves little room for growth in the relationship. You *think* you know them; you tend to finish their sentences. And you don't learn anything new. Instead, allow yourself to listen and refrain from making snap judgments. You might be pleasantly surprised, as in this humorous example we plucked from the Baby Whisperer forums. Lana's mother-in-law (MIL) arrived to stay with her and her "dear husband" (DH) on her due date. Lana, desperate to go into labor, finally suggested to her husband that they DTD ("do the deed"):

> *DH flat out refused, and on the night of day 6, we had a full-out fight about it in front of MIL at the supper table. DH was beyond embarrassed. I at that point didn't care. So MIL looked right at DH and said, "You know, I don't have many days off left. This baby needs to get here so Lana doesn't end up 2 weeks late with a C-section and I'm long gone home. Man up, and go have SEX." DH almost fell on the floor, and I burst out laughing. BTW, MIL never ever says the S word, doubt she even says "making love" out loud around her own husband! Needless to say DH "manned up" and I went into labor around 6am!*

It's impossible to know how Lana felt about her mother-in-law before this amusing scene. But it's not a stretch to imagine that she now has a fuller picture of, and greater respect for, her MIL. The more we know about someone, the easier it is to find common ground.

Look at the person through another family member's eyes. When your father-in-law breezes in with pastries you'd rather not keep in the house or shows up with a too-large bicycle for your child, remember that he is your partner's father and your children's grandfather. Instead of indulging your own annoyance, try to see him as they do.

Your partner grew up on those pastries, and in his eyes, Dad brings comfort food. From the looks on their faces as they devour the sweets, both guys are delighted, perhaps even transported to a time long ago. Meanwhile, all little Johnny can see right now is the new cool bike that Poppa brought him. It doesn't occur to *him* that it's "impractical," and "a waste of good money," or that he can't reach the pedals yet.

In a similar vein, watching your kids play with your brother or sister might evoke bad memories, but that's *your* past. It's not what your children see. Your son is deliriously happy when his "awesome" uncle comes around. Your daughter feels special when her aunt does "grown-up" things with her.

Seeing what others see helps you stay grounded in the present. You might be more generous about giving second chances. You'll also be more compassionate and understanding when others have trouble with family members *you* favor. For example, when your husband isn't as excited as you are to learn that your parents are flying in from Phoenix to stay for a week, looking through *his* eyes will help you understand his reaction. You've known and loved Mom and Dad all your life; they've been in his universe for a relatively few years.

Step into the other's shoes. We can't say this often enough: Empathy is vital to all relationships. Your parents and in-laws, for example, are inching toward older age. Their becoming grandparents—a new life passage—was spurred by *your* decision (to have a child), not theirs. They might be in relatively good health—many baby-boomer grandparents are—and probably love being with their grandchildren. All the same, they are now in a position of less importance, less visibility, and less control. As artist Jennifer Wane sums it up, "Inside every older person is a younger person wondering what happened." Your elders remember other times—better times—when they didn't have to ask permission or depend on anyone. Have compassion when you deal with them. (This, of course, goes both ways, as we point out in "Words to the Wise.")

Words to the Wise (Elders) about Adult Children

Building a relationship takes work on both sides. Below are some pointers for the older generation. Younger-generation readers might use the information to seed authentic and constructive conversation with their parents:

Be someone your adult child <u>wants</u> to consult. Learn about new parenting trends and about child safety, which probably wasn't as much of a concern in "your day." If you read the books your adult child is reading, discuss them, but don't dispute them. Your own life and parenting experiences are different from theirs. Don't be dismissive ("Why are you making such a big deal out of toilet training? We just let *you* run around without a diaper!") or insulting ("You're *still* breast-feeding?"). Don't constantly point out how well you do with the baby/child ("He went right to sleep for me," "He never talks back to me"). And as the grandchildren get older, forge a separate relationship, but don't collude with them ("Mommy and Daddy can't know that we do this").

Don't invade. When problems crop up in their family, hold back. Rather than rush in with your solutions and "expert" opinion, wait until you're asked. Don't assume that you know better. When you're consulted, spend most of the time listening and acknowledging how hard it is to run a family. Often, all they need to know is that Mom or Dad is solidly in their corner. Keep your response short, and let go. Your adult children might or might not do it your way—that's their prerogative. Don't push, even if you feel justified ("I am only telling you this because I love you"). Trying to shape your adult child's family is a lose-lose proposition. It will position you as the bad guy *and* (accidentally) send a message to your daughter or son that she or he is not competent.

Don't take it personally when they don't want to talk to you. A son or daughter might sound angry or stressed out, dodge your phone calls, or make excuses for not wanting to have a particular conversation right now. Ask before drawing conclusions. It's not always about you. Before you react, think. Modern parents are very hard on themselves. Are you being sensitive to their plight? Is this the best time—and way—to approach a particular topic? Will this conversation help or hurt your relationship? If the latter, back off for now.

Take the high road. Reflecting on her resentment toward her daughter's in-laws, a sixty-something says in all seriousness, "I wish she had married an orphan!" Jealousy and competitiveness between "sides" affect—and infect—the whole family. Even the little ones feel the tension. The solution: Acknowledge, but don't act on, such feelings. Barbara Graham, author of *Eye of My Heart,* an anthology of grandmothering, is convinced that "admitting them—if only to ourselves—makes us much less likely to behave like self-centered teenagers out to win a popularity contest. Awareness confers . . . the power to behave like a grownup."

With sisters, brothers, and siblings-in-law—your contemporaries—perspective taking is also important. Try to understand why they've made certain choices and how their particular lifestyle, different though it might be from yours, serves them. What led your sister-in-law to become a big-shot lawyer? What motivated your brother-in-law to buy a farm and take your sister to a foreign country to grow olives? See these "stories" from *their* perspective. Their life path might not be what you've chosen or find appealing, but it isn't better or worse. It's just different.

Focus on what's good for the whole family. If you enjoy being with your parents and in-laws and find solace in your various sibling relationships, it's great for everyone. In some homes, though, that's not the case. For example, Edy, Carl's mother, feels left out and upstaged by the other grandmother. She makes offhanded comments to Amanda, her daughter-in-law, such as, "When Carl was a baby, I didn't do it that way." Amanda, annoyed at the unsolicited advice, is now less inclined to visit Edy or invite her to stay. Carl feels guilty and fights with his wife *and* his mother. Amanda thinks Carl is sticking up for his mother; his mother sees her son as Amanda's puppet. None of the adults gets what they want, and ultimately the grandchildren also suffer.

Similar scenarios play out with siblings. Carl and Keisha, Amanda's little sister, also lock horns. Carl complains to Amanda that Keisha is demanding and entitled. He resents how she flits around the world and then comes to "crash" at their house. "But she's my sister," Amanda insists. "You wouldn't say that about *your sister!*" The children adore Aunt Keisha, but they're also confused when they hear their parents argue about her.

Circling the wagons and viewing extended family members as outsiders tend to isolate your family and upset the children. Tracy often told parents, "Put your emotions on one side, and know that your child has *two* sets of grandparents. To deprive your child of them is selfish." The same goes for aunts and uncles. But it's not just for your children. Diversity is good for your family. You can usually find *something* redeeming about your other significant others. And there's probably one thing you can all agree on: your love for the children/grandchildren/nieces and nephews.

FYN Is Your Deal Still Working?

Whether or not we say it out loud, we have a "deal" with each of our close adult relations. It might be anything from "I'm here for you, and you're here for me" to "I'm stuck with you, but I'm never going to like you." The problem is, time and life change us. Every so often, therefore, "re-view" your adult relationships, and ask yourself, "Is the deal still working?" The following questions can be applied to your partner, your other significant others, or any long-term relationship.

- Has time changed *you*? If you're different in some way from how you once were, does it affect the relationship? Are you being your authentic self with this person?
- Is what you once hoped to get from this relationship still relevant? Are you seeking a different kind of emotional or practical exchange now from when you first met or when you were younger?
- Does he or she usually live up to your expectations? If not, are you continually disappointed by the same thing? That might give you pause; perhaps it's not a realistic expectation. Are you really seeing this person as he or she is today?

Notes on Adult Family Ties

SIX

CONTEXT: YOUR FAMILY'S ROUTINE

The Zones

*God grant me the serenity to accept the things I
cannot change; the courage to change the things I
can; and the wisdom to know the difference.*

—SERENITY PRAYER

Let's take a moment to recap. We've shown you how two of the Three Factors make your family what it "is." When the *individuals* get REAL and become more mindful about their *relationships,* they make better choices, which, in turn, helps keep the family strong and secure. And now we turn to the role of *context,* the element over which you have the least control.

Of the Three Factors, we can work on our relationships and with consciousness and willingness, change them for the better. You can't fundamentally change another person—he is who he is. At the same time, a Spirited baby can become a leader or a bully, depending on who's around her and what she experiences. Context is far less shapeable.

For example, you can't stop a hurricane, an epidemic, or a recession from happening. You often have no choice about living next to quarrelsome neighbors or relocating to a country where the culture is not in sync with your values. And you can't easily change your child's teacher, the way your boss treats you, or the prevailing views of your church or ethnic group. Indeed, most aspects of context fall under the umbrella of "things I cannot change," described in the Serenity Prayer, a favorite of Tracy's. However, there is an important environment that you and your family *can* control: the immediate context, your household.

In almost every interview for this book, we asked, "What was it like growing up in your household?"

"We had dinner at seven in the pantry, and my parents ate at eight in the dining room. Sunday was the only day we were allowed to eat with my parents."

"My best memory is of my father coming home from the office every night at six and watching *The Flintstones* with us. My mother would be sitting there with a book, but he'd get into it. I loved it when he laughed at the parts I laughed at."

"I grew up as a Mennonite. But my parents were also very curious about the world. As a family, we took many trips—every year, two or three—a camping trip to one coast or the other."

"My parents were hippies. It was chaotic—I certainly don't run my house like that today—but we had fun. I don't remember ever being told to make my bed or eat at a particular time. Every year, around Christmas, we had to fill at least one box with toys we would then give away—only good toys, not broken ones."

In each case above, the person—now a parent "running" a family—is remembering aspects of his or her family routine. The daily comings and goings, the way the household is managed, and how time is allotted and actually spent all reveal a lot about how a particular family functions.

Your family's routine can be left to chance or consciously designed.

Granted, the words *design* and *family* aren't usually found in the same sentence. But they should be. Not as in "designer" jeans—true design doesn't have anything to do with style, money, or class. And not as in "genetically designed," which implies tinkering with nature. By design, we mean done with consciousness and planned. In a perfect world, everything we use, live in, or practice would be well designed, carefully thought-out, safe, and emotionally comforting. Why not our families?

When good design is incorporated into any context, it has a positive effect on how we feel as individuals and how we interact with one another. Patients in hospital rooms designed to maximize sunlight, for example, need less pain medication. A well-designed neighborhood makes you feel safe, more likely to slow down and connect. And so can a well-designed family routine.

A Routine for the Whole Family

Tracy's first order of business was always to help families establish a consistent and structured daily routine. Babies and toddlers do best when they know what to expect. Thus, we prescribed EASY in our earlier books—recurring cycles of **E**ating, **A**ctivity, **S**leeping, and time for **Y**ou. A structured routine gives the day markers and makes it easier for parents to tune in to their new baby's rhythms. They get to know their child and learn how to interpret her cries. If every day they feed her, more or less, at 9:00, when she cries at 10:00, they know it's not hunger. But EASY wasn't designed solely for the baby's benefit. It allows Mom to figure out when she can fit in a shower or take a walk and when it's best to get Dad involved, especially if he works outside the house.

A family never outgrows the need for a structured routine, a plan that guides how time is spent. Like EASY, a routine for the whole family arms you with information about what just happened and what's supposed to happen next. You can test out options. Most important, you can put difficult moments into perspective, just as you did as a new parent, when the baby woke you at 2 A.M. and again at 5 A.M. He won't be a newborn for the rest of his life.

A well-thought-out routine helps you keep track. Family members know where they have to be and when and what's expected of them. They make informed choices. However, a routine for the whole family has to accommodate a tangle of distinct and sometimes conflicting personalities and needs, not just those of one baby. It can't be captured with four letters. As your family grows, you also spend time outside the house—contexts you can't control—which means that some portion of your routine then has to conform to schedules over which you have no say.

Admittedly, the word *routine* initially scares some parents. They assume that it means watching the clock. Or they hear "routine," and they think *dull*. They fear that structure will take the surprise out of life. Nei-

> ## The Best Family Routines Are Designed with the Three Factors in Mind
>
> *The individuals.* Part of your family routine should allot time to nurturing family members' strengths and meeting their needs, including each one's need for time alone and time with friends.
>
> *The relationships.* Your routine should provide opportunities for time together, as duos and trios, as a family. If no one tends to relationships, they wither.
>
> *The context.* Good routines are flexible enough to withstand whatever life throws at your family, from everyday glitches (a child coming home from school with lice or an unexpected demand at the office) to big upheavals (divorce, a job loss, a promotion that takes you out of the country, a bad year financially).

ther is true if you are flexible and if you design and modify your routine with your whole family in mind.

The fact is, everyone, young or old, thrives when there's a sense of predictability. A review of studies on family routines shows that they are linked with marital satisfaction and good parenting, children's health and adolescents' sense of personal identity, parent-child harmony, and academic achievement. This all makes sense. Routines ensure that our basic needs are met. We get the nourishment we require to go about the day, we have time for family and friends and activities that make life interesting, and we, ideally, get a good night's sleep. Not so incidentally, we learn a lot about ourselves and our loved ones by paying attention to how the day goes.

No two family routines are the same. Like the families who design them, they run the gamut from rigid to wildly complex and creative. The details don't matter if the plan works for *your* family. What does matter is having an awareness of how you function together in your household—and when things go wrong, mustering the "courage" to change the things you can.

A Day in Your Family's Life: The Zones

Observing how you function as a whole family can yield a gold mine of information. Tracy lived with, traveled with, and visited hundreds of families in the U.S. and the U.K., some with babies and toddlers, others with older children as well. Every family had its own unique rhythms and logistics. She always asked questions about their routine, because, as she put it, "You can tell a lot about a family from the way it gets through the day."

To see what Tracy saw, set aside a day to look at *your* routine. Pick a typical weekday in which the kids have school and the adults have work or other responsibilities. Think of it as an assignment to put on your architect's hat and observe your clients in their natural habitat. Your job is to help them design a routine that works for them.

To help you focus, we divide the day into ten daily "zones"—periods and categories of responsibility that most families move through, or do, every weekday:

prep work
wake up
breakfast

transitions
reunions
caretaking
home maintenance
dinner
unscheduled free time
bedtime

The daily zones help you maintain a family-think perspective.* Whereas parenting books make you focus on your child or children, in this family book, we want to help you keep your eye on the whole—how your household runs and who does what. The zones involve everyone.

The best way to design a family is to pay closer attention to the critical periods and responsibilities all of you face every day.

Being aware of the zones won't guarantee that family life will always go smoothly. Still, knowing what it takes to get through the day will give you information that, in turn, will help you figure out whether your family is working as well as it could. If you already sense that your family needs a bit of a redesign, being familiar with your routine will help you come up with a new blueprint.

Keep in mind:

- The zones are listed in logical order but not necessarily in chronological order. For example, in some families the *prep work* zone occurs in the morning; in others, it's the night before. *Unscheduled free time* and *transition* zones also vary across families.
- Some zones occur more than once a day or not at all. If you have young children, you probably find yourself in *caretaking* and *home maintenance* zones throughout the day. If you have a job that requires you to travel, you might have more *transitions* than a parent who works at home. If your family has a roster of recurring activi-

---

*There's no lunch zone listed, because lunch is rarely a family affair, and once kids attend school full-time, it's a meal typically eaten outside the home. We also didn't include a weekend zone, because the focus of this chapter is your daily routine, but we cover weekends on page 149.

ties, work/school-related or extracurricular, there might be no *unscheduled free time* zone.

- Zones can overlap. When you're driving your child to school, for example, both of you are in a *transition* zone and *caretaking* zone. Also, technology has led to a blending of zones, because you can be in two places at once—Skyping your kids from the office, for example, or texting them to stay in touch throughout the day. Of course, it's not the same as being together, but you are in touch.
- Zones are of different durations. Some are very short—*reunions* after school or work take only minutes. It all depends on the family. Children's *bedtime* can eat up an entire evening in many households.
- Zones are subject to change. You're humming along, and suddenly one of the Three Factors changes. It might be one of the individuals (a child joins a new team), a relationship (the parents separate), or the context (school officials decide to start an hour earlier). Such shifts in family life require everyone in the household to adapt. A particular zone may be dominant in your schedule today and far less significant a year from now. As the kids move through their tweens and teens, they spend increasing time on their own. The nature of the *caretaking* zone then becomes more about supervision and monitoring, which usually don't require as much time (but, often, even more energy!).
- Family members are more depleted in certain zones. Everyone's reserves tend to be low when parents return from work and kids from school. Instead of having an important talk with a loved one or trying to make a decision during these *transition* zones, wait until everyone is, say, in an *unstructured free time* zone, when you can all kick back a bit, have a snack to replenish the glucose levels in your blood, or take a walk to energize yourselves. The *bedtime* zone can be tricky, too, if there's been a lot of homework or drama or visitors. A quiet space before bedtime—a bath, a story, a board game—allows reserves to build up again.

On the next page, we describe the various zones in detail. Keep them in mind as you consciously travel through a day in the life of your family. Pay attention to the daily comings and goings in your household (or two households if you're divorced and co-parenting). Remember that routine is as much about anticipating needs as fulfilling them. So look not only at what you do but also how you plan and execute and how you adapt when things don't go as planned.

Promise yourself that for those sixteen or so hours—from the time your household swings into action until the last person goes to bed—you'll pay close attention to the small moments of everyday life that unfold and fly by in each zone. Notice:

How choices are made and how responsibilities are divvied up.

How family members express themselves (verbally and nonverbally) and deal with distress.

How you connect with one another and what kinds of activities make you feel like a family.

At the beginning of the discussion about each zone, you'll find a box describing "The Challenge"—what's unique about it and what you might want to strive for. To help you focus on how your family moves through that zone, we offer "Some Questions." We can't peer into every household, so some of the questions might not apply directly to your situation. You don't have to answer every one, nor do you have to answer the questions as written. Let them spark your imagination.

You'll see the **FYN** symbol before each set of questions. Remember that this chapter is about information gathering, not problem solving. You don't have to write down the answers in your family notebook, but you'll get more out of this chapter and a better sense of how your family runs if you do. Even more important, you can reread your answers later.

Compare notes with your partner, assuming you have one. If you have different answers or different perceptions of what goes on during the day or how your routine should go, talk about why you both feel as you do. But remember that there are no right or wrong answers. The questions are there to make you think and to help you see what your family needs, not to judge or fight over who's right. If you're a single parent, answer the questions on your own, and then talk about what you learned with someone you trust—a parent, a close friend, your family mentor.

Your Family's Style

As you read about each zone and answer the questions that follow it, consider your family's "style." Individuals and families have different levels of tolerance for chaos. In our first book, we provided a short quiz to determine your Wing It/Plan It quotient, your WPQ. The idea was to help new parents gauge their household's readiness to create a structured routine. Now we apply the concept to the whole family. "Winger" families tend to organize their households on the fly—no two days are the same—whereas "planner" families are more likely to carefully orchestrate family life, at the extreme, by religiously sticking to their routines no matter what. Take the WPQ quiz.

What's Your Family's WPQ?

For each question, fill in the number that best describes your family during typical times, not holidays or special occasions. The word "we" refers to all the members of your family. Of course, each of you is different, and sometimes only one person (often the planner) does a particular job. Still, try to answer for the whole group, based on how you usually function as a family.

5 = always   4 = usually yes   3 = sometimes   2 = usually no   1 = never

We eat meals at roughly the same time every day. _____

When we walk in, we put items such as coats, keys, and backpacks in a designated place. _____

We live by a predictable schedule. _____

We plan ahead. _____

We prioritize what's most important and tackle that first. _____

When we go shopping, we immediately put things away. _____

We use a family calendar to help us see what's coming. _____

We are known for arriving on time. _____

Before we start a project, we lay out everything we need. _____

We do regular cleanup projects to cut down on the clutter. _____

When the laundry is done, we immediately put the clean clothes away. _____

When life gets chaotic, we try to figure out what we can do differently to make it less so. _____

Total = _____

To compute your WPQ, which will give you a sense of where your family sits on the Wing It/Plan It continuum, add up the total score from the quiz, and divide by 12.

5 to 4: Your family is extremely organized. You have a place for everything, and everything is put back in its place. You probably don't have to work at having a structured routine, but you might want to think about whether you have enough flexibility in your day.

4 to 3: Your family falls on the "Plan It" end of the continuum, but you're probably not fanatics about neatness or structure. Eventually, though, one of you notices that the house needs straightening or that you'd better plan more carefully next time to make life less stressful.

3 to 2: Your family tends toward the "Wing It" end of the continuum. Routines are a challenge, and you might find yourselves rushing around in the morning or whenever someone has an appointment. The good news is that flexibility isn't a problem for your family, but it might be helpful to put some systems in place to help you all become a little more organized.

2 to 1: Your family barely has a sense of order and organization. If that works for you, fine. But take a second look. If there is tension in your household or if you're constantly putting out fires, a little planning goes a long way.

In moderation, neither winging nor planning is inherently bad. What counts is whether it works for your family. If you fall somewhere in between the two extremes—a score between 2 and 4—you've at least given some thought to planning and organization, and you are somewhat flexible.

Now, consider how you bring your style into the various zones.

Prep Work

In order to get through the day, *someone* has to look ahead to figure out what needs to be done, by whom, and when. Let's be clear: Adults are in charge of prep work, but it's also good to get input from the children. Needless to say, in most families today, it doesn't work that way.

> **The Challenge:** Work with what you've got; design a routine that takes the Three Factors into consideration: who's in your family (the individuals), how they interact (their relationships), and where the drama plays out (context).

Some families are better at planning and maintaining routines than others. In part, it's a matter of your family's WPQ. It also depends on how your Three Factors interact. A family made up of strong, healthy individuals who cooperate and support one another and who have significant resources in their environment generally has an array of choices, which probably makes it easier to anticipate each day.

At the other extreme are families in crisis. The individuals might have serious personal problems. Their relationships might be tainted by disappointment, sadness, or conflict. They might worry about how to pay the bills, or they lack a support system. Maybe no one has taught them how to anticipate, organize, or cope when plans fail. For these distressed families, it's hard enough to get through the day, let alone prepare for it.

FYN Some Questions about Your Prep Zone

- Is there a principal "administrator" in your family who keeps track of appointments and school dates, is responsible for writing it all down, makes the telephone calls, or writes the texts needed to coordinate with others? Or are these tasks shared by more than one adult? Is one or both of you resentful or angry? Are there fights over prep work?
- Are the children part of the planning? Are they expected to fall in line? Both?
- In planning, are you mindful of recent changes in a particular family member's life or in your context that might require tweaking the routine—illness, a child's difficulty in school, a new baby, a salary change, a move?
- Do you have house rules and systems—procedures for coming home, hooks for coats and backpacks, and specific places for other gear, a shelf or corner of a desk where permission forms are deposited so they can be noticed, signed, and later, easily found? Do family members actually use these tools? Does the "gathering of the stuff" happen in the morning, or is it handled the night before?
- Who's responsible for meal planning? Shopping? Whose job is it to make adult and/or child lunches, or is it every person for him/herself?
- Are things written down, or is everyone expected to keep track mentally? Do you keep and coordinate a calendar mainly with your partner? Or is there a big wall calendar that everyone uses and can see?
- Do activities outside the house dominate the daily routine? Do the adults share equally in the responsibility for children's appointments and schedules? Is time with family compromised because of homework, practice, or other individual activities?
- Do cell phones play a role in keeping tabs on one another? When plans change, who gets the call? Who forgets to call? Who gives permission? Are there rules around cell-phone use and internet-connected devices? Are these checked by parents?
- Other than the parents, who else is part of the family's day—baby-sitters, household help, coaches, friends, parent(s) in another household, grandparents or other relatives? Do you consider them when you plan?
- Have you noticed that certain recurring occasions—birthdays or holidays, the beginning of a new school year, vacations—disrupt the everyday pattern? Do you anticipate and plan for such times?

Wake Up

How we start the day sets the tone. Morning is when individual personalities play out. It's also a first look at who does what in your family. In some households, anyone who's old enough to sleep in a big-kid bed is responsible for his or her own wake-up; in others, it's a daily strug-

> **The Challenge:** Use *wake up* to better understand the members of your family. When your eyes pop open, each of you reveals your basic temperamental morning self—chirpy, grumpy, all business, or slow to rouse.

gle. Especially if you or your partner is not a morning person and prefers to sleep until noon, the kids might not be the only ones who need to be coaxed into action.

Many families have a "morning cuddle." In households we surveyed, the kids frequently headed for their parent's or parents' bed, even as they inched toward adolescence. The frequency varied from occasionally to always. When the little ones climb in, you might try to coax them back to sleep, or they might coax you out of bed. If the latter, a moment of sweet sibling togetherness often gives way to "Hey, you're hogging the covers!" and battles over who gets to watch their favorite show.

To be sure, some morning traditions make the wake-up more pleasant or at least somewhat predictable. Take the Perlman family. Greg has been performing songs and skits for his daughter, Sadie, since she was born, adapting them over the years. "Wake-up usually starts with a song mentioning events of the day, sung to the same tune every time. Then it's followed by a little skit," he explains. "One of her favorites is 'The Wake-up Machine of Dr. Wakenstein,' where I play a mad scientist testing his invention with Sadie as the subject, turning up the machine higher and higher with tickling, rolling, shaking. Another one has her stuffed animal discovering a hole—Sadie's ear—and trying to dig in to find out what's in there."

Sadie always enjoys it, Greg says, but she is also a child who is dependably cheerful when she wakes. To be sure, temperament plays a big part in the morning drama. We know some kids who'd hide under the covers if their parents started singing and some parents who'd have to get up an hour earlier to be in the mood to perform. In any case, a lot has to happen in a very short time, especially if both parents also have to get ready for work.

Wake-up also depends on what the expectations are. Kids might be allowed to pad downstairs in their pajamas and dress after breakfast. Or they have to bathe, get dressed, make beds, and straighten up first. In our small survey, it's more often the former, which usually involves nagging as well ("You're not dressed *yet*?").

If you're not sure how much time your family's wake-up takes, pay attention to the clock. With children younger than three or four, helping them dress has to be factored in. With older children, there might be questions about missing clothing ("Where's my Jets shirt?") or battles over bathroom time.

FYN Some Questions about Your Wake-Up Zone

- What are your first interactions of the day like? How do you greet one another?
- Whose body clock kicks in automatically? Who requires an alarm? Do you wake your spouse/kids, or do they wake you?
- Who needs coaxing? Who's comfortable talking right away? Who can barely speak until he or she has had [food, a particular beverage, a shower, at least thirty minutes without talking]?
- Is everyone responsible for himself or herself, or is there a lot of monitoring going on just to get family members started? Is there nagging and resentment?
- Are there rules around the wake-up—for example, dress before breakfast—or do you just leave it to chance whether everyone gets out of the house on time?
- How do family members' individual temperaments play into wake-up? What kinds of moods and behaviors are typical for each person? Are issues of temperament accommodated (you anticipate and act before a mood takes over), or is the outburst merely tolerated (you internally roll your eyes and say to yourself, *Here he goes again*)?
- Is there a "family bed"? If so, is it by choice or by default? Is it a source of joy or dread?
- Is there fighting over possession, space, or attention? What do good mornings have in common—an adequate night's sleep, more/less parental involvement, anticipation of common problems and strategies for diverting them? What do bad mornings have in common?
- Is screen time allowed/encouraged in the morning? Are there limits to it, rules that govern how much time can be spent and what has to be finished before [dressing, cleaning, breakfast, etc.]?
- Has there been a recent change in the wake-up routine—a toddler now in a day bed, a middle-school child taking on more responsibility, a parent's schedule change? How has this new circumstance affected everyone else?
- Is there something that bothers or worries you about these first moments of the day? Something that makes you proud?

Breakfast

All meals are important, of course; they literally nourish the family. But each meal has its own significance. Breakfast is the first coming together as a family. It can be stressful because of the clock. Everyone's

The Challenge: Nourish—with food and attention—more than you nag. Have the day start on a positive note.

on the way to somewhere else. It's a time to consciously keep your eye on the goal, to give everyone a good launch into the day.

But don't expect to look like the families you see in cereal commercials, with everyone passing the box around, happily engaged in cheerful banter. In real life, breakfast can be a minefield. The one who leaves for work first grabs a slice of toast, barely says good-bye, and flies out the door. Two kids are fighting over chairs. And the surly teenager says to her mom, "I'm not hungry, and if I was, I wouldn't eat *that*."

Food issues can make it worse. One's on a diet; another is a poor eater; another has strict rules and preferences—eggs can't be runny, cereal is never eaten with milk, toast can't be too dark, vegetables can't touch one another. In some households, Mom or Dad functions as a short-order cook, and the kitchen becomes a diner that accommodates everyone's culinary needs. At the other extreme are families in which one meal is prepared, and everyone eats what's served. Most of us do a little of both.

Breakfast rituals can defuse morning tensions. Saying grace feels right in some families, corny or forced in others. Nevertheless, pausing to be thankful and acknowledge one another's presence—in whatever way you choose—ensures that, for at least those few moments, everyone sits still, symbolically saying, *We're a family starting our day.*

Breakfast can also be a time of teaching new skills and allowing the younger members to stretch and experiment by doing age-appropriate jobs. Kids who participate in cooking are more likely to eat what they produce. Even at three, Melinda's son Jeremy would stand on a step stool, scramble his morning eggs—with her at his side—and then gobble them up with pride. He was a skinny kid; his parents worried about his weight. Allowing him to cook made the meal his and made breakfast a lot more palatable for everyone.

Tracy, herself a picky eater as a child, often reminded parents that kids don't die from eating the same breakfast every morning. Although

---

FYN Some Questions about Your Breakfast Zone

- Is the table set? Do you sit down together, or does everyone casually eat when ready?
- Do you have assigned seats at breakfast? Are you unconsciously imitating your own parents, or did you make a deliberate decision to do it this way? If so, why?
- Who cooks? Who helps? Does everyone eat the same thing, or are orders taken? Are the kids encouraged to help prepare breakfast, or are they served?
- Is there conversation—for example, about the day ahead? Do you discuss nutrition ("You can't just eat sugary cereals. You have to have some protein") and/or food preferences ("You've had waffles every day this week").
- Does everyone have to eat well, or is it OK to run out without finishing or eating at all? Do different rules apply to the adults?
- Is one of the adults the designated breakfast nag, urging the kids to eat, to finish, to clean up after themselves? How's that working out?
- What does a good breakfast (the experience, not the meal) look like in your household? What about a bad one?

---

we don't recommend it, they can also survive no breakfast—they eat when they're hungry.

Transitions

The Challenge: Even over the course of a typical day, transitions require physical, mental, and emotional shifts that affect your comings and goings. Help family members become mindful when traveling away from and back to your household.

The household is an island, but we venture out in our dinghies every day. Adults have to get to work, kids to school, and then everyone has to come home. Parents sometimes feel torn. "When I'm at the office, I think about the family," one mother commented, "and when I'm at home, I think about work." Even parents who work at home, either as homemakers or work-at-home entrepreneurs, find that it can be tricky to shift from one role to the other. The transition zone can be very small (the ten minutes it takes you to shuttle the kids to school) or quite large (a long, tiresome commute). Either way, transitions are costly, because they involve physical and mental work.

That is, aside from the tangible resources that transitions require, such as car, gas, garage, money for public transportation, there are also human costs involved. For example, you must be alert and vigilant about schedules, act as chauffeur and make your own commute, deal with unexpected delays, and juggle it all in your head. Even if you run a home business and all you have to do is go to your desk after everyone leaves, the mental leap is enormous.

Whether you're accustomed to a particular transition or it's forced upon you, it's easier to shift gears when you're mindful.

Think about where you are and where you're going.

It's surprisingly rewarding—and effective—to say out loud what you have to deal with next. If transitions are stressful, share your feelings. For example, most evenings during her postwork drive, Sara Stern calls a good friend who works at home. "It gives me a way of recapping the day and talking about what I have to do when I get home." For the friend, a writer who talks to very few people during her work day, the daily conversation is a welcome social break.

Although it's not common and possibly not doable for many families, Viola and Paul Vardoni, parents of very active, capable teenagers, figured out a way to deal with their work-family transitions *together*. They leave at different times in the morning, but most evenings, they take the same commuter train home, which gives them fifty minutes to share what happened at work, to talk about Manny and Theresa, and to place bets on whether the kids started dinner.

In the best-run families, transitions are adapted to each member's temperament. Remember that Grumpy toddler who screamed when it was time to eat, despite your best efforts to coax her away from her Play-Doh? Today, as a middle-schooler, she probably still needs a significant reentry break when she comes home from school, whereas her little brother has never had a hard time with transitions.

With young children, repeating certain actions or phrases helps prepare them to accept a transition. For example, one father we know used to sing, "Hi ho, hi ho, it's off to work I go" (to the tune of the Seven Dwarfs song) when he kissed his little ones good-bye. Other families have a special phrase, handshake, or high-five.

FYN Some Questions about Your Transition Zone

- Which family members have to leave the house each day for school or work (paid or unpaid)? What does each transition involve?
- Are your family transitions generally peaceful or problematic? Why? Do you have trouble getting out of the house? If so, what seems to be the reason—lack of proper planning, general chaos, one particular adult or child?
- Do aspects of your commute—rushing to a train, dealing with traffic, hassles from others—add stress? Do you consciously use your commute to make the mental transition from home to work and vice versa?
- Is your transition different from your partner's (if you have one)? Are transitions a source of difficulty in your relationship?
- If you work at home, do you have a ritual that helps you shift gears, such as coffee with a friend, the gym, a brisk walk? Or do you just move on to the next item on your to-do list? Do you have—or do you feel the need to create—an area that is yours, a work space, instead of merely inhabiting family space when others are not home? If not, what do you do to make the mental transition? When everyone returns, do others respect your work space, or do you feel invaded when your desk turns into the dining room table?
- Do one or both of you take the kids to school? Do you carpool or trade off with other parents to get the kids to school?
- If you and your partner commute together, do you use the time for family issues, to reconnect as adults, to talk to each other about the day ahead?
- What kinds of conversations do you have with your children during their transitions between home and school? Do you dominate the conversation or use the time to listen? Do you remind, instruct, give directions? Do you help them prepare mentally for the day ahead and what might happen in school? On the way home, do you discuss what's going to happen once you get there, such as homework, a special guest, snacks, chores?
- Has a recent change altered a family member's transitions? How have the new circumstances affected the family?

The Challenge: Reunions reinforce relationships. Each time you reconnect, even after a short absence from your partner or children, give yourself a few minutes to smile, listen, hug, and be unquestionably present.

Reunions

"Hi honey, I'm home!" is another sitcom staple we love. In the early days of television, the line was delivered in earnest by a returning father who "knew best." More often now, it is said sarcastically as way-cool teenagers enter an empty house. Either way, it represents a reality of family life: During the day, everyone is off doing his or her individual thing, and at some point—or at various points—you come together again.

Exits (departures, drop-offs) and entrances (homecomings) are relational transitions. When we separate from family, we go from being-with to not-being-with. Reunion is the being-with again. Kids come from school, after-school activities, or a sleepover, adults from work, travel, or social outings. Reunions can be joyful, chaotic, confusing, upsetting, surprising, overwhelming, or all of the above. They're little moments—a greeting doesn't take long—but they're filled with meaning.

Studying greetings, as anthropologists and psychologists often do, tells us a lot about the greeters and the state of their unions. In the space it takes for a hello, a peck on the cheek, or a welcome-home hug, pay attention. On any given day, you might be happier to see certain family members than others. It's not always the same person. It depends on how that child or adult acts toward you in general, what happened earlier, what else is happening on your return that diverts your attention, and— significantly—what *you* need at that moment.

Sadly, family reentry rarely resembles a Hallmark moment in most homes. In one study of middle-class families, family members greeted each other "warmly" less than a third of the time. What happens in the Sherry family is typical: Like three-quarters of the mothers surveyed, Clarice, whose work day ends at four, is first to greet the kids. Clarice and Ted have talked with Jarred, age nine, and Dale, fourteen, about how important it is to stop what you're doing and say hello when someone walks through the door. Still, when Ted comes home at six, Jarred is on his DS, Dale is doing homework, and Clarice is busy with dinner. Each manages an unenthusiastic "hi." It could be worse. At least the Sherrys aren't among the 10 percent of families who are either negative toward one another or businesslike, leading with impersonal "logistical talk" about what needs to be done. Still, the Sherrys are, like many families, distracted 50 percent of the time, which does not bode well for relationship building.

Caretaking

The Challenge: Be with, or at least accessible to, your children when you're "on duty." Do your multitasking in a no-child zone.

If you have children, you're in the *caretaking* zone from the minute they arrive until "ever after"—happily or not. But for the purposes of this discussion about your daily routine, we're referring to times of day when you are mentally and physically devoted to taking care of children. If they're young and still dependent, you bathe, dress, and (until they're old enough to eat on their own) feed them. You supervise them in play, take them to doctors and playgrounds, buy them shoes and clothing. As they get older and negotiate increasing freedoms, time continues to be spent teaching, explaining, demonstrating, waiting, chauffeuring, monitoring, coordinating, advising, chastizing, and soothing.

It doesn't matter whether your time involves diapers and *Barney* or bullying and baseball practice—or how much you enjoy your children or love being a parent. When you decide to have a family, you recognize that, for a long time, children need your care. Still, let's be honest. The childcare zone can be a tiring, lonely, stressful place. You're never off duty when you're a parent. Many adults find relief by participating in play groups, where they can share war stories. Some also have a partner, a mother or other relative, a neighbor, or a paid childcare worker whom they can count on to lighten the load in this zone.

Parents in the childcare zone are prone to multitasking, because of both the tedium and the time crunch that plagues so many modern families. Here's a mother reading a book while she shovels strained pears into her baby's mouth. She then plops her into a bouncy chair and squeezes in a few yoga poses. There's a father getting a stock quote and then calling his office at his son's Little League game. Everyone does it, we rationalize. But we have to wonder how all this multitasking affects family relationships.

We hasten to mention that if you're a member of the so-called sandwich generation, adults who care for aging parents even as they care for children, you have a double dose of responsibility in this zone, which can add stress to your family's daily routine. As much as we might anticipate that someday our parents will probably need us, when it actually happens, the reality hits hard. Having to step in and to oversee various aspects of an aging parent's life is quite different from childcare—a job you signed up for when you decided to start your own family.

FYN Some Questions about Your Caretaking Zone

- How big a chunk of your family routine involves caretaking? Is any time and energy put into elder care?
- Who's in charge of caretaking in your household? If you are the only adult in residence, do you have outsiders—volunteer or paid—who help with caretaking? If there are two adults, is childcare shared? Is it a cause of ongoing conflict?
- Do you hire anyone to help in this zone? If so, does the cost strain the family budget?
- On a continuum from "very stressed out" to "enjoying every minute," how do you feel most of the time in this zone?
- Do you multitask in the caretaking zone—catch up on phone calls, squeeze in a few minutes to review a work project—or do you try to give your full attention to the child or adult in your care?
- Is there a former spouse or grandparent in another household who shares responsibilities in this zone? Do these arrangements generally work well for you, or does the coordination of schedules and logistics complicate your family routine?

(continued on next page)

- Does one (or more) of your children have special needs or a talent that requires more childcare time?
- How do sibling relationships affect your childcare time? Is it generally harmonious or contentious? Do you referee or let them battle it out?
- Have your caretaking circumstances changed over the last year? The last five years?
- If your children now require something different of you—say, help with homework when you get home from work—how has this affected your day? The household? Has a child's desire for more independence placed new or perhaps unexpected stress on your family routine?

Home Maintenance

The Challenge: Look past your "chore wars" to see how issues of personality, power, and gender are negotiated in skirmishes over who does what. "Making a home" should be a *family* responsibility.

Having a family involves maintaining a home. It's not just a matter of planning. Someone has to *do* the food shopping, cleaning, laundry, gardening, repairs, and touch-ups. Home maintenance might be the province of one adult, all the adults, or the whole family or a set of tasks you pay someone else to do.

It's important to look carefully at home maintenance, because it's a zone that leaves many women angry and, potentially, drives a wedge into the adults' relationship. Fathers and kids often feel good at home on a typical weekday evening, because their "primary activity," according to a recent survey, is leisure. Mothers, who tend to chores after work, feel— not surprisingly—"mostly negative" at home. And no wonder. They do the boring, repetitive tasks that no one wants to do. Often, no one even notices, no less thanks or praises the person who does this grunt work. When is the last time you heard, "Good job changing that light bulb" or "Wow, these clothes smell great," other than in a commercial for laundry detergent? In contrast, the one who cooks or teaches a child a new skill, such as bike riding, often earns excessive praise.

Discussions about this subject make it clear that the issue is often far deeper than who takes out the garbage. Who does what and how you and your partner negotiate housework are influenced by your upbringing and personality and whatever notions about marriage, family, and fairness each of you brings to the table. Consciously or not, each of you has a sense of how men and women are supposed to think, what they are capable of doing, and who should be responsible for what.

Then you also have to factor kids into the equation. Whether they're first enlisted to help around the house at two or twelve, they will react to rules and requests according to their own personalities and whatever attitudes they've picked up from you and your partner. As we pointed out at the beginning of this book, we ask very little—sometimes nothing—of our children, and we often underestimate what they can do. Not surprisingly, then, home maintenance is not just a zone; it's often a battle zone. (Chapter 8 offers you a family-focused solution to "chore wars.")

FYN Some Questions about Your Home Maintenance Zone

Note: We have attempted to pose the following questions in gender-neutral terms.

- Are there chore wars in your household, or have you reached a peaceful agreement about who does what? If you're cooperating, how are chores divvied up—according to likes and dislikes, gender, abilities, negotiation, all of the above?
- After meals, how do the dishes find their way into the sink? Does someone wash them or put them into the dishwasher? Who will unload the dishwasher and put everything away when it's clean? Does everyone assume he has a part in cleanup? Or do family members follow the orders of the one person who takes charge and, often, cares the most about how clean the house is?
- If housework leads to battles and resentment, what's the beef? Does one adult feel she (or, rarely, he) is doing more than the other? Is that true?
- Does one adult have more rigorous standards than the other? Is one generally critical of the way the other handles chores?
- If one of the adults takes over the chores, is it to avoid a battle or because that person thinks he is better at it? Or is it by default?
- Do the children share in the housework? Do they take on responsibilities routinely and without prompting, or is a lot of reminding and harping going on? If the children are not expected to help, do you worry that they should be doing more?
- Do you pay someone else to do housework and other types of home maintenance? Is it a good solution for your family? Can you afford it?

Dinner

The Challenge: Make family dinners a priority and a requirement, a time to regroup, to feel like a family, and to share the cares of the day.

Research only confirms what we already know: Families who eat together—at least three nights a week; even better, five—are more likely to be strong, resilient, and better at communicating and dealing with problems than those who don't. Breakfast tends to be a rushed affair. Lunch is often out of the house. But dinner is about physical *and* emotional nourishment. It's the meal where we take a little more time, at least in theory.

Plenty of us sit down as a family at dinnertime. Between 43 percent and 74 percent eat together "all the time," depending on which poll you believe. But we're also more distracted. In a 2010 survey conducted by CBS, when asked whether their TVs were on during dinner, a third of viewers checked "always," and another 27 percent answered "half the time" or "sometimes." Ten percent admitted that they text, email, or use their cell phones during a meal. A small number, perhaps, but the net effect is that instead of communicating, many of us are staring at a screen or "talking" to people elsewhere, even as we spend time with our families.

Dinner is the aspect of family life we're most likely to recall. What happens at the table tells us who dominates the family, how family members communicate, whether people listen to one another, whether they care about what someone else has to say. Unfortunately, in many households, conversations are one-way, because the spotlight is solely on the kids—how *their* day was. Asked whether he talked about his day, one father said what many feel: "I don't think she's very interested in what *I* do."

How could she be? She's spent ten years holding forth. At what point does she turn to her dad and say, "So, Dad, how was *your* day?" Maybe never—unless her parents start teaching her how.

Ironically, many of today's parents grew up in a less child-centered era. Families viewed dinner as a time when the adults talked and the children behaved themselves. Some were expected to let the grown-ups talk; others remember their parents engaging them in discussions during dinner, but children rarely monopolized the conversation as they often do now.

Looking at your dinnertime—talk, manners, appreciation of food—tells you a lot about your expectations in general and what kind of family you want to have. In many households, it's different from the parents' childhood. For example, Yale law professor Amy Chua, the self-proclaimed "tiger mother" whose exacting standards made headlines in 2011, ate and watched television news at her childhood dinner table. Her parents always stressed the importance of education, but dinner was not for conversation. Everyone sat in silence and listened to the TV. Today Chua and her husband, Jed Rubenfeld, also a law professor, keep the TV off during meals. They strike an equal balance, she recently told a *New York Times* reporter, between listening to their children and asking them to weigh in on "moral dilemmas." She offers an example of a question she might ask her kids: "If one of us committed a crime, would you turn us in?" Whether you agree with this family's approach, you at least have to respect the idea that the parents have put thought into this zone: "I felt like, let's not just gossip about stupid stuff. I wanted them to be more cultured and have deeper thoughts."

Parents often use strategies to get the conversation going—for example, asking about each person's "rose" (the best part of the day) and "thorn" (the worst or hardest). It's important to figure out what works for your clan. "I have two boys," said one mother who liked the idea of a best/worst prompt, "but we use root-beer floats and Brussels sprouts instead!" She passed the strategy on to another mother, whose family changed it to spaghetti and eggplant. Regardless of how you designate the best and worst, the important point is that the adults also have to participate and talk about their day.

FYN Some Questions about Your Dinner Zone

- What's your orientation to food? To cooking? Do you enjoy putting food on the table? Does it feel good when you see the family eating together? Or is this a time you tolerate because you know you all have to eat?
- Do you stress the importance of family dinners in your home? How many nights a week do you eat together? If you rarely do, what stands in the way?
- Are several different choices offered to cut down on mealtime complaints, or is everyone expected to eat what's served?
- Is a blessing said before dinner? Is it a rule to wait until everyone is served before starting? Are manners and civility important? What happens to anyone who is not civil—are they reprimanded, asked to leave, banished without dinner?

(continued on next page)

- Is the dinner table a place for conversation? Do people really listen to one another? Do adults and children have equal talk time?
- Does your clan favor a conversational free-for-all, or do you try to give everyone a turn to talk. Are you hoping to hear news of each person's day, or are you hoping to stimulate their minds? Do you regularly use a specific strategy to get them going?
- Are dinners generally rushed? Pleasant? Emotionally taxing? What do you think contributes to this atmosphere?
- Are there troubling issues around dinner? Is one child a poor or picky eater? Is she reprimanded for pushing food around the plate, for eating too slowly or not finishing? Is someone on a diet? Are certain foods or substances (such as sugar) considered bad or forbidden altogether?

Free Time

The Challenge: Look at free time as a window into family members' needs and choices and as a way to determine whether and how you spend time as a family.

This zone refers to any period of time at home that's not spoken for or required. It's about making choices—and those choices tell us a lot about each person and about the family. You might argue that doing homework or putting the finishing touches on a report is not optional. That's true, but when, how, where, and whether those things make it into the family routine *are* a matter of choice.

For families with school-age children, free time at home tends to occur—if it happens at all—after school, before dinner, and before bed. In most families, mornings are hectic, but one of the adults might enter this zone by slipping out for a run or taking time on a treadmill.

Free-time zones depend on homework load and extracurricular activities, how independent the kids are, whether the adults work at home or bring their own "homework" from the office. It is also a matter of how time and responsibilities have been negotiated—the expectations, the rules, and whether it's even OK to take time from the family to snag a moment to yourself.

Free time often flies by, barely noticed. When we ask people, for example, "How are your evenings at home spent?" they often have no idea. It's just a blur of kids and homework, baths and negotiation. It certainly doesn't feel like free time. Most women rarely find themselves in this zone during the evening—they're busy with chores. Free time also can be eaten up if you're still dealing with lingering sleep issues. Fretful babies often turn into toddlers who, a decade later, become teens who continue to have trouble getting to bed.

Increasingly, families' free time is spent on digital devices. Parents catch up on email, take turns in Words with Friends, and trade links with Facebook friends, while the kids are off in a corner with *their* gadgets. It may be free time, but it's certainly not family time.

Here's the saddest irony about free time. All family members, including mothers, feel happiest when the whole family is together. The problem, research suggests, is that it rarely happens. Families devote relatively little time to joint activities. In one survey that looked at working parents with adolescents, the family was together *as a family*, on average, four hours a week—mostly at the dinner table or watching TV together. In another study of middle-class working families with slightly younger children, families were observed "in the same home space" only during 15 percent of the evening, and some never were. Granted, family members might have spent time together when the researchers weren't watching. Still, those are sobering statistics.

FYN Some Questions about Your Free Time Zone

- In general, is weekday free time about connecting or doing your own thing? Do you each carve out your own corner? If so, do family members generally announce their intentions ("Tonight I'm paying bills," "I'm going upstairs to work on my airplane model")? Or do they silently wander off?
- How does the issue of screen time play out in your household? Do children need permission, or can they just flick on the switch? Are there rules? Limits? Are all types of screens lumped together, or do you distinguish between TV and hand-held digital gadgets? Are there different rules about how close to bedtime children are allowed to be in front of a screen? Do adults have to abide by screen rules, too?
- Do family members pair off regularly, sometimes, or rarely? Does one usually invite the other ("The Eagles game is on in fifteen minutes—want to watch with me?" "C'mon, let's go build a Lego house")? Are invitations quickly and eagerly accepted, or is coaxing involved?

(continued on next page)

- During the week, does the whole family engage in games, sports, screen watching, or other activities? Do you have a family project? Even if you're all off doing your own things, is there still a sense of togetherness? What does that look like in your household—members conversing and relating even though they're differently involved?
- Is the adults' evening cut short because of chores, homework helping, a child's drawn-out bedtime routine? Are there disagreements over such things? Is one adult more disgruntled about "having no time to myself" than the other?
- Is one family member resentful about not having time with a particular person ("I don't see enough of ———")? Does he or she actually say this? Have you discussed it?

Bedtime

Bedtime is the doorway to a good night's sleep, which apparently not many of us get. In our 2005 book, we drew on the National Sleep Foundation's annual 2004 Sleep in America poll, which showed that:

The Challenge: Bedtime should be a special time of intimacy and sweetness that leads to a peaceful night's sleep. In an ideal world, no child or adult would go to bed crying or angry.

- Children were sleeping less than experts recommended.
- Two-thirds of kids experienced frequent sleep problems.
- Because of children's nighttime waking, parents lost around two hundred hours of sleep that year.

A good night's sleep is still hard to come by. More than half of the Americans between the ages of thirteen and sixty-four polled by the NSF in 2011 experienced a sleep problem every night or almost every night—snoring, waking in the night, waking up too early, feeling unrefreshed when they got up in the morning. Part of the problem is technology. Almost everyone surveyed (95 percent) used some type of electronics in the hour before trying to sleep (television, computer, video game, or cell phone) at least a few nights a week.

Bodies need to rest. Lack of proper sleep results in learning problems and poor performance at work, erratic mood swings, and difficulties with relationships. Bedtime, therefore, should be sacred—a time for winding down and letting go of the day's responsibilities. Good habits can be started early. It's why we included three chapters on sleep in our third book.

Bedtime should take time, both for children and adults. It must include a wind-down period, a critical part of Tracy's "sensible sleep" ritual, which was designed to help babies and toddlers. However, switching to calming activities, like reading books instead of having screen time, works at any age—and for the whole family. The goal is to help everyone get enough sleep (see sidebar), a problem in many households. The wind-down ritual is a good start; it sometimes includes a bath. Also, the room always should be darkened and the shades drawn—a physical act that both inspires rest and symbolizes a shift from activity to sleep.

How Much Sleep?

The following are just guidelines; some people need more or less sleep, depending on their own body clock, lifestyle, and health.

Ages 1–3:	12 to 14 hours
Ages 3–5:	11 to 13 hours
Ages 5–10:	10 to 11 hours
Ages 10–17:	8½ to 9¼ hours
Adults:	7 to 9 hours

Source: National Sleep Foundation.

Parents put children to bed or at least oversee the process even as the kids inch toward their teens, because it can be a time of special closeness. But there's a difference between having a moment together and adults' *over*involvement. The latter drains the parent and robs children of their independence. Sometimes the child *wants* to be more independent, and it's hard for the parent to let go.

If you've been helping your child learn to make good choices and become increasingly independent, at some point you'll allow her to monitor her own bedtime. "She goes to bed after us now," said an otherwise vigilant mother of a fourteen-year-old girl. "It was taking too much energy to constantly check on her, so I said, 'OK, you have to learn to get yourself to bed. You'll see that you're tired if you don't get enough sleep.'" Wise mother!

FYN Some Questions about Your Bedtime Zone

The children:

- When your children were younger, did you allow time for winding down before bed to set the stage for sleep? Did you practice a consistent bedtime ritual? Did the little ones develop self-soothing skills and learn to fall asleep on their own?
- Do you have a predictable bedtime ritual now? What does children's bedtime look like in your family—reading, cuddling, talking, screen watching, fighting?
- Do the children have fairly consistent bedtimes? If you have more than one child, do they all have the same bedtime? If not, what determines bedtime—age, willingness to sleep, other?
- Is bedtime problematic, something you dread? How long has this been going on? What have you done to correct the problem? Do children's bedtime issues cut into adult time?
- Do the children sleep through the night? If not, do they wake you? Do you take them into your bed?
- Do the children get enough sleep? Do you know what they look like when they don't?
- If there are two adults in your household, do you agree about bedtime practices? Have children's sleep issues become a point of contention—one believes in a more consistent bedtime, one is more likely to give in to a child's endless requests after lights-out?

The adults:

- Do you and your partner, if you have one, go to bed at the same time?
- Do you have an evening ritual that involves reviewing the day and renewing your intimacy? Do you share about your own lives, focus mostly on the kids, or both?
- Even if you don't actually make love every night, are you consistently intimate with each other in some way—snuggling, spooning, kissing, anything that suggests that you're more than just friends?
- Do you ever/often go to bed angry, or do you have a rule that you must try to talk things out? How's that working out?
- Do you sleep through the night? If not, what do you do when you get up?
- Have your own sleep issues been the result of a long-term pattern in your life, or did they begin after you became a partner? A parent?
- Are you getting enough sleep?

Weekends

Weekends are a window into family life, too—a weekly occurrence rather than a daily zone. Once upon a time, you could tell the difference between weekends and weekdays. Weekends used to be for doing things in your own time. There were fewer obligations and scheduled events. But in many families today, the weekend means an even more crowded calendar. The adults have catch-up errands and projects they couldn't get to during the week, along with social gatherings, dinner dates with other couples, and if they're lucky, a date night. The kids have Little League, classes, recitals, and an endless stream of classmates' birthday parties. If there's time, the weekends are also for movies and family outings and special occasions with the extended family.

> **The Challenge:** Clear the calendar to leave room for family time. Weekends should also give each family member at least a small chunk of down time.

Your weekends speak volumes about what your family is like—and what your family likes. So pay attention. Before answering the questions below, review the V indicators, as suggested on page 21: your family's *values* (what's important), *venues* (where you go), and *vulnerabilities* (what gets to you).

FYN Some Questions about Your Weekends

- When you think about your family weekends, do you actually frequent the venues your family prefers—the ones you listed in your Family Notebook in response to the "What's Your Family Like?" exercise? Are you true to your values? Does the weekend bring out particular vulnerabilities?
- When you enjoy a weekend, what, exactly, makes it pleasant? How is a great weekend different from a weekend that leaves you drained?
- What do you find disruptive on weekends—traveling, overscheduling, too little time for yourself, too little time together as a family?
- Do you have weekend traditions, such as pancakes on Sunday, a special regular outing, dinner with the extended family, or anything that leaves you with a lingering feeling of family?
- Do you consciously build in down time on weekends?

So What Does It All Mean?

We have only touched on the basic highlights of a day in the life of your family, the times that everyone shares—waking and sleeping, mealtimes, exits and entrances, how you share responsibilities, how you plan. Don't be surprised if this felt like hard work. Most of us have pretty full plates nowadays, and it's enough to get through the day without adding a heaping serving of introspection. Thinking about every moment *is* hard work. Especially if you took notes (and we hope you did), you might be feeling a bit overwhelmed. That's because you've just recorded and taken in a lot of information about something you normally don't analyze.

However, you now have a better overall sense of how your family gets through the day. Don't expect to come to any tidy conclusions, though. Instead, think of what you've learned as baseline information, a snapshot of your family at this point in time. It's there for you to review when your family has to deal with new circumstances and especially when problems emerge. Information is power. Looking closely at your family will change the way you see it and enable you to make changes when necessary. It will also give you clues about how to inspire everyone to "invest," as we explain in chapter 7.

FYN How's Your Family Routine?

Take a few minutes to jot down whatever ideas popped into your head after reading the previous questions about the ten zones and your weekends.

- Did this exercise give you new insights or confirm what you already thought about your household?
- What do you wonder about? Worry about? Feel good about?
- Are there things you'd like to do differently?

Notes on the Zones

SEVEN

STAKEHOLDERS IN THE FAMILY CO-OP

Strengthening the **We**, Supporting the **I**s

Members of strong families feel good about themselves as a family unit or team; they have a sense of belonging with each other—a sense of "we." At the same time no individual gets lost or smothered; each family member is encouraged to develop his or her potential.

—NICK STINNET AND JOHN DEFRAIN,
IN *SECRETS OF STRONG FAMILIES*

Lanie and Bill Allen, both forty-two, met in college and now live in a small town in the South with their four children: Peter, sixteen, Kyle, fourteen, Tom, twelve, and Hannah, ten. Lanie and Bill grew up south of the Mason-Dixon Line. Both wanted children and a rich family life, but their respective visions were the result, in part, of very different childhoods.

"He comes from a family with traditional roles and expectations of what Mom and Dad should do," Lanie explains. "I come from a family with no expectations about dinner or how the laundry should be done, or *if* it should be done!" She imagined that her own family would be loud and loving. "I envisioned wonderful holidays together. I also thought everything would be perfectly perfect. We're not! At times, we're downright disorganized and haywire. I've had to learn over the years to not fight it, but let's face it, I'll never be a 'magazine mom.'"

"Zany Lanie" was working on her doctorate when the first Allen child, Peter, was born. She was already on a different road from Bill's stay-at-home mother. Although she took time off to be with her four kids, when Hannah, the youngest was two, Lanie told Bill she wanted to work part-time. "He hit the roof at first, because he was worried about how it would affect the family," Lanie recalls. "He had a really hard time. Nontraditional is tough for him; so is change."

Eight years later, she's still her, and he's still him, but their similarities have helped sustain them through their differences. "We're pretty much in line as parents," Bill agrees. "Church is important and community service. We're fairly strict, and we demand excellence, kindness, and doing the right thing." The Allens guide their children, says Bill, to "have a lot of fun, work hard and play hard, and be good community members."

Most important, they remind their children day after endless day that they are part of something bigger. When one of the boys gets into trouble, they frame it as a family issue, not an individual shortcoming. For example, Kyle was caught drawing a "body part" on a classmate's hand. Bill acknowledged that "it was the same kind of mischief we did as kids. He's going to do things like that. But I wanted him to understand that his actions reflect on the Allen name, so I told him, 'You have a responsibility not only to uphold yourself and your actions but also to uphold the family.'"

That message has gotten through. Certainly, there are times when the Allen kids, like all children, want what they want, lie or get into trouble, and tease one another, but they are also capable of being loving, responsible family members and good citizens.

The Four Requirements

What inspires family members to want to be part of something bigger and, at times, to put their own needs aside for the sake of the **We**—the family? The short answer is that each person sees himself or herself as a "stakeholder," someone who cares about the family, wants to protect and sustain it and help it "run."

Being a stakeholder is a form of what psychologists call "social investment." Your personal growth as an individual comes, paradoxically, by putting your energies and commitment into something bigger—in this case, your family. Individuals who "invest" in this way—it could also be a company, a cause, a team, or a spiritual community—tend to have more desirable personality traits: warmth, conscientiousness, openness. They are more organized and less depressed than people who are isolated.

Does social investment cause you to develop these more agreeable personalities, or do you possess those traits to begin with, which would make you more likely to invest in the first place? For most of us, it's a little of both.

It *is* easier for some people to step up to the plate because of the qualities they possess. You can see it in nursery-school classrooms. Some children are more engaging, kinder, and more easygoing than others. They join in and are the first to act when the teacher asks for volunteers or shouts, "Cleanup time!" They're likely to comfort or help when another kid cries.

For others, social investment involves more of a learning process. Being around people who are conscientious and committed—and, importantly, *expecting* something of them—inspires them to invest, too, and to become willing stakeholders.

The best families take care of business the way a cooperative does. Everyone is a member of the co-op. Everyone pitches in. Everyone gets cared for. Everyone has a stake in the family's welfare. The adults have a "good enough" relationship that nurtures each of them. And like a responsible board of directors, they set policy. But when it comes to making plans, major decisions, or changes, they also seek the input of the "membership" (of which they, too, are a part). In a single-parent family, one adult is the sole director and confers with the members, but he also has a range of "consultants"—extended family and close friends, acquaintances whose opinion he respects, and in the case of a well-managed divorce or separation, an ex-spouse with whom he coordinates.

In a well-run family co-op, the adults and children are consciously aware of caring for the **We**. In a sense, the "by-laws"—the family's overriding values and beliefs—create an environment in which every member has a role. To the best of their age and ability, everyone is a stakeholder. And at the same time, family members know that each **I** is important, too.

Every family's **We** is unique. But those in which family members are more likely to act and feel like stakeholders have four key characteristics in common. Think of them as the Four Requirements of family stakeholding:

- **The We values its members.** Each person knows that she matters to the rest of the family. Each one's **I** is respected and accepted for who he or she is and as an essential part of the **We**.
- **The We is cared for.** The adults oversee it, the children help run it, and everyone pitches in to protect it.

- **The We is fair.** The family's resources—money, energy, and time—are spent thoughtfully and divided fairly.
- **The We is loved.** Everyone puts energy into planning good times together, noticing little moments of joy and connection, and savoring important occasions, all of which makes the family a good place to be and to come home to. The Is enjoy, and are grateful for, being part of the **We**.

There's no particular order here. The Four Requirements work together. In the pages that follow, we discuss the Four Requirements in greater detail and show you how to meet them.

The **We** Values Its Members

There *is* an *I* in *family*. And in the best families, each person is seen, accepted, and supported for who he or she really is, which strengthens his or her commitment as a stakeholder. Family members recognize that the **We** holds and heals them. Why wouldn't they want to better it? When they bolster the **We**, it becomes stronger and better able to care for them. It's an *auspicious cycle*.

"The needs of the many outweigh the needs of the few—or the one," Mr. Spock famously said in the movie *Star Trek II* when he sacrifices himself to save the ship and its crew. At times, a family is like the Starship *Enterprise*. Everyone pulls together for the greater good. But at other times, the needs of the one might outweigh the needs of the many—or at the very least, must be taken into consideration.

Whether your **We** has two or ten members, the reality of family life is that someone always wants something. It's not always easy to see, because we're caught up in the thick of it. But if you could rise above—view your family from a more distant perspective—you would see how the Is assert themselves and, sometimes, collide.

We can't possibly know what your family is like—who your partner is (or if you have one), how many children you have, how far apart they're spaced, or how the Three Factors have shaped you thus far. Therefore, we've constructed a make-believe family for you to borrow and to observe. Even if your **We** is considerably different, the scenario might feel familiar.

As you magically fly above your kitchen—a room in which everyday family dramas often play out—you'll see your two kids, eight-year-old

Grace and five-year-old Calvin, and your seventy-nine-year-old father. Your mother died several years ago, and Dad, who lives in a senior residence nearby, often eats dinner with you. Grace grabs a Slinky from Calvin. He pulls back, clutching one end of the metal coil, which is now almost three feet long.

"I just want to see it!" she insists. "Don't be such a baby."

He screams.

You don't intervene. You've been here. *Let 'em work it out.*

A few minutes later, Calvin runs out of the room, shouting, "No, no, no!"

You have no idea what's going on. You're busy preparing dinner and have tuned them out. But when you call out to remind Cal to wash up for dinner, he doesn't budge from the couch.

"Oh, you were just like that as a kid," your father offers. "Just leave him alone. And what's the big deal if he doesn't wash his hands? It's not like he's been digging ditches."

"Daaaaad," you say between clenched teeth. You want to add, "Butt out!" but you don't. He seems to read your mind, anyway, and shrugs accordingly. You've been *here,* too.

Enter Roger, your partner. It doesn't occur to you to lead with "Hi, honey" or ask about *his* day. Instead, you say, "Did you remember to buy milk?"

"You forgot to text me," he says accusingly.

You shoot him "the look." *Why is it my job to remind him?*

When you rise above the fray like this, you might notice things you miss when you're on the ground, being a member of the **We**. You see how the **I**s bump up against—and affect—one another. It's like watching a family ballet. Every action, interaction, and emotion that sweeps through the family ecosystem changes you and changes them. You seep through one another's pores. At any given minute, one (or more) of your **I**s seems to be screaming "Look at me" or "Leave me alone."

This view from above allows you to see that Roger, now sitting at the table, is glancing into space. His hands are balled into fists. Angry about your greeting, he avoids your eyes and looks at the children instead, heaving a loud sigh that says, *I hope they don't start, too.* Roger would just as soon take his **I** elsewhere. For that matter, so would you.

Each gesture and exchange is rich with information. The kids look at each other and then back at you and Roger glaring at each other. It's brief, but their eyes go wide—a stress response. Calvin glances in your direction after he shouts at Grace *again*. "You're in my chair." He wants to make sure you're listening. He wants you to help him defend his I. That Calvin is so easily ruffled by his sister today could be business as usual. Or perhaps an incident earlier in the day with a classmate or his teacher left him feeling a bit vulnerable. Either way, his I needs attention.

During dinner, you sit next to Calvin, coaxing him to eat his peas, and you catch Grace smiling. She leans toward her father and grabs his arm. Grace's smile and body language suggest that she's trying to align her I with Roger's. You might wonder if that horrible Marianne Pierce is still taunting Grace at school. When her I feels safe, she's kind and considerate to Cal and enjoys being Big Sister; on her bad days, she wishes you'd give him back. At this moment, she seems almost delighted that Cal is on the hot seat!

What You See You Can Change

In one family scene, it's all there: your individual personalities, your relationships, and whatever the world has flung at you so far, separately and together. Roger's suppressed anger is all the more intense because his I wanted to get closer to you last night. Instead, you gave him a quick peck on the cheek and rattled off a list of repairs that needed doing. Factor in today's less-than-warm greeting, and it's not hard to see why Roger's I feels dismissed, unappreciated, and exploited at the same time.

Looking down at yourself, it's easier to tell yourself the truth: Your I felt as if it was under siege *before* Roger walked in. The kids were going at it, Calvin was being uncooperative, and your father seemed to be judging you. You also realize that urging Calvin to eat his peas had more to do with your I than his. You were a skinny kid, forced to take "tonics" to improve your appetite, and you swore you'd never do that to any child of yours. At the same time, when Calvin doesn't eat well, you somehow believe you're a bad mother. If you could fly even higher, above your household, and watch what's happening in other homes, you'd see that you've absorbed those beliefs from several bigger contexts—your community, class, the culture, your ethnic group—all of which have given you ideas about motherhood.

But it's not only the past or the context that affects you at this moment. Dammit, your I wants control over *something*. Meanwhile, your father is sitting right there, witnessing the whole thing. You imagine the car ride back to his apartment, when he tells you once again that you "make too much of everything."

There's nothing out of the ordinary in this scene. Even on a good day, the family ecosystem is a tangle of individual needs and desires, the Is jockeying for position, reacting to one another, and at the same time, vying for their piece of the family pie. No surprise here. The family is where we first learn to mediate our own needs with what others need.

In the moment, as we explained in chapter 3, it's important to tune in—be mindful—a basic tenet of family whispering. You can use the TYTT mantra (page 87) to help you rise above it all. The story of Harriet and Gretchen in chapter 4 shows how important it is to slow down, monitor what your own I needs, consider the other person's I, tell yourself the truth, and then *do* something.

For example, in the midst of this kitchen scene, you might have taken a momentary PTO (personal time-out) before you let your father's comment and your kids' squabbling get to you. Had you spent even ten minutes taking a walk, reading, or having a quick shower, that "breather" (a perfect term because it allows you to breathe again) would have made a difference. When Roger walked in, you might have taken another deep breath and not allowed feelings from those interactions to spill into your partnership. You might have taken him aside and told him what was happening. You might have given him a hug and said, "I'm sooooo glad you're home, hon. But I'm really sorry. Between my kids and my father, I'm about to lose it."

If you were honest at that moment, presenting your authentic self, and if you also let your partner know that you needed him just to listen, not to fix the situation, that might have changed the scene. You might have felt you had an ally, someone who understood what your I was going through—and that, too, would have helped you recharge. In a perfect world, your partner would have asked, "What else do we need to do for dinner?" Then you would have been able to cool down, instead of letting your feelings ratchet up about the kids and your father. You would have had the energy to spend a few minutes with each child before dinner to ask about their day. And you might even have remembered to ask your dad about the sculpture he is working on.

Of course, the world is not perfect. But any action or word in which an I in need is cared for usually changes the scene for everyone. The fact is, if any one of your Is feels deprived or invisible, you can't have a solid **We**.

FYN Instant Replay

Think of a recent family moment, and replay it while watching all the actors in your family drama.

- What is each I doing? Do you feel pulled at? What does that person's behavior make you feel or awaken in you?
- Who is vying for family resources? Be specific. Does the person want time and attention? Does his or her demand require more energy than you can, or are willing to, give?
- Was anyone being ignored? Does this happen frequently with that particular family member?
- Ask yourself if you're willing to learn from this replay and apply the same questions to future family moments. If you're not, try to figure out why. Does it feel like too much work? Are you too angry at other family members? Especially if it's the latter, you might be in one of the early stages of chore wars (see "The Chore Wars Progression," page 185).

Valuing the Is: Let 'Em Know They Matter

At the end of her senior year in high school, Carlie Reynaldo's life was changed forever by a drunk driver. A middle child and only daughter, she was in the passenger seat when the young man careened into her mother's blue Camry. Her mom was killed instantly, and Carlie, a good student and talented athlete, was left with serious multiple injuries. "I had a broken hip and pelvis and was bruised all over."

Aunt Laurie, her mother's protective older sister who had no children of her own, had always been a part of Carlie's life. As a kid, Carlie would get on the bus in New Jersey with her two brothers, and Aunt Laurie would meet them at the Port Authority Terminal in Manhattan. Laurie took them to the movies or out to dinner and shared family stories. Years of trust had accumulated even before Bernadette was killed. After the accident, Laurie rushed to the hospital and let her niece know that life had to go on.

"She was very frank and straightforward," Carlie recalls. "I remember her telling me that my brother Jason was coming to visit—he was ten at the time—and that I'd better look my best for him."

Looking back, Carlie credits Aunt Laurie for setting her on the right path. Carlie thought it would be better if she lived at home, so she could help her father out with Jason. Her plan was to reject the full scholarship an Ivy League university nursing school had offered before the accident and enroll at a local college instead. "Nothin' doin'," Aunt Laurie said when Carlie shared her plan. "You're going, and you're going to do well. It's going to be hard, but you can't pass up that kind of opportunity."

"She believed in me, and she had high expectations. She wouldn't let me screw it up!" Carlie explains. "She was not an enabler after my mom died. She expected all three of us to do for ourselves. But she was *there* for us."

In effect, because her sister was no longer around and her brother-in-law was preoccupied with his own grief, Aunt Laurie's stepping in gave Carlie and her brothers a **We**. She told them, "We need to face what happened. We need to say it out loud and then do something about it." She let them know that even though Bernadette was gone, there was still a **We**—and that the three of them mattered.

The concept of *mattering* was first used in the late 1980s to explain why some students weather the transition to college better than others. Those who perceive that they matter feel as if they are part of a bigger **We**. They are more likely to hunker down and do whatever it takes to get past the hard stuff. They know they have support and that others care about them. In contrast, those who feel marginal—as if no one notices or cares—often become self-conscious, irritable, or depressed in the face of change.

It works the same way in families. Mattering is a win-win. When you feel that you matter to your family, you believe that others are proud of your successes and sympathize with your failures and that you'd be missed if you were gone. That sense of being cherished makes you want to give back and to let others know that they matter to you as well. You're more willing to strengthen the **We**.

The sense that she mattered so much to Aunt Laurie helped Carlie Reynaldo believe in herself. It enabled her to push through her grief, spend several months using a walker, and cope with four years at the more rigorous nursing school. In the long run, being part of a **We** paved a path to her own family. Today, Carlie is married and has a family similar to the one of her own childhood, two boys and a girl. "There are things I do like my mom—holiday stuff, mealtimes—but Aunt Laurie really taught me how to parent. I'm the same way with my kids as she was with me."

Mattering is not the same as self-esteem, which comes from within.

It's a sense, a confidence, that you derive from your relationships, especially from family members.

To whom do *you* matter? Do other family members think *they* matter? This simple five-item "mattering" quiz can help you find out.

Do You Matter to Others?

Sociologist John Taylor uses a simple five-item quiz to gauge mattering. You can take this test several times if you like, keeping a particular family member in mind or the family as a whole. Use the following rating scale:

1 = not at all   2 = a little   3 = somewhat   4 = a lot

1. How important are you to [name]/your family?   _____
2. How much does [name]/your whole family pay attention to you?   _____
3. How much would you be missed if you went away?   _____
4. How interested is [name]/your whole family in what you have to say?   _____
5. How much does [name]/your whole family depend on you?   _____

Your score is the total divided by 5. Most people report high levels of mattering, usually around 3.5.

The following are a few things to remember about letting family members know they matter.

Say good things about them out loud and __to__ them. We often boast about family members to relatives, good friends, and acquaintances: "My husband is such a dear. I don't know how I'd get by without his support." "My middle boy is the helpful one. I can always count on him to clean up." But do you remember to say it out loud and thank *that person?*

"I can know in my own heart that I would do anything for my wife and kids, but if I don't say that to them, I'm living a lie," says sociologist John Taylor, who studies mattering and promotes it in his own family with his wife, a dermatologist, and two sons, ages ten and thirteen. "I don't leave the house without kissing everyone good-bye. I understand that parents are overwhelmed, and kids are so busy. But you have to do the little things that let people know they're valued."

Take the time to notice. When your partner or children are helpful, tell them how much you value their input ("I followed your advice about talking to my teacher, and it really worked out"). When they carry through on a promise or take over a particular responsibility, even if it's something they're supposed to do, let them know they're appreciated. Thank them, but don't overdo it. Letting someone know they matter is not the same as doting or smothering. Praise and appreciation should be doled out when others deserve it and when you really mean it.

When you're not together, let them know that you're thinking about them ("I met a little boy today at the volunteer center, and he reminded me of you, because he was so good at building Lego houses"). These little authentic statements take almost no time, but they have a big impact, and they inspire family members to reciprocate. Mattering is also conveyed when you respect each I and when you listen and are present, when you are patient and don't jump to negative conclusions about the other person's intention, as in "You're doing that to drive me crazy!"

Tailor your appreciation. The way you let someone know that he matters differs from person to person. Don't necessarily use yourself as a gauge. For example, you might feel that you matter when your partner takes you in her arms. But she might perceive that she matters when you unexpectedly call her at work to say, "Honey, I gather you've had a rough day. Why don't you go to the gym instead of coming straight home from the office?" Likewise, one of your children might feel valued after a cuddle, while the other knows he matters because you let him come along when you go to the gym.

Abby Porter, the mother of two boys, is aware of the fact that her I figures into the equation when it comes to paying attention to her sons' respective interests. "Zane just happened to fall in love with something I also love," she explained, referring to her older boy, an inveterate jock who likes to watch sports as much as compete in them. When Abby goes to Zane's games or watches the playoffs with him, he knows he matters. She has to find a different approach with Levi, who isn't into sports. "His interests—meteorology, geology, trucks—are harder. It's not that I'm *un*-interested. I'm a nonfiction thinker, so I can go there, but it takes a little more effort. Thank God it's not superheroes, though. *That* I'd have trouble wrapping my head around!"

Sometimes we do things for our loved ones simply because it makes their I feel good. Liz Weil camping out with her family. Abby Porter taking Levi to a monster truck show. More than kind words or praise, an action has great power. Andrew Solomon recalls his own childhood in his recent book, *Far from the Tree*, and his fascination at age ten with "the tiny principality of Liechtenstein." A year later, when a business trip brought the family to Switzerland, his mother carved out time to visit Liechtenstein's capital, Vaduz. "I remember the thrill that the whole family was going along with what was clearly my wish and mine alone." Andrew knew he mattered.

Maintaining a healthy **I/We** balance—meeting individuals' needs and the family's—can be especially challenging when one person's condition necessarily overshadows the others. But if the **We** has been nurturing the **I**s all along, family members at least recognize the intention to be fair. For instance, Jack Reynaldo (Carlie's older son) was diagnosed with leukemia at seventeen. During Jack's chemo sessions, he rarely had an appetite. Every night, Carlie asked what he felt like eating. "One day," Carlie recalls, "when Jack said 'spaghetti and meat balls,' Nora piped up, 'What if *I* don't want that for dinner?'" Carlie explained to her that Jack rarely even ate dinner or had a yen for something in particular. Nora, then ten, listened, and when her mother stopped talking, she said, "But sometimes *I* want to be the one who picks out what's for dinner." Of course, Nora didn't really care about dinner. She needed to know that she mattered, too.

The **We** Is Cared For

"We knew our grandfather loved us, because he always gave us work," Stephen Klein recalls, speaking of his mother's father, a "major figure" in his childhood, especially after his parents divorced. "He made it clear that he needed our help, whether it was picking up dog shit, painting, or moving something for him." By asking Stephen and his siblings to "work," his grandfather was essentially asking them to help care for the **We**. He wasn't making busy work so they wouldn't get into trouble; he genuinely needed their help, wasn't afraid to ask, and knew it was good for his grandsons to pitch in.

Caring for something outside of yourself, knowing that you make a contribution that benefits the whole family, makes children and adults feel good and want to do good. The **We** becomes stronger. The Sargent-Kleins started when their four children were barely out of diapers. "We might be getting ready for the holidays, and the house needed to be cleaned. We'd say to them, 'Hey guys. We need your help.'" Stephen adds that it's not just important to say you need help. "You actually have to allow yourself to be a little helpless."

No **I** is an island. Promoting cooperation isn't simply because we all *need* help or because we *should* get children involved. More than one head is better than one. Each brings a different way of seeing and thinking to the table. Increasingly, we humans are being relied on to participate, co-operate, and co-create, not just to show off our phenomenal individual selves. Today, virtually every business, institution, and cultural and civic arena is undergoing a major shift that requires people to work and think together—to share. What better place to learn this than in our own families?

Don't mistake taking care of the **We** as a discussion about chores. It's a much bigger and more important issue. Think in terms of what roles need to be filled to sustain your family. Instead of "The patio has to get swept," the family needs a *sweeper*. Instead of "Feed the dog," we need a *dog feeder*. Instead of "Who's going to make school lunches?" we need a *lunch maker*. We also need assistants, like a *bed maker's helper* or a *reminder* (a role little kids love and are usually better at than busy adults).

This is not just clever word play, a way to disguise chore assignments or make them more palatable. It's family-think. Families are built on mutual obligation. Remember the *R* in REAL. We're all *responsible* for this entity that is our family. How do we care for it together? And remember that if your child is old enough to attend school, she's already been asked to step into various roles. In most preschool classrooms, you find line leaders and snack helpers. Often, the only place young children's skills aren't tapped is at home!

"Role doling" (which we discuss in greater detail in the next chapter) is not about making family members responsible, although it does that. When you're part of any organization that rewards participation and independence, you become more conscientious. It's also about increasing everyone's skill set and knowledge. You gain confidence and competence when you wear different hats. In short, the **We** thrives, and so do you.

Family Check-Ins: KISS

Taking care of the **We** requires thought, planning, effort, and follow-through, not just the completion of tasks. The needs of the many keep changing. The **I**s grow, their relationships shift, and new cards are dealt. The many have to have a simple yet effective way of staying on course as a unit. Weekly "check-ins" allow family members to be in it together—

talking, sharing, supporting, learning, exploring new ideas, planning, helping each member find ways to pitch in.

Don't confuse a check-in with a "family meeting." Otherwise, you might stop reading. When you ask parents today about whether and how often they have family meetings, they hesitate. A rare few say, "Of course—every week." Most have to think about it, and in that moment of silence, they look a tad guilty. Some will even say out loud, "I know we *should*, but . . ." This is followed by:

"The kids are too young."
"Who has the time?"
"We did for a while but couldn't seem to stick to it."
"We're not sure how to do it."

Having a family meeting sounds like a big deal, a grave undertaking in which problems are aired and important decisions are made. The very idea of adding an extra "should" into the family routine is enough to put many modern parents over the edge.

Tracy loved to remind people of KISS: "Keep it simple, Stan."* A check-in is the KISS alternative to family meetings—something easier, tailored to your family in particular, and more fun. And less daunting.

What is it? A time to look at what the **We** needs and to also see how each of the **I**s are doing. A check-in makes everyone feel like a stakeholder. It's mostly about enjoying and encouraging one another, but it also delivers certainty and support when times are tough. It is a time to make decisions and solve problems and to solidify the sense that we're a unit. The check-in acknowledges that each of you is an independent thinker and doer. It helps everyone notice subtle change—each day, we become a little more capable and competent—and to be rightfully proud of ourselves. The biggest payoff is that the whole family is stronger, a place everyone wants to come home to and help.

Who's in charge? The parents are the executives—the board of directors—who make the rules and have the last word, but the children have input. They can communicate their desires and feelings, complain

---

* KISS, which Tracy picked up in twelve-step meetings, actually stands for "Keep it simple, stupid." But Tracy didn't believe in calling anyone stupid, even in jest. Who Stan is will forever remain a mystery.

about something that is unfair or impractical (from their point of view), contribute their ideas and solutions.

Who takes part? Everyone. In fact, if your only child is young, start now to get in the check-in habit. She can just listen at first. She's probably not going to come up with meaningful suggestions, but including her acknowledges that she's a stakeholder, too.

How do we prepare? Bring up the idea first with your partner. Agree to at least try. Then talk to the kids. Do it at dinner one night, a time when you're together and off screens, or on a long car ride. You might say something like this:

> *We're going to start having "family check-ins." Every week, we'll find a place to sit together—maybe right here at the table, maybe on the porch, wherever we decide. It will give us a chance to talk about ourselves and our family. Let's first pick a day. And then let's figure out how to have some fun with this. Maybe we could combine it with ice cream, or maybe you have some other ideas.*

But what if the children resist? "My kids will never go for it," one mother lamented. Many parents probably have similar concerns. The notion of check-ins might not be well received at first. Expect them to say it will take too much time or that the whole idea is "lame." They might feel awkward, too, depending on how old they are, how the idea is presented, whether the execs are in sync, and what else is going on in your family. If you're the only one on board at first, make the suggestion and start small. Convince the **I**s to commit to six check-ins for the good of the **We**, at least three if they really balk. But let it be known that *not* trying is unacceptable. Start with very brief check-ins and modest intentions, at least until they become a natural part of your family's routine. Be open to suggestions.

If your kids are five or younger—*and* you're committed to the idea (kids sense parents' ambivalence)—getting them on board will be relatively easy. Older children, especially teens, might give you a hard time. In that case, insist. Use words that feel comfortable to you, but let them know that it's not negotiable.

> *You might think this sounds dorky or inconvenient, but it's good for our family, so we're going to do it.*

If a teen asks, "Why now?" or accuses you of having just read this new "technique" in a book (older kids are incredibly savvy about self-help), explain:

Yes, I know we haven't done this before. But now that each of us is so involved in our own stuff, that's all the more reason to make sure we have these weekly check-ins. Let's at least try it, and if it's working, great, and if not, we'll see what we can do to make it better.

Your children might still roll their eyes and groan, but the important part is that they show up.

This is not meant as a punishment. It's a time when we can all be together. And each of us can help make it a good time.

Stick with it. Most children, even teens, end up appreciating the experience, because it's fun and fair, and they have their parents' undivided attention.

What materials do we need? Use a chalkboard, a white board, or an oversize pad of newsprint to record questions and suggestions. Some weeks, you'll write very little. But if, for example, you're using a family check-in to discuss new rules, write them down.

When do we schedule these check-ins? Write them into your routine, ideally at the same time each week and at a time when you're all home together anyway. It could be after dinner on a particular weekday night or during the weekend. If having ice cream doesn't appeal to your family, ask what does. One family of foodies decided to use the time to sample a new food.

How much time should we allot? A check-in can last from five minutes to thirty, which is definitely on the long side. At first, especially if you have mostly children under five, keep them short, no longer than ten minutes. Older kids get bored, too. So if something "big" is going on, such as a proposed vacation or a family project, it might be necessary to add another check-in later in the week. It's more important to keep everyone's interest and make the experience pleasant than it is to handle everything at once. Simply say, "Let's talk about our summer plans next time. But thank you, Wendy, for bringing it up. It's a great idea."

What's the format? Light a candle, ring a bell, or designate a particular item to signify that the check-in is about to begin. One family uses a large conch they found on a family vacation. Every week, a different person gets the shell. When he or she sets it on the middle of the table, it's time for everyone to gather 'round. Mark the beginning by an action. For example, you might hold hands, close your eyes, and take a few breaths together. Such deliberate gestures create "sacred" family space.

What do we discuss? What you put on your agenda to talk about depends on your family and will evolve over time. You might go for a very loose structure—a few minutes of everyone telling jokes. Or you can have a set agenda that has several components— opening, new business, old business, close. You can ask, "Who wants to speak first?" and then go around the table.

One check-in might be the time to plan an outing, another to deal with a problem or for members to choose what roles they want to play during the week. You might have a check-in just to review house rules or to come up with a "family mission" that reflects what's important to your family (see sidebar).

Regardless of your particular agenda or how the conversation flows, keep these ground rules in mind:

What's Your Family's Mission?

Steven Covey, author of numerous books about being "highly effective," suggests coming up with a "family mission statement" that reminds us of "the things that matter most" and guides our decision making. Covey practices his own advice:

In our home, we put our mission statement up on a wall in the family room so that we can look at it and monitor ourselves daily.

Mission statements are unique to each family and must be "reviewed and reworked" twice a year. If you need help, go to http://www.franklincovey .com/msb.

- *Each I has an opportunity to speak and to offer ideas.* Recognize who needs encouragement and who needs a timer. Everyone *can* speak; no one *has to* speak. Don't allow interruptions. Some families use a version of the Native American "talking stick"—it can be a rock, a stuffed animal, a piece of silverware. Whoever holds it has the floor and, most important, the respect and attention of everyone else.
- *Don't allow complaints to degenerate into tattling.* Siblings can talk *about* each other—to share information or ask for help—but tattling is not allowed. What's the difference? Frequency and patterns. Tell on your brother once, we pay attention. Tell on him twice, and we begin to wonder. Tell on him three times, that's tattling (more on how to handle sibling squabbles in chapter 10).

- *Get and give feedback.* Esteemed Israeli psychologist Daniel Kahneman points out that "true intuitive expertise" is learned from prolonged experience with good feedback on mistakes. We get better at anything—relationships, tasks, a particular role—by learning, trying, sticking to it, and suffering the natural consequences of our mistakes. It also helps to have people who accept who we are and how we do things, even if it's not their way.
- *Use check-ins to congratulate and to correct with kindness.* "We know it takes a while to get used to that lawn mower, Jake, and it's not easy to push. But you've been giving it your all, we can tell. Maybe next time, go back and forth in the same direction. That might make it easier for you." If an older sibling has done the same job, perhaps she can help, too.
- *Shine a light on new ideas.* "Stan, it was a very good idea to separate your toys into two piles and give the ones for young children to Maya's school and the rest to the homeless shelter. I was just going to bring it all to Goodwill. Good for you for being so thoughtful and taking the time." In a sense, you're applauding Stan for taking care of the **We**. His idea handles a job that needs to get done (decluttering the household) and at the same time connects your family to other families.

Why keep at it? Check-ins help create what Daniel Pink, author of *Drive,* calls "Type I" people. They feel competent, independent, and connected. The *I* stands for *intrinsic motivation*—that is, doing things because something inside drives us, not because we're afraid of punishment or because we're looking for rewards. Pink argues that we have evolved into a society that requires Type I people who are self-motivated, willing to collaborate and cooperate in service of the greater good—in this case, the health of your family. Everyone is motivated from within, because all are part of a mission, and it feels good to belong to the pack. In chapter 8, we look at how to involve even the youngest members in the family "co-op."

The **We** Is Fair

No family has an endless reserve of resources, especially when it comes to time and money. Arguably, time is the most precious commodity—we need to spend it wisely. And money is the resource we have the most trouble talking about.

Let's start with time. Building trust and intimacy takes time. Running a family takes time. How we use time, therefore, says a lot about what we value, or at least it should. By taking charge of your time, you make it work for you. The problem is, most of us go through our days with only vague notions of where our time goes.

Become more aware of how your family spends time. Keep a log, and pay attention to what's happening in the zones. Tracy prescribed her EASY log to keep track of babies' feeding times, sleep periods, diaper changes, and bath hour. Writing down the various times helped new parents understand and get to know their child.

Monitoring how time is spent in the hubbub of the daily comings and goings in your family is much harder. There are more **I**s to track. Also, we often put ourselves on automatic pilot to get through the day, and it takes effort to be mindful instead. Monitoring the zones heightens your awareness. Each one is rich with information about how the various **I**s bump up against one another. Watching your family in the zones will give you clues about whose **I** needs attention and where you might have to make adjustments—to spend more time with a particular family member, to put more time in or spend less time on a certain activity.

Many types of **We/I** conflicts are related to time issues and can be headed off at the pass, as the old cowboy movies put it, by looking at who needs what and when. Perhaps you are already tuned in to the different types of time in your family—**We** time, alone time, one-on-one time. Are these various types of time built into your daily routine or negotiated, or do people grab moments spontaneously when they can? If you can't readily answer those questions, the Time Log on the opposite page will get you started. You will find a blank version on page 182. Make a copy and paste it into your Family Notebook. Ideally, spend a week keeping track. Use the "Take Note" exercise on page 172 to guide you.

Family Time Log

Time is one of your family's most vital and scarcest resources. To see how you "spend" it, fill in the simplified, blank version on page 182. Use the one below as a sample. We left out "prep work" but list the remaining nine zones below, asking that you note of what kind of time you spend in each zone, what's good, and what needs adjustment.

W **We time** (when everyone is present/participates)
C **Child time** (could be one-with-one or one-with-several)
A **Adult time** (your partner or another adult)
I **Individual time** (alone, with nonfamily member(s), or engaged in solo pursuit, such as a soak in the tub, working at a desk—an adult paying bills, a child doing homework—when others are also at home)

Note: We didn't include "S" for screen time, but if it's an issue in your family, you might want to note how much of each person's time is spent in front of a computer or gadget, especially if it's at the expense of other kinds of time.

The Zones	WHO GETS THE TIME?	WHAT'S GOOD?	WHAT NEEDS ADJUSTMENT?
WAKE UP	C	Kids dressing themselves	Nothing; works well these days
BREAKFAST	W, C	Bob's new schedule has him home in the am now	I'm still making the meal and the lunches
TRANSITIONS (to and from work/school/other)	I	Bob takes the kids to school	Feels like I waste this precious time
REUNIONS (reentry after work/school)	C	Children are at the same school; p/u is easier	Noah needs at least a half hour to recover
CARETAKING (child/ elder care)	C, A	The kids are doing more for themselves these days	Mom broke her hip; I feel like I'm always in the caretaking zone
HOUSE MAINTENANCE	I	Hired someone to help with the outside work	All my time is eaten up by this zone
DINNER	W	Our best time of day as a family!	We need to work on cleanup
UNSCHEDULED FREE TIME	A, C	The kids are getting better at doing their own homework	I still have no time for me
BEDTIME	W, C, A	Bob and I take turns reading a chapter book to both kids	Willie gets out of bed often after lights out

---

FYN Take Note—Literally

Once your family log is completed, answer these questions about how your family spends one of its most precious resources: time.

- If a stranger were to enter your home, what kind of time would she most likely see? Family members off doing their own thing? One-on-one activities? Family time? Or does your family do all of the above?
- Do all the duos (adult-adult, adult-child, child-child) get one-on-one time? Do they seek each other out? What is the quality of one-on-one time? What effect does it have on the two? Do siblings fight frequently? Are the adults like ships passing in the night?
- Is the importance of decompressing from the stresses of the day acknowledged in your household? How do people spend down time—with one another or on their own? Do the adults get to relax or only the kids?
- What kind of time is spent playing—individual time, one-on-one, or family time? Is play usually cooperative, or does it end in fights?
- How much and what kind of time is spent on electronic gadgets and screens? Phone calls? Do these activities calm or rev up family members? Are there rules about television, computers, video games, or other screens during family time?

Bringing Up Money

Discussing money is off-limits in some families. Sometimes partners have a difficult time talking about finances with each other. And it doesn't even occur to them to share financial information with their children. One or both adults might be secretive or reluctant because they believe they alone should worry about cash flow or because it's none of the children's (or the partner's) business.

The problem is, *not* talking about money is not fair to the **We** and, ultimately, can damage it. Money is a family resource. It is everyone's business. When you sweep financial issues under the rug, you tend to buy things without considering the impact. Family members learn nothing about saving, spending, or making decisions for the greater good. Besides, giving children information and making them responsible about money is not the same as burdening them. When no one talks about how much hard work it takes to buy "stuff" or the responsibility of owning it, possessions are taken for granted. No surprise, then, when expensive sneakers are forgotten ("I think I took them off at the pond") or an electronic gadget is left out in the rain. There's more where they came from.

Check-ins provide a great opportunity to talk about the family's needs and wants and about what's fair and right. But, first, you and your partner, if you have one, should ask yourselves the following questions.

Do we talk about money and spending openly? Don't assume that children understand the relationship between value and spending. "Katy told me one day she thought we were poor," says Sara Green, who lives a solid middle-class life. "When I asked why, she told me that Mike and I are always saying, 'We can't afford this. We can't afford that.' I had to explain that when we say stuff like that, we really mean, 'That's not where we *choose* to put our money.'" Sara then pointed out where the Greens do spend money and why: on books and schooling because they believe knowledge and education make for a more informed and richer life, on lessons because they want to nurture their kids' talents, on food and entertaining because socializing is important to them. They might say no to some electronic gadgets or to expensive trendy sneakers, but they are certainly not poor.

Do your children have a clue about money? Or are they misreading your financial situation, as Katy Green did? If you think they are unaware of money, remember that once children go to school and begin visiting other kids' homes, where they see how other families live and spend, they begin comparing. They won't know how to talk about it at home unless their parents create a space for such discussions. Don't be afraid to make comments or ask questions ("What was it like for you to be in Sally's big/tiny house?"). If a child asks about material possessions ("Why can't we get a big swing set like Debbie has?") or a lack of them ("Susie has hardly any toys"), answer truthfully.

Does our consumption reflect our family's values? Refer to the notes you took in response to the "What's Your Family Like" exercise at the end of chapter 1. If you listed or should have included overspending as one of your family's vulnerabilities, you might have to work especially hard. Ideally, you spend wisely and use money to support the values you hold and to attend the venues you enjoy as a family.

So, for example, if enjoying nature is important to your family, do you consider the eco-consequences of what you buy and do? You always have choices. You can invest time and energy in composting, buy recycled products, and figure out other ways to be environmentally responsible. You can also decide to buy books and magazines to learn more and keep up with news about the natural world. You can send your kids to nature camp or allot funds to family trips that involve outdoor activities. You can choose to rent, swap, barter, or share possessions with other families, rather than buying everything for your own private use—both to cut down on your own expenses and to reduce your carbon footprint.

Are we honest about our finances? If you're at the shoe store and you need to stick to a budget, say it out loud. If you can't afford certain purchases, let them know. "I know that some kids at your school have Air Jordans, but our family can't afford to buy $150 sneakers for everyone. You can choose one of these pairs because they're in the family price range."

Do we weigh our choices out loud? Help younger members of the family see that you spend in different ways—sometimes money, sometimes effort—even better if your energies go to helping someone else. Link your values to what you spend. Have discussions about the pros and cons of an activity or a big purchase. Relate it to how it affects the family. For example, if one child wants to play on the soccer team, talk openly about the costs—not just money and energy but also the loss of family time. This is not to say that individuals should not be allowed to pursue their separate interests. To be sure, for many families, watching one kid play a sport does qualify as family time, and everyone enjoys it. The point is, make these decisions mindfully and as a family, so that everyone's I is taken into consideration.

Do we review our choices after spending? Was that trip to the museum—the admission fee, the car fare, the time and energy spent, the experience of being there—worth it? There's no right answer, but at least check in to see what everyone got out of the experience. That information can guide future outings. The same review should be applied to purchases. Was a toy or gadget forgotten a month later? Did you use the item as often or in the way you imagined? You can apply similar questions to an activity. Do the participants continue to eagerly anticipate and engage in it? Again, knowing these answers will hone every family member's decision-making skills and guide you in the future.

Do we deepen our everyday awareness of real value? When contemplating a new purchase or activity, the adults have to first ask themselves, "Do I/we/the kids really need it? Is this appropriate? Is there a way to do this for less—for example, hire a talented teenager to introduce your child to guitar rather than investing in costly lessons. Is this an authentic choice or something we're considering just to keep up?" Whether it's a toy or a game, a pet or a boat or plants for the garden, is the item or activity something that a particular individual or the whole family has the time for owning/doing? Is it something for which you're ready to take responsibility? Will it enhance or detract from family life? Does it speak to who you are as a family? If spending leads to anxiety or stress, or if it sets your teeth on edge when the kids now seem ungrateful about something they lobbied for a month ago, it's time to reorder your priorities.

The **We** Is Loved

"McLing" is not their real last name, explains Maxine Ling, age forty-eight. "That's our term for us." The made-up surname is a nod to Maxine and Liam's mixed heritage. Her parents are from China, and his McTavish clan is mostly still in Scotland. The two met in Chicago. Right from the start—out of respect for each other and good "familying"—they incorporated rituals and traditions from both sides that would give little Brenna a sense of continuity and certainty. Without realizing it, they were creating a **We** worth loving.

"We're a small family, so we're very aware of one another. Every Friday night is dinner out as a family. We did a McLing website," says Maxine, "and even a Chateau McLing wine. We do things together, we sit down together. It's the glue that keeps us connected."

Two years ago, the McLings moved from Chicago to England for a family adventure. Bringing their rituals, traditions, and a strong sense of family with them helped ease the transition.

The adventure also happened to coincide with what Maxine calls "that whole emerging adolescent thing." Brenna is now fifteen. "We try to do things together, like we've always done, but it's getting harder. She sleeps 'til 12!" Brenna also wants to spend more time with her friends. "This whole year is going to be like this," says Maxine, who, to her credit, is telling herself the truth about Brenna's changes.

"She has to practice violin. She has homework," Maxine says, "and she wants to spend more time with her friends." Accordingly, the McLings have come up with a new ritual that honors Brenna's busy schedule and at the same time creates a space in which the three of them can connect. "Every Saturday, we have lunch together at this great little pub which happens to be very close to a library. Then she can go do her work there.

"We see that she's starting to pull away. Some parents just let it happen, but we're trying to steer her. She's still hearing us. She's hearing less, but I'm very happy that she's hearing us at all! Our job as parents is to guide her and at the same time make her independent."

As it turns out, Brenna is a willing participant. The McLings—the entity that is her family—is a good place to come back to.

When families build in rituals and traditions and make time for spontaneity and special times together, it's like putting good memories into the bank. When we look back on those times, it makes everyone love the **We**. We think of it as "memory-banking."

This isn't a new idea. We wrote extensively in our other books about the importance of "R&R," recurring routines and rituals that provide security for your children. Tracy always advised parents to try to "stick to your routine" during travel or crises or in the face of any out-of-the-ordinary event. A decade later, many of her clients say that the EASY routine turned out to be a gift for the whole family. As fifty-year-old Dale O' Grady, now the mother of an eight-year-old and a six-year-old, put it, "It wasn't just a matter of organization. It gave us something to rely on, a sense that life has some degree of predictability."

R&R is doubly important for the whole family. Memory-banking is the broader umbrella. It includes all family interactions that result in feelings of joy and togetherness, anything from participating in community events, such as a street fair or a charity walk, to everyday occurrences that make the **We** happy. Whether a fleeting moment or a momentous occasion, the formula is the same: Everyone is involved, positive feelings are generated, and the memory becomes "ours." Best of all, the process is cumulative and compounds over time, just like money in the bank. Memory-banking builds a reserve of family strength that we can draw from during hard times.

You're probably already doing it. When asked, "What routines, rituals, and/or traditions does your family practice/honor, and why are they important?" most of our interviewees rattled off a string of examples. Many mentioned spiritual practices (attending a house of worship, taking part in family programs there), vacations, holiday rituals, meals together, special Sunday outings, movies, games (playing them, watching them), and tucking in. They also stressed the importance of recurring one-on-one moments.

Memory-banking is not only about savoring the fun and the triumphs, but it's also about keeping track of the challenges. At regular family check-ins, for example, we might take time to review, say, "how we got through Billy's illness" or "how scary it was after the hurricane." We might also revisit a disappointment with new insight ("You were so upset when Yale rejected you, but look at how you blossomed at Syracuse") or talk honestly about a tragedy ("It has been five years since Marie died, but I can still see her face. I don't ever want to forget her"). Sometimes parents are afraid to bring up unpleasant events long past, let alone "bank" them. They think they're protecting the children. But the opposite is true. Just because we don't talk about something doesn't mean it is forgotten. Disappointment and grief are part of life. Indeed, another reason Carlie Reynaldo appreciates her Aunt Laurie is that she helps keep her mother's memory alive, frequently telling Carlie, "Your mother would have been proud!"

> *Memory-banking allows us to consciously honor the times we bent without breaking. Knowing we've fought a hard-won battle also tells us we're prepared for the next time.*

Here are some ideas that can help you keep a good supply of memories on hand.

Review your family's R&R. Build predictability and accountability into your everyday life. Celebrate the good you create and the bad you overcome. It doesn't matter whether you have lavish birthday parties or go all out with holiday decorations, as long as you observe occasions, transitions, and milestones in some way. Routines, rituals, and ongoing traditions give a family a sense of identity, a kind of security that says no matter what *I* go through, *we* still exist. No matter how hard something is for *me*, I can look to *us* for strength.

Build time into your everyday routine that brings you together. Take a moment to slow down as a family. Learn from the Buddhist teacher Thich Nhat Hanh. When asked, "What do I teach my children to prepare them for this world?" he tells parents:

> *We should teach our children how to be calm, and how to be able to be in the present moment. How to come back when they have strong*

emotions, how to be able to handle their strong emotions, how to be able to come back to breathing exercises or walking mindfully so they realize their emotions are not in control of them, so they can handle their emotions.

Borrow from both sides of the family; involve everyone. The rituals you practice and the traditions you uphold should be a mix of your and your partner's childhoods, along with what your family creates. Rather than argue over your respective traditions, as some couples do, make room for both, keeping in mind that R&R helps give your **We** an identity. We are a family that says grace before dinner. We are a family that reads before sleeping. We are a family that does Halloween in a big way. We can count on us. Remember, too, that R&R sometimes involves trial and error. See how everyone responds, and correct course when necessary. What works for your family this year might have to be revised twelve months from now as jobs, grades, and other circumstances change.

Notice simple moments of connection. Creating memorable moments doesn't require a trip to Disneyland. It's about cherishing conversation and small moments. Be aware of the little things: how a child's small hand feels around the back of your neck when you're carrying her, how intensely blue your partner's eyes are. Pay attention when one family member's **I** connects with another's. Little Sister walks toward Big Brother, who's sitting on the couch watching TV. Instead of telling her to scram, he pats his lap, as if to say, "It's OK—come be with me," and she lies down and puts her head in his lap.

Such moments convey mattering. "I love it when I have just one child left in the car, and we have the conversation we want to have, no interruptions," says Lanie Allen, the mother of four whom you met earlier. "I hear about their day, their ideas, what they're worried about, what they're happy about." The Allens also try to allow each child to share about his or her day at family meals, but Lanie admits that "it doesn't always happen that way."

Holly Burbank, one of Tracy's clients whose son is now twelve, recalls one piece of advice that had the "biggest long-term impact" on her family. "Even when Danny was the tiniest infant, Tracy told me, First, tell him what you're going to do, as in 'I'm going to change your diaper now.' Even if he doesn't understand the specific words, the conversation will help the two of you develop a relationship." Holly has never stopped talking to Danny. Today, her best talks with him happen at pickup from

---

From the Trenches: Don't Underestimate the Car Ride

A car can be a great place to talk and to build memories, a sacred space of connection for families-in-perpetual-motion.

Parent-child: Go for the "oboe moments" (page 82). So-called by a couple who knew that their son had long become bored with his oboe lessons. They never suggested his giving them up, though, because in those brief rides to and from his teacher's house, he invariably opened up about his life.

Couples: Connect on long trips. No doubt, couples can have oboe moments, too, but they tend to happen on longer trips, alone or with the kids in the backseat, asleep or amusing themselves. Either way, the car can be a good time to have longer-than-usual adult conversation. The goal is not necessarily to make a weighty decision or resolve a problem, although that might happen. Rather, think of it as a time to reacquaint and share new insights.

Siblings/the family: Create car rituals. Don't immediately plug in the DVD player or allow the kids to play video games with headphones on. Sing at the top of your lungs, play a game of "I Spy" or "Geography." Do what you did as children, or invent new games. Get everyone in on the adventure. Share maps, look for landmarks, allow rotating seats if that works for your family. Incorporating predictable elements—fun, especially—will make long trips something kids look forward to taking.

　　All things being equal—no one's sick or overtired—siblings tend to fight less when they're having fun. They also complain less when they feel they have some power, which is why we like what one family did. Knowing that nagging was an inevitable part of every car trip, Mom and Dad let their four kids know that if they were hungry or needed to stop for any reason, they could call, "Next nag!" You might think that granting children that kind of power would result in a stop every ten minutes, but because the kids felt they had a say in the trip, they rarely abused the privilege.

---

school. "He's a boy who talks anyway, but he talks more because I ask him questions, like 'Did anyone make you laugh today? Did anyone get into trouble?' Then you wind up hearing about the little things."

Compile a visual family history—and savor it. Thanks to the digital revolution and all the gadgets we own, there has never been an easier time to document the good times: your little one going off to nursery school, sporting a backpack that's as big as she is; the Halloween costumes you made (or bought); the time your partner surprised you; the Thanksgiving you all spent in a soup kitchen. Modern parents sometimes don't know what to do with it all. Many upload photos and videos to their own blogs or to social-networking sites. That's fine for sharing, but make sure you remember to savor the memories *together*, too. Make scrapbooks; put the best photos in frames (the old-fashioned kind or digital). When you take videos of vacations and important moments, view them and review them. Some families also save artifacts—a bit of sand from a trip to the Bahamas, an interesting twig found on a family hike. Tell the story that goes with the object.

That said, one family's cache of souvenirs might be another's clutter. Experiment, and figure out what works for your family—and know that your needs and desires might change. For example, by the time her third child came around, a mother who dutifully shot pictures at every occasion and collected them in scrapbooks realized that she was drowning in memorabilia. Now she makes special-occasion books a few times a year, rather than try to keep up with everything.

Regardless of how you do it, these various forms of memory-banking also showcase family members' talents and attributes. Poring through the scrapbooks, we fondly look back. "Remember when Luis got his blue belt?" "That was when Paul swam with the dolphins." It's also a way of keeping everyone current. "Let's watch the fortieth-birthday video about Mommy again so Chase can see it. He was just born then."

Take on a shared project. Activities energize the **We** and give family members something to look forward to and to look back on. When Seth Sargent-Klein became interested in baking and was already getting good at it, he and his father, Stephen, decided to build an outdoor wood-burning oven together, just like the ones Seth first learned to use on the Indian reservation. The project consumed them for months, as the two researched, planned, shopped for the materials, and finally built the oven. Today, every time Seth bakes in that oven, it's a reminder of what he and his father did *together*.

Your family project might involve one or two members or the whole family. It doesn't have to be complicated or expensive or very time-consuming—a collage of a recent vacation, baking brownies for a local shelter, cleaning up the yard after a storm. If you take on something that requires ongoing effort, like a garden or a building project, take the time to plan, to experiment, and to make mistakes. Bite off small chunks of tasks rather than getting overwhelmed. The so-called end product is not the best part of the reward. The process is. In doing something as a **We**, everyone's **I** becomes stronger.

Remember, too, that the **We** thrives on novelty. Surprise one another.

We grow by stretching ourselves, opening to unfamiliar ideas and experiences, and trying activities we have to practice to become good at. Doing it together sweetens the pot.

In the long term, by cultivating positive experiences, as memory-banking does, the **We** thrives, and the **I**s "broaden and build"—a phrase psychologist Barbara Friedrich used to describe the expansive effect of good feelings: Positivity enhances your sense of self, improves your relationships, and makes you more open to new experiences.

FYN Does Your **We** Meet the Four Requirements?

- Does your **We** value its members? Does everyone in our family know that he or she matters to the rest of us? Is each member's **I** respected and accepted for who she is?
- Is your **We** cared for? Does everyone pitch in, protect, and work for the **We**?
- Is your **We** fair? Are our family's resources, especially time and money, spent thoughtfully and divided fairly?
- Is your **We** loved? Is everyone involved in planning good times together, noticing little moments of joy and connection, and savoring important occasions? Is your **We** a good place to come home to?

If your family is having difficulty meeting any of the Four Requirements, read on. In the last four chapters, we look at chore wars, change, and other challenges to the **I/We** balance.

The Family Time Log

On page 171, we gave you a starter version of the Family Time Log. Fill in this one to get a better idea of how your family "spends" time. Try to keep track for at least a week. Tell yourself the truth about the kind of time you *predominantly* spend in each zone. If during breakfast, for example, you're mostly herding the kids, don't count five minutes with your partner as couple time! Likewise, if you're all sitting at the dinner table, but you keep jumping up to answer work calls, that's not family time. If your partner and older children are willing, give each one a clean copy to fill out on their own. Then share your perceptions at your next family check-in.

The Zones	WHO GETS THE TIME?	WHAT'S GOOD?	WHAT NEEDS ADJUSTMENT?
WAKE UP			
BREAKFAST			
TRANSITIONS (to and from work/school/other)			
REUNIONS (reentry after work/school)			
CARETAKING			
HOUSE MAINTENANCE			
DINNER			
UNSCHEDULED FREE TIME			
BEDTIME			

Key: W = We time; **C** = Child time; **A** = Adult time; **I** = Individual time

Notes on Our Family Co-op

EIGHT

CHORE WARS
A Family-Think Solution

*Nobody can go back and start a new beginning, but
anyone can start today and make a new ending.*

—Maria Robinson

*It's where we go, and what we do when we
get there, that tells us who we are.*

—Joyce Carol Oates

"You *still* didn't call the plumber?"

"Why is this living room such a mess?"

"Why can't you just hang up your coat when you come in?"

"Why don't you put your socks in the hamper instead of leaving them on the floor?"

"Why don't you *ever* do something the first time I ask?"

"Why are those dishes still in the sink?

You've been there; we all have. The details may be different, but it's the same story in many, if not most, households. Fights erupt over dishes, dirty socks, who's doing what, and how it's done. Since the 1970s, when families have had to readjust to new roles for Mom and Dad, writers and researchers have referred to the problem as "chore wars." That we are still reading articles about these annoying everyday skirmishes tells us they haven't gone away.

Chore wars emerge as a minor disturbance at first. They don't *have* to get worse. Household hassles are not the result of forces beyond your control, such as a hurricane or an infectious disease. They are not caused by something happening *to* your family. Rather, they are the result of what's happening *in* your family. That's why, at least in the early stages, you can control them. And you should.

Chore wars are a signal that the body—in this case, the whole family—is ailing. Most advice about sharing the responsibilities of running a family focuses on what's happening between the adult partners. Do they need to communicate better? Does the problem go deeper than housework? In part, that's appropriate. The adults are in charge; they're the directors. Chinks in their relationship can harm the children, who absorb their parents' negative emotions. But helping the couple can take you only so far. A strong **We** needs adults *and* children to be stakeholders.

To minimize, even end, chore wars: Apply family-think.

Every family is susceptible to occasional disagreement over who does what and whose turn it is. Certain zones might be particularly problematic—times when there's a lot to do and less energy to get it done.

- Is there a particular zone in which you and your partner tend to argue or when you tend to yell at the kids? (If necessary, refer to the discussion about various zones, pages 124–150.)
- Is there a time of day when you feel pulled in six different directions?
- Is there a zone in which siblings invariably lock horns?

In each case, try to figure out whose needs aren't getting met. Rough spots happen, but if the adults are in sync and in charge as co-directors, and all members—including the kids—are stakeholders, someone is likely to notice what's wrong, talk about it, and figure out the best medicine. Everyone might have to communicate better or include more family time in the daily routine or give one member extra attention or help. But they heal the family *together.*

If the signs are ignored, the infection spreads, and the whole family gets sicker.

The Chore Wars Progression

As you may recall, in the early years of Daria Wilkerson's marriage, she often ranted about her husband Conrad's lack of initiative around the house (page 101). Luckily, she realized that her anger and resentment only made the problem worse and caused her to plunge into depression. Looking at what she brought to the table, she began to see (with a therapist's help) that Con's behavior was not directed at her. His personality and his process were simply different from hers. Had Daria allowed their relationship to get stuck there, she might have continued to seethe and blame. Every unfinished chore would have become another fight. Daria and Con would have become increasingly resentful. In time, they would probably have ended up in end-stage chore wars, at which point the gloves come off. Passive-aggressive questions ("Why are these dishes still in the sink?") turn into sweeping accusations ("You never do anything around here"). By then, the arguments go far deeper than housework.

In such cases, the parties become polarized: the Designated Doer versus the Shirker. She thinks about and actually *sees* what needs to be done. He—sometimes rightfully, sometimes by comparison—is positioned as the one who avoids responsibility. At first, the DD, exhausted from reminding and cajoling, might make excuses ("He works so hard," "He's so ADD"). Eventually, she blows up. The Shirker strikes back or withdraws (literally or by tuning her out). Both parties feel angry and betrayed, each convinced that it's the other's fault. Negativity permeates the household. Seemingly innocuous statements, such as "I'm in here, reading the paper," can spark a full-blown argument.

At worst, chore wars *violate* the Four Requirements of family stakeholding.

- **The We is not cared for.** When you a see a couple arguing over who does what and/or harping on kids to "clean your room," it's a sign that everyone is not pitching in. It takes a whole family to care for the **We**.
- **The We does not take care of the Is.** Chore wars tell us that someone's **I** needs attention. Anger and seething resentment mean that something bigger needs to be addressed and fixed. Battles over housework are, of course, not the only reason negativity seeps into family life, but they are often front and center.
- **The We is not lovable.** Chore wars pollute the air families breathe. Instead of being a place where family members "broaden and build," everyone becomes narrower, more self-focused, and less able to handle what life throws at them. The **We** isn't fun to come home to.

- **The We is not fair.** In many households where chore wars rage, the woman is the Designated Doer. The arrangement often starts when the partners first become parents, say psychologists Phillip and Carolyn Cowan: "She's doing more than she thought she would, and he's doing less than he said he would." When the **We** is not fair, it becomes a breeding ground for chore wars.

Chore Wars: Where Do You Stand?

A change in your relationship can be a signal that you and your partner are descending deeper into chore-wars territory. You might skip one stage altogether—many couples go right to reconsidering. You might also bounce back and forth.

Awakening

"It's your turn." You begin to see that running a family isn't what you once imagined. You try to figure out what's fair, but when life gets in the way and things don't get done, someone gets blamed. You won't have to undo any bad habits at this point, but you will have to look at your differences. The challenge is not to take them personally and to work out an equitable way of getting things done.

Reconsidering

"I didn't have time." As the responsibilities of family life increase, your differences, and social conditioning kick in. If you feel you do enough, your response might be a string of cat-got-my-homework excuses. If you feel like you do it all, you might try to manipulate the other person. The challenge, in either case, is to tell yourself the truth and to attack the problem together *before* resentment takes hold.

Polarizing

"You never do anything around here!" You and your partner have squared off in opposite corners. The Designated Doer feels burdened and resentful; the Shirker unfairly accused. If no one takes steps to balance this lopsided arrangement and to engage the children as stakeholders, the whole family will feel it. The challenge is to see what's happening to your relationship and in your household and to be willing to take concrete steps to change *your part* in it.

Is Gender the Problem?

"I can't believe she's having the same kind of arguments I had with her father," says a sixty-five-year-old woman, reflecting on her adult daughter's complaints about how little her husband does around the house. "Has nothing changed?"

Actually, things *have* changed. Recent studies in which couples are asked to keep diaries of how they spend their time suggest that the "gender gap" at home has narrowed considerably. When both partners work, women log in only twenty minutes a day more paid and unpaid work than their partners.

And yet women *feel* as if they're doing much more. One reason for the disparity, says journalist Ruth Davis Konigsberg, is the *mental* energy women spend. "Time diaries don't take into account the stress [of] keeping that precisely calibrated family schedule in their heads at all times or knowing what's for dinner, what ingredients are required and their exact location in the refrigerator."

Another reason is that sexist images and messages seep into our households and continue to promote outdated attitudes about gender roles. Most of us know better, but culture is a powerful and pervasive force. That's probably why the YouTube video of four-year-old Riley hit a nerve. As we go to press, more than four million people have tuned in to hear her indignant rant about the fact that girls are expected to buy princesses and "pink stuff" while boys get to buy superheroes (http://www.youtube.com/watch?v=-CU040Hqbas).

You can hear Riley's father in the background, which led some to wonder whether the pint-sized feminist was coached. She wasn't. We tracked down her mom, thirty-three-year-old Sarah Madia. She is a lawyer, and her husband, Dennis Barry, is in school, studying special ed. The two share responsibilities based, for the most part, on each one's availability. "He has a more flexible schedule," Sarah explains "To tell the truth, he does more of the jobs my mother did." At school and in the toy store (where the video was shot), even a four-year-old can see that the world isn't as gender-neutral as her household.

Yes, males and females have different bodies, brains, and hormones, which influence their physical capabilities and emotional responses. There *are* well-documented gender differences. But just as temperament—the emotional package we come in with—isn't destiny, neither is gender. As one family researcher concluded, the "many differences observed in household research do not appear to be biologically inevitable, but socially enforced."

In other words, we *learn* to "do" gender because of what we see around us. If in your childhood household, your or your partner's mother cooked and cleaned while Dad sat in front of the TV, despite your intentions to have an egalitarian family, you might unwittingly slip into similar roles—they're what you know. It's also a matter of what you were allowed and encouraged to do as a child. One of you might have done laundry; the other had it done for her. One of you might have grown up with siblings or baby-sat as a teenager; the other rarely spent time with young children. No surprise, then, when you find yourselves at different points on the household and parenting learning curves.

Gender differences don't have to translate into gender disability.

The fact is, everyone is "differently able" in some ways. Gender doesn't have to be one of them. "I was clueless about how hard it would be after our son was born," admits one dad, who believes that "women are more aware and better prepared." It took some adjustment on his part, but today he's a true co-parent. And remember Stephen Klein's experience after Ellie, his firstborn, arrived? Nancy wasn't "naturally" better at tuning in to their baby or getting food on the table. Once Stephen stepped into those roles, he *became* just as proficient.

At the same time, chore wars aren't always about male/female differences. If gender was the sole culprit, then you would expect *not* to see partners squaring off in families headed by two men or two women. And yet gay and lesbian couples also argue about who does what and how it's done, because imbalances can happen in *any* relationship.

Same-gender partners do seem to have an edge over male/female couples in one respect: They are freer to *choose* their respective responsibilities. Dan Savage, a gay Seattle-based journalist who writes about his family dynamics, notes: "[We] do hew to some pretty strictly defined roles in our house, roles that pretty neatly parallel the male/female roles. . . . It helps that these are roles we play willingly, not roles we're obligated or expected to play because of our gender. . . . We borrowed these roles from straight people . . . mostly because they work for us."

The fact is, partners often have different ways of looking at life and taking care of (family) business. Opposites attract. As the Wilkersons' story illustrates, personalities, individual preferences, and a host of other differences cause couples to clash, not just gender. If the adults are not mindful or accepting of each other, willing to share strategies instead of criticizing, their battles intensify, accumulate, and become harder to reverse.

The challenge is to deescalate, *before* you get to that point, by focusing not only on what your partner does or doesn't do but also on the messages you're inadvertently sending your children.

From the Trenches: Strategies for Stretching

These tips are a mash-up of family-whispering ideas and the wisdom of the members of the Baby Whisperer forums. They apply to children and adults.

Set a great example. If you don't want your kids to be gender-typed—or even worse, gender-disabled—as one mother wisely proposed, "Set a great example. So next time something needs drilling, ladies, don't get hubby to do it, get him to show you how to do it, or get DH ["dear husband"] to pack the school lunches."

Treat adults and children as individuals. Expect the best of their individual abilities, regardless of gender.

Don't give up. "In one of Tracy's books it is stated that it is important to let kids put their toys away and in order, even though it is quicker and easier to do it yourself. OK, men are not kids, but the concept is the same." And it's not just men. Some women act helpless when it comes to checkbooks or mowing the lawn. Everyone should strive for versatility.

As a family, actively and critically analyze what you see in media and marketing. When you're spending time alone with your partner and/or children, watching a show as a family, reading a book, or at a toy store or sports arena, don't just point out stereotypes. Also, take notice of good role models: girls, mothers, and grandmothers who handle responsibility with strength, guts, and smarts (Hermione Granger in the *Harry Potter* series) and guys who are not afraid to show their sensitive side (the boy who helps nurse a dolphin in *Dolphin Tale*).

Engage in guerrilla tactics. "I frequently change the gender in my son's books so there are more girl characters in them (he can't read yet, so he doesn't know!). I also look for books with female characters, rather than the standard princesses and witches." To heighten adult awareness, sit with your partner and check out gender-equity resources on the internet, such as the Geena Davis Gender in Media Foundation (http://www.seejane.org).

Accept that sometimes family members will act true to gender, but don't let it define them. "In addition to not pigeonholing boys as boys and girls as girls, we also need to let boys be boys and girls be girls. If your son is great at bashing stuff, making stuff, and generally being (the stereotype of) a boy, make the best of it, and embrace him for it. But also try to teach/expose him to housework, encourage him to be kind, empathetic, and nurturing." Likewise, if your daughter is all about princesses and pink, encourage her to get outside and get dirty.

Allow no excuses. "If I teach my kid to put his plate in the sink or to clean up his toys, I want him to learn that it's his responsibility and that he needs to do it even if he would prefer doing something else."

Involving the Children: Start As You Mean to Go On

Giving children a real role in running the family—not just busy work or jobs to "build character"—is a hedge against chore wars. It's also a challenge in most households. As we pointed out in chapter 1, when women complain that men don't do their fair share, it rarely occurs to them to ask their children to contribute.

In some families, parents try. They put up charts, offer rewards, but a few weeks later, it's back to business as usual. They might lament, "I know I should be better about that." But they give up anyway. And children quickly get the message that helping is optional. Parents also underestimate *what* their kids can do. A preschool teacher can get twenty three-year-olds to pick up their toys, but many parents can't reinforce the lesson at home. They seem to need a good reason for asking children to step up.

For example, Anne and Arnold are the forty-something parents of five-year-old Oliver, a doted-on only child who has minor developmental issues. At a parent conference, Oliver's teacher suggests that Anne and Arnold encourage their son to be more independent at home—dress himself and take responsibility for cleaning up his room. Expecting any less of him, she suggests, might impede his growth. Mom and Dad know they "should try harder." Anne admits that Oliver is calmer and acts more responsibly in school. But she can't really own the idea of fostering independence at home. Listen to how she breaks the news to Oliver: "Teacher Stacy told Mommy and Daddy that we wouldn't be a good mommy and daddy if we didn't let you get dressed on your own."

Anne puts it on the teacher. Other parents practically apologize when they ask kids to help, explaining to their children that it's for their "future." Of course, that's true. What you learn in your family helps you become a more competent adult. But does it really make an impression on a six-year-old when you tell him, "I want you to watch your baby brother, because one day you're going to be a dad"? Of course not. The future is not a major selling point for kids. More important, that's not why children should be given responsibilities in their family.

The message to children should be: You need to pitch in, because you are part of this family.

In some households, the "pity problem" stands in the way. Many parents we talked with "feel sorry" for the "burden" their kids carry at "so young an age"—homework, lessons, teams, practice, and other extracurricular activities. "The poor kid is so exhausted," Dan, a work-at-home father, said of his only child, Adam, who is fifteen years old, a budding musician and actor. "All he wants to do is collapse." Dan and his wife, Roberta, often let him.

If you are a fan of baby whispering, you probably already know that one of the main pillars of the philosophy is to *love and let go*. Tracy urged new parents to "start as you mean to go on." In other words, know that every choice you make has consequences. When parents don't think about where a particular practice might take them, they risk "accidental parenting," creating a bad habit and, often, teaching an unintended lesson.

Accidental Parenting

Accidental parenting often starts when a baby comes home from the hospital. For several nights, you rock your fussy infant to sleep. You hate it when he cries, and rocking seems like the easiest way to calm him. Most nights, he falls asleep in your arms. What you don't realize is that you're inadvertently teaching him to associate rocking with sleep. Several months later, when he's too heavy to rock or you're just too tired, you put him in his crib instead. Because he has no idea how to get to sleep without rocking, he cries. You didn't mean to, but you never gave him a chance to learn how to self-soothe and to fall asleep on his own. You've done it for him. Instead of strengthening his I, you have unwittingly made him rely on you for sleep. And we all know how *that* turns out!

As children get older and family life becomes more complex, accidental parenting can take many forms, but in each instance, parents inadvertently impede kids' ability to become stakeholders by doing for them what they can, and should, do for themselves. Adam's parents chalk up his lack of participation to his many activities—he has no time to pitch in. They "try" to get him to do a few "chores," because "we know it's good for him." But after years of not having to do anything around the house, he resists and wears them down. They have accidentally taught him that helping out is optional and that if he objects, they'll do it for him. They rationalize that he's "very responsible" when it comes to schoolwork and performing—all those lessons and rehearsals are "preparing" him for his career. But where will he learn how to be part of something beyond his "self"?

The answer: in his family. Parents who start as they mean to go on make choices that gradually lessen their children's dependence. They give them a real role in running the family. Be assured, though, we're not suggesting that you throw your kid in the pool to teach her to swim. You need to be there, to guide, and to build trust—but not to take over.

Some parents have trouble walking that fine line. When Nathan's daughter Yoli talks about her fourth-grade science project that's due next week, he offers to help. He doesn't want her showing up with something that looks like a nine-year-old did it. It's as if *his* I is on the line. She's delighted. And why not? She gets Dad's undivided attention, and he does all the work.

The following week, when Nathan drops Yoli off at school with her masterpiece—that is, *his* masterpiece—they run into a mother whose ten-year-old is carrying his child-made cardboard construction. "Isn't it amazing," the mother says, looking right at Nathan, "that Yoli can already use a buzz saw?"

Nathan could not care less. He laughs about it later with his wife, dismissing the mother as "jealous" and "bitchy." They convince themselves that their daughter "came up with all the ideas" and "supervised from start to finish" and is "really proud of her work." Isn't that all that matters? What they don't stop to consider is that it isn't *her* work to be proud of. Nor are they aware of what Yoli accidentally learned from the experience: To get something done, get other people to do it. Even worse, Yoli also might conclude that she herself is incompetent. She knows her project was adult-level work, a standard she can't possibly meet.

Most important, Nathan has subverted the goal of the assignment, which would have helped his daughter grow. Yoli hasn't learned how to do a project on her own, to lay it out and take the steps to complete it. She hasn't learned that you can make mistakes. And she hasn't learned that things don't always come easily or turn out perfectly—unless you're a fifty-year-old man doing a fourth-grade project!

Give Them Real Choices

Another form of accidental parenting is asking when you mean to tell. Some parents justify giving their children endless choices in the name of being "democratic" and "respectful." In such households, you hear Mom or Dad ask, "Do you want to take a bath now, Maisy?" or "Willy, don't you think it's time to clean up your toys before dinner?" or "Alice, wouldn't it be nice if you cut the grass today?"

Tracy was all about respect and giving kids choices, as in "Do you want OJ or apple juice?" But don't *ask* when you mean to *tell*, unless you don't care whether or not your child actually takes a bath, cleans up his room, or cuts the grass.

Otherwise, this is what happens. You get an answer you don't like: "No! I don't want to!" You then order your child to do it. Why ask if you're ultimately going to force her to do what you wanted in the first place? You have accidentally taught her that her input doesn't matter. And just as damaging, if you take the other route and let *her* decide if and when to take a bath, clean up, or mow the lawn, you accidentally teach her that every privilege and responsibility is subject to negotiation.

Parents who tell when they need to and give children *real* choices when they can are what we call HELPing parents. They don't sweep in and take over; they encourage children to explore on their own. They don't try to limit kids' frustration or clear obstacles from their path, a practice some educators have dubbed "snowplow parenting." Because HELPing parents are keen observers, they are aware of what their kids can do, and they give them many chances to try.

HELPing the Parent/Child Relationship

One way to strengthen your relationship with your child is to remember the letters in HELP, an acronym from our toddler book that works well with kids of any age:

Hold back before you rush in. Wait a beat. If your child is engrossed in a building project, for example, take a moment to look at what he's doing and talk to him, before you come at him with *your* agenda.

Encourage exploration. Your child's **I** grows through discovery. Know what's age-appropriate, and let her venture forth. At times, you can take the lead—show her something you do well or loved doing as a child. But don't take over.

Limit them. You—the adult—know how much sugar he can eat, how much sleep he needs, how much time he should be allowed to stare at a screen. Limit her emotionally and socially, too—say no to tantrums or to the way she talks to you, give her guidance about how to act around siblings and friends.

Praise their competence and confidence. Be authentic. Don't say "good job" when it isn't. Not everything is praiseworthy, and kids see right through you. Insincere praise erodes trust. Praising the effort, not the end result, helps children appreciate the process, tolerate frustration, and learn from their mistakes.

Know What Your Kids Can Do

Noelle is shocked when her young sister, visiting from out of town, tells her what a "savvy" chess player little Freddy is. Noelle had no idea that her son *could* play chess, let alone that at eight he knew the game well enough to be savvy. She also doesn't realize he's capable of making his own bed, sewing on a button, or oiling his own baseball glove. Nor does she suspect that he can use a knife, wash out the trash cans, or clean up after the dog. She's never asked him. She's never let him try.

Many of us are blind to our children's growth. We see them getting taller, having real conversations, solving math problems, learning to ride a bike, but we don't realize all the other things they can do. Sometimes it's because we're not aware of what they've learned elsewhere, say in school or at a friend's house. Sometimes it's because we freeze them in time. Sometimes we're too busy trying to mold them, so we concentrate more on the talents *we* appreciate. Sometimes it's because we don't ask them to try things beyond their comfort zone. Most of the time, it's a mix of many reasons. The bottom line is that children's capabilities are often far greater than we imagine.

To "prime" children to participate, know what they can do—and let them. Start when they're young, if possible. Between eighteen months and two years, when children literally and figuratively find their voice, they have specific tastes and a budding sense of identity and independence. Use it—don't fight it. Toddlers and young children love to help, and their capabilities improve every day.

If your children are older, start now. At any age, if you are conscientious and consistent and allow them to be stakeholders, they will develop skills, attitudes, and habits that will serve them well throughout life. Giving children real responsibility turns them into competent, confident, caring people. Most important, they'll want to be part of the **We**.

Don't underestimate your children. As you read through "Toddler to Ten: What They Can Do," below, your first reaction might be, "I'd never ask my child to do *that*." We're not suggesting that you make your kids indentured servants. They don't have to do all the tasks listed. For that matter, neither do you. Depending on your standards and your tolerance for disarray, maybe you dump socks into a drawer without sorting them. But we're not showing what your child *should* be doing as much as what he or she *could* be doing. (Besides, *you* don't have the time to do it all.)

In chapter 7, we introduced the idea of having roles in the family, as opposed to assigning chores. Therefore, our list is divided into broad role categories, such as "good citizen" and "pet caretaker." Each role naturally requires certain skills and physical capabilities.

As you read the various categories, remember:

- We are all differently able. Some kids are more responsible and competent than others. It depends on their small and gross motor skills and impulse control, their track record, what they've been taught, and how much they've been allowed to practice.
- Ability spans a broad age range; kids get there in their own time. For example, "Play without adult attention or supervision" might generally happen around age three. When kids have older siblings, it can happen earlier. But by five—except in cases of serious accidental parenting by adults who think it's their job to constantly entertain— most children are capable of independent play.
- Skills tend to build new skills. If you have a seven-year-old who has trouble tying her shoes, you might need to help her work on that before suggesting that she try to sew on her own buttons.

Every day, take small steps that help your children build a repertoire of skills. Nudge them toward independence. Someday, when they go off to college or to pursue other dreams, you'll be proud that they're not "teacups" or "Twinkies"—the terms college admissions officers sometimes use to describe fragile freshmen who've never had to take care of themselves.

Toddler to Ten: What They Can Do

Good citizen (practices common courtesy, is considerate toward others).

- *Younger than 3:* Can greet and see off; says "please," "thank you," and "excuse me." Sharing and managing own emotions is tricky at this age, but parents can help by identifying feelings ("You're angry") and ignoring whines and tantrums.
- *Ages 3–5:* Can draw pictures for someone else; dictates birthday, thank-you, and get-well notes; shares toys with friends; knows to ask permission ("May I go outside?") and inform parent of intentions

("I'm going to play in my room"); is willing to give away toys to children who need them.

- *Ages 5–7:* Can carry out own responsibilities and begin to offer help in new arenas (helping on computer, offering a neighbor assistance); observes phone etiquette, can make calls, answer phone courteously, take messages; by age 7, can write simple letters and thank-you notes, create birthday cards.
- *Ages 7–10:* By now, politeness, courtesy, sharing, and respect for others are default reactions; welcomes and cares for guests; plans own birthday and sees it as an occasion to be grateful and to do something good for others; increasingly helpful with younger siblings (changes diapers, helps with bath and bottle, will entertain sibling when adult is out of the room, helps with simple homework); helps others with their responsibilities when asked (sometimes even offers); volunteers in the neighborhood or community; can handle self in public, alone or with peers, or when staying overnight with a friend; packs own suitcase.

Independent doer (responsible for self).

- *Younger than 3:* Can handle simple (parent-sanctioned) choices ("Cereal or waffles for breakfast?") and follow somewhat detailed instructions in the house or yard ("Bring Daddy that bucket" to "Take this paper towel and put it in the garbage").
- *Ages 3–5:* Can play for increasingly longer periods without adult attention or supervision; keeps room neat (with reminders); has gotten better at handling morning routine (by age 5, dressing on own, cleaning room); assumes reg-

---

Find the Sweet Spot: Don't *Overestimate* Your Child Either

Ironically, the same parents who think their child isn't old enough to use a knife often expect more when the kid takes up a sport or an instrument. It might be because Mom and Dad view learning as the child's "only job," so she'd better do it well. One parent might have played as a child—or always wanted to. Or, he had a similarly demanding parent himself. Regardless of the reason, parents who tend to push their children often give mixed messages ("You played very well, but next time . . .") in the name of "helping."

Admittedly, there's a fine line between encouraging and discouraging, and it's important to be authentic. But when your child is learning *anything*, it's better to praise improvement ("You've gotten much better at the guitar") and hard work ("Your batting practice has obviously paid off"). Especially if you've entrusted (and are paying) someone to coach or teach your child, go to that person first. Discuss whether your concern is appropriate given your child's age, how long she's been at it, and her natural ability. If your child is lagging, let the coach or teacher address the problem. Let the professional guide you about how to help.

ular responsibilities around house (see other categories); capable of gradually more complex decision making about meal choices, outings, time with friends (at age 3, "Would you like the red or green shirt?" and getting closer to five, "Would you like to go to the playground or have a play date with Billy?"); speaks on the phone; knows phone numbers and address; puts away laundry.

- *Ages 5–7:* Can wake to an alarm; picks out own clothes, dresses independently, ties shoes; strips bed sheets and puts them in the laundry; makes bed daily and cleans room on own; knows appropriate clothes (play vs. school vs. Sunday best); shops for and selects own clothing and shoes with parent; does many unsupervised chores (wash out trash cans, shake rugs, gather wood for the fireplace, rake leaves, weed); saves money (from allowance, gifts, earnings) and decides how to spend it; carries own lunch money and notes back to school; still limited use of electronics but aware of dangers; changes school clothes without being told.

- *Ages 7–10:* Can take increasing responsibility for self; keeps own appointments; receives and answers own mail/email; is savvy about internet (with parents' knowledge of child's password and sites visited); gets up in the morning and goes to bed at night on own; changes sheets; prepares own school lunch and snack; crosses streets unassisted and increasingly ventures out on own; runs errands for parents; works for neighbors and earns own money on weekends and at summer jobs (lawn mowing, dog/baby/plant-sitting, painting fence or shelves, other odd jobs) with parents' help; is thrifty and trustworthy about money (handles, learns about banking, and does own financial planning, including allotments for saving, donating, gift giving); by age 10, can be alone at home for short periods.

Self-cleaner (takes care of own body and personal hygiene).

- *Younger than 3:* Washes hands before meals; cleans body in bathtub; begins to undress self and learns to dress.
- *Ages 3–5:* Can use the toilet; brushes teeth; washes and dries hands and face and brushes hair.
- *Ages 5–7:* Can take a shower or bath independently; washes own hair (more easily in shower); has the wherewithal to come in when

cold or overheated; cares for own minor injuries (Band-Aid, ice, rest), if necessary. Boys (should) put the toilet seat down.

- *Ages 7–10:* Has basic knowledge of first aid; can run own bath or shower; leaves the bathroom in order after using it.

Clothes/equipment maintainers.

- *Younger than 3:* Can throw dirty clothes into a hamper.
- *Ages 3–5:* Can sort dark and light clothes (with supervision); helps empty the dryer; matches socks; can fold simple items, such as dish towels and pants.
- *Ages 5–7:* Learns how to use the washer/dryer and measure detergent; can fold clean clothes and put them away; by age 7, can be unsupervised with laundry; is careful with sports equipment and other gear.
- *Ages 7–10:* Does own laundry; irons clothes, when needed; folds large items (blanket, tent); does simple sewing (buttons, seams, hems), uses sewing machine, and, if interested, learns other skills (weaving, knitting, macrame); maintains own gear without being asked (oils baseball glove, cleans cleats).

Food-service workers (shopping/cooking/meals).

- *Younger than 3:* "Helps" by handing parent or older sib items (in market or at home to be put away); carries light bags from the car; executes simple cooking tasks such as mixing, sprinkling, adding premeasured ingredients; cleans up what is dropped or spilled during meals.
- *Ages 3–5:* Helps plan meals, compile grocery list, shop, carry from car, and put away food on low shelves; sets table; improved cooking skills to help prepare family meals (stands at stove with supervision, holds a mixer); fixes part of own meal (spreads butter on sandwiches, prepares cold cereal, simple dessert); helps clean up, puts items in refrigerator, scrapes dishes, and disposes of uneaten meal; loads dishwasher; washes light dishes.
- *Ages 5–7:* Writes or contributes to shopping list; in supermarket, finds items on list (while in same aisle as adult); carries heavier items from car; makes own sandwich and pours own drink or prepares

simple meal for others (breakfast for family); increasingly handy with small appliances and cooking skills (makes own toast, scrambles eggs, cuts with blunt knife, bakes, peels vegetables, mixes frozen concentrate to make beverage); prepares own school lunch.

- *Ages 7–10:* Buys groceries using a list; does comparative shopping; can take on more complex kitchen projects, including meal planning and preparation, baking; chops and slices, using sharp instruments; measures and organizes ingredients; uses appliances; cleans up mess afterward; helps defrost and clean the refrigerator, with supervision; gets grill or campfire ready for a cookout (by age 10, lights fire).

Home maintenance staff (house/plants/garden/lawn).

- *Younger than 3:* "Pretend" cleans with child-sized items or dustrag; puts books and magazines in a rack or on a low shelf; helps make bed by handing pillows; waters indoor or outdoor plants (premeasured in an easy-pour cup); picks up toys and trash in yard.
- *Ages 3–5:* Vacuums, sweeps (not perfectly but good-enough); helps wash the car, take out trash, dust furniture; needs help to make a completely unmade bed; smooths covers to make bed look "straightened."
- *Ages 5–7:* Uses cleaning supplies properly; eventually can clean sink/bathtub; polishes furniture; cleans mirrors/windows; takes out trash and recyclables; learns the purpose and beginning usage of tools and helps with home maintenance; waters plants and flowers.
- *Ages 7–10:* Complete responsibility for own room (bed making, dresser drawers, closet, vacuuming); handles more difficult cleaning projects (scrubbing kitchen floor, windows, cleaning appliances); oils and cares for bike; sweeps and washes patio area; washes out garbage containers; cleans out inside of car; does yard work without supervision (lawn mowing, edging, cleanup, gardening).

Organizers.

- *Younger than 3:* Can put toys away after playing, eventually sorting into categories (ball bin, truck shelf).
- *Ages 3–5:* Puts backpack, equipment, clothes, and other personal items in a particular place; knows where family items belong in various rooms of the house.

- *Ages 5–7:* Hangs up and puts clothes in drawers, with help; devises systems for collecting, storing, and sorting.
- *Ages 7–10:* Makes to-do lists, keeps an appointment book or assignment notebook; does chores and homework without being reminded; handles big "projects" (reorganizes own closet, "weeds" toys and gadgets no longer used, helps parent configure a new work space, straightens or cleans out silverware drawer); helps reorganize family storage areas.

Pet caretakers.

- *Younger than 3:* Puts down pet food; notices whether water bowl needs filling.
- *Ages 3–5:* By age 4 or 5, takes over pet feeding (with supervision).
- *Ages 5–7:* Feeds own pets and helps clean their cages, litter box, or living area; trains and walks dog.
- *Ages 7–10:* Bathes pet; cleans up pet messes in house and yard; becomes more knowledgeable about own pet's habits and health by reading, going to vet, etc.

FYN Reality Check

After you read the list of "What They Can Do," be honest about where you stand. Unless you tell yourself the truth, your own attitudes and feelings might get in the way of your children becoming stakeholders.

- Do I underestimate my child's capabilities?
- Am I willing to take the time to help my child learn new skills?
- Is there something in me that prevents me from allowing my child to be all she can be? A parent who ignored me as a child? A reluctance to let go for fear that she'll grow up too fast? The sense that I'll be a bad parent if I don't do *for* my child? Other?

Role Doling: Running the Family Together

Now we get to *role doling*, which is at the heart of our family-centered approach to chore wars. The concept is simple: Divvy up responsibilities in a way that is both fair and appealing.

Start by figuring out what roles are needed to keep your family running. If you're new to the idea of stakeholding, devote a series of family check-ins to figuring out what kinds of doers and thinkers your household needs. List the various roles on a board or large piece of paper.

> *Discussing roles is as important as volunteering for them, because everyone gains knowledge and learns how to think about what it takes to keep the family running.*

Allow family members to choose what roles they'd like to play. If two people vie for the same job, suggest taking turns or, even better, sharing the role. Alex might be Dad's assistant on homemade-pizza night. Do the same with chores no one likes to do. Suggest that siblings work together as gerbil-cage cleaners. With younger children, you might make suggestions ("Mikey, would you like to be the table clearer this week?" "Suzy, how about helping Derek with the dish-drying?"). Be creative, especially with the little ones. "Waker-upper" could be a great job for a toddler who has older siblings, especially if he's an early riser himself.

Factor in what each role requires. "Dinner maker," a daily role, could be quite labor-intensive. Should you consider job sharing? Allow for individuality in each role. This week's dinner maker might have a completely different approach from last week's, because of his culinary tastes and skill in the kitchen. Encourage him to ask for help if necessary.

Link roles and responsibility to capability, not gender. A seven-year-old girl is just as capable of being "trash taker" as a seven-year-old boy. If you actually ask what everyone likes to do, you might be surprised—Tracy discovered that her husband loved to iron. She hated ironing and happily offered to take out the trash instead.

The point is, every family member deserves, and should have a chance, to try anything and to step into roles that go against type. At the very least, don't perpetuate the stereotypes. Mom isn't the only one who can tie a ponytail or soothe a scratched knee. Yes, girls mature earlier, but they

A Word of Caution to the Designated Doer

If you and your partner are already in polarized positions and your children do little or nothing at home, role doling will be a challenge at first. You might have trouble envisioning others doing what you usually do. But consider the downside: Playing the martyr or hurling accusations will only escalate your chore wars. Instead, try the following.

Let family members know you need them. We made this point briefly in chapter 3, but it bears repeating here. Needing is not only more effective than nagging, but it lets everyone know they matter.

Phrase requests so that you explicitly say what you need. Being needed makes a partner think twice about saying no and reminds him that you're on this journey together. It motivates children to become increasingly responsible and also makes them feel as if they're making a real contribution.

Listen to yourself before responding. Let's say you walk into the kitchen after someone else cleaned up. Before you say anything out loud to that day's kitchen cleaner, say the words in your head. If you're about to compliment the person, go for it. But if you're about to correct or criticize, and explain how you would have done it, stop yourself. Otherwise, family members begin to believe that they *can't* do the job (certainly not as well as you), and they lose interest in trying.

Don't expect family members to read your mind. Lead with "I need your help," as one grandmother did with her six-year-old grandson. "I don't think I can put all these chair covers back before it starts to rain. They're also a little heavy for me. Could you please give me a hand?" Her grandson not only willingly helped, but he was also genuinely proud of himself when the task was completed. He knew he mattered.

Be honest with family members. Kids have a keen eye for bull———! They know the difference between real work and busy work. Never make up things for them to do. Even better, ask for help doing things you can't do at all (a tech task) or have trouble doing on your own (heavy lifting). Authenticity is important with your partner, too. Some women purposely test their mates by leaving a particular job undone, and then when the partners don't notice, they pounce. That kind of tactic will only inspire more arguments and, usually, more resistance. Remember that you're *both* unhappy. Better to position yourself on the same side with a common goal: running the family.

are no better than boys at baby-sitting and cooking when both are given the opportunity. Your son can be the decorator during the holidays. Your daughter can be the hedge trimmer if she's strong and capable of wielding the shears.

Allow one another to grow—and be patient. If you (or another family member) initially feel uncomfortable or inadequate in a particular role, try to understand what's holding you back. What ideas are floating through your head? Has the past or the culture taught you that you can't or shouldn't do it? Talk about your experiences and attitudes out loud. Try some of those strategies for stretching yourself on page 190. Practice and venture beyond your comfort zone—and encourage your children to do so, too.

Discuss duration. Decide how long family members stay in a particular role—a day, a week, a month? It doesn't have to be the same for all roles. You're more likely to volunteer for a less popular role if you only have to do it for a short period. Remember, too, that "good" and "bad" are in the eye of the beholder and can change over time. One teenager admitted that when he was younger, he relished being "garbage person," because he got to go outside alone every night, and it made him feel "really grown-up." Now he'd rather take turns at being the cook.

Talk about frequency. Does the role recur once or several times a day, a week, a month, or—this is tricky—"as needed"? Birdseed refiller, for one, is an as-needed role. In such cases, talk about how often the container usually needs to be filled. The previous birdseed refiller might offer input here ("When I did it . . ."). Someone else might point out that the season matters, too. Welcome everyone's suggestions. Family members might have different ideas about how often the car washer or the vacuumer needs to show up.

Recognize that there's rarely one right way. Hash it out; listen to suggestions. You might have a different agenda but not necessarily a better one. If you disagree, try it one way this week, evaluate, and then revise next week.

Keep track of who's responsible for what. It can be a list or a chart—anything that is easy for everyone to see. One family we met uses a to-do basket instead of a wall chart. They make a list and write each role on a different index card. The person who's doing a particular job that day or week gets to keep that card and puts it back after the job is done. Whatever system you devise, make sure it's something everyone understands. With young children, substitute pictures for words.

Rehearse new roles. Life—in general, not just in the family—is an ongoing series of challenges and risks, for both children and adults. In our toddler book, we introduced the concept of staging "rehearsals for change" to help little ones get accustomed to new situations and develop new skills. The strategy works for the whole family, too.

Marnie, for example, allowed her teenage son Cary to rehearse living on his own. He wanted to take on a summer internship in another city between his junior and senior year, and she needed a preview of how he might handle himself. So when she and Cary's dad went off to celebrate her birthday at a bed-and-breakfast two hours away, she left their son in charge.

"Some friends thought I was crazy. But he is eighteen. And I told him that a lot was riding on this." Cary did well; he managed to care for and feed himself, and the house wasn't a mess. "He commented on what 'hard work' it was to be on his own!" Marnie recalls. The rehearsal gave him a dry run at living without Mom and Dad and gave her the peace of mind to let him do it.

A rehearsal for change is like standing in shallow water—a less intimidating, more manageable context—and allowing time to get used to it before swimming to the deep end. Start with an easier version of the job—wastebasket emptier before garbage person. Don't lecture; have a conversation about the what-ifs. What if the bag rips on the way out? What do we do to prevent it? How do you clean it up? Because jobs rotate, you can also bring your partner or a sibling into the conversation. Get their input, too. Gradually, as your children gain confidence, they'll become willing to take on harder challenges if you let them try.

The principles of rehearsing apply to adults, too. Taking on a new role almost always requires patience and practice. The only difference is that partners (we hope) already know what running a household involves. Children need to be shown. Start when they're young, talking to them and showing them what you do and why ("I'm double-bagging this because I'm afraid it might leak").

If housework sounds like a strange or unpleasant topic to include in everyday banter with your kids, is it any different from teaching them about a sport—the plays, the rules, the techniques? Knowledge of the game makes your son more eager to participate and practice. A few months later, watching a game on TV, your daughter says, "That was a great play," and she knows why. Why shouldn't they also learn what it takes to run a household?

Be patient; don't remind or micromanage. Be there to help and encourage them to ask, but once roles are assigned, let go, and step away. Teach, but don't overteach or take over. This is not school. This is family, a group of children and adults who help and learn from one another. Step in only if you're asked or it's an emergency. Say "thank you" often.

Each family member is an independent worker who gets to decide when and how to get the job done—and whether he or she wants help.

Afterward, have the doer reflect on the experience and evaluate his own work. Was it hard? Was the doer satisfied? Would he do anything different the next time? Whether it's with your child or your partner, if you're the seasoned pro, and the other is venturing into a new or less familiar role, you're not the boss. A rehearsal for change is not a lesson in how *you* do things. For example, you go off for a weekend with your college chums, leaving your partner "on duty." Provide instructions *only when asked.* You might offer support: "Is there anything I can do to help you prepare for the weekend?" But don't leave directions or lists unless your partner requests such guidance. When you return and things are not done to your liking, before launching into a critical tirade, ask yourself, "Is this really bad or simply not the way I'd have done it?"

If something goes wrong, troubleshoot together. Say this week's garbage person drags the bag out to the curb and leaves a messy liquid trail. Don't jump to the conclusion that she was being careless or lazy. Instead, ask yourself (and her), Did I explain that part? Has she had enough practice? Might the bag be too heavy? Should she job-share with an older, stronger sibling? Don't bring up past mistakes ("This is exactly what happened last week when you didn't pay attention to what you were doing"). It will give her performance anxiety, and she'll be less eager to try something new for fear that she'll disappoint again.

Also resist saying what *you* would do in this situation; they already know. Your child has been watching you all his life. He watches as you wipe off the bottle before putting it back into the refrigerator. He listens to your conversations and hears what you say about yourself ("I can't believe I didn't get that promotion," "I really don't care if I win, I just enjoy playing the game," "I don't want to make a mistake"). Trust us, he also knows what you would do when it comes to housework!

Learn from one another. Thirty-five-year-old Daniel Rose, originally from Chicago, is now one of the most celebrated chefs in Paris. Eating a meal at Spring, his current restaurant, is impressive in every respect—meticulous presentation, superb flavors, and an incredibly warm and friendly ambience. Daniel, a new father who splits his time between home and restaurant, is hands-on in both places. At home, he co-parents with his wife, and at Spring, he's a dependable presence, interacting with staff and patrons. But even more unusual is the chef's humility. "I am fortunate to have good people, and when they tell me they can do something better, I let them."

Let's apply that lesson to our families. *Let them.* We're all familiar with "teachable moments" in which you impart a bit of wisdom or common sense. But family relationships go both ways—you have an impact on other family members, and they have an effect on you. So it's important to be equally open to others' ideas. Otherwise, you're constantly advising, instructing, and correcting, and you miss those magic "learning moments" when the other person shows you a better way or a different perspective. Even if you don't think theirs is a better way, listen. Try it. *Let them.*

Writer Beverly Willet describes one such learning moment in a blog for the Huffington Post: "Years ago, when my youngest daughter was in elementary school I'd often find myself egging her on to keep up with me as we walked to school each morning. 'You're just walking too fast,' she told me one day. 'That's why I seem so slow. Don't worry,' she added, smiling. 'We'll get there.'"

Learning moments enrich you and widen your view of the world. They let your children know they matter. Slow down and wait a beat when your child or partner makes a suggestion, rather than always rushing in with your own ideas or agenda. As Willet reminds us, "We know what happens in life without the necessary pauses. A baby not quite ready to walk, tumbles. The teen-child who still needs her mother's guidance becomes a mother herself. We step out from the curb before spying the bus."

In learning moments, the benefits also go both ways. The ones you learn from feel heard and respected. Be open to them. You might be surprised at how good you feel afterward and how willing *they* are the next time to pitch in.

Give "us" a break. In some families, orders are issued, and everyone is expected to fall in line. "Growing up in my family," Bart proudly recalls, "being tired was not allowed. My mother used to say, 'Idle hands are Satan's tools.' We were never allowed to slack off. It gave me a sense of pride to do a job well." His wife, Laura, who came from a more laissez-faire family, wishes she could soften his attitude. "He's like a marine sergeant! I feel sorry for the kids and worry how it's going to affect them. Sometimes I secretly let them off the hook, even if I have to do their chores for them, because you've gotta give 'em a break sometimes."

Try to land somewhere in between Bart and Laura. Let them all know they're expected to participate for the good of the family, but accept that at times, someone might be too tired, too upset, too busy, or too sick to pitch in. But it can't always be the same person or a secret that's hidden from other family members ("Don't tell anyone I did this for you").

Have fun with responsibility. When you look for ways to break up the monotony of the everyday grind, adults and children are less likely to look for loopholes. Give everyone a scheduled day off—once a week, once a month, whatever works for your family. Call an unexpected break ("Tonight no one has to do anything"), and turn it into family time instead—go for a walk, get ice cream, watch a family movie.

Be creative, even a little crazy. Ellen Lefcourt, mother of four, had a recurring "Pig Night" when no one was allowed to use utensils. She also came up with a bizarre-sounding game, "Pretend Mommy's Crippled," that put the kids in charge.* Instead of their being horrified—after all, she wasn't really disabled—they rose to the occasion and felt proud of themselves for being able to take over. Granted, Ellen's approach is not for everyone, but if you have trouble cutting family members some slack, give it a try. Imagine the worst: a debilitating disease, total incapacitation. Then giving them a day off won't seem so extreme.

What Happens When Things *Don't* Get Done?

Admit it, didn't that question pop into your head as you read about role doling? Especially if you're the Designated Doer and the idea of stakeholding is new to your family, you're bound to have moments when you're sure that it's not possible. Running a family and managing a household are complex and never-ending challenges. Some days, hard as you try, you'll encounter resistance (including your own). One I will want something that another is not willing to give. Family members will argue over roles no one wants to play. But at least you'll be aware of what's happening and, therefore, more likely to push through these difficulties, because you have designed a "good enough" family that supports everyone's growth. These troubleshooting ideas will help.

Ask yourself if you're really letting them. Even if you don't think of yourself as the DD, are you stepping in to save time or because you don't have the patience to watch a family member learn how to handle a particular

---

*This was in the early 1970s. A more politically correct parent today might call the game "Pretend Mommy Is Physically Challenged."

role or because you do it better? (If the latter, reread "A Word of Caution to the Designated Doer," page 203.) Are other family members standing in the way? For example, does one sibling make fun of the way another does a job? Does the man of the house secretly seethe when his son sweeps, because that's a woman's role?

Do you need to tweak the routine? Does your partner or child have time to pitch in? If family members spend a great deal of time away from home or are involved in time-draining pursuits, perhaps some activities need to be evaluated or cut back.

We need to do for our family members what we (ideally) do for ourselves in order to get through the day with a minimum of stress: analyze, plan, execute, and, if necessary, revise. Sit down with your partner or child, and mentally walk through his day. Especially with a child, it helps to list responsibilities. Time management might be the issue, in which case you can offer to help him plan—but don't assume the role of reminder.

Each of us has a particular tolerance for "busyness"—some need more down time than others. Talk about what each of you can handle. Also, circumstances and family members' (especially children's) capacity for responsibility changes over time, so it pays to review this issue regularly.

Don't take it personally. Keep an open mind, and try not to overreact. Take a breath, and recognize that a chore forgotten or done differently is just that. It's not directed at you. We all forget and overlook our responsibilities at times.

So if the cat is mewing and you notice that his bowl is empty, instead of getting angry, you might say, "Kitty looks like he's hungry. Megan, I see that you're the cat feeder this week." When you have Megan's attention, calmly find out what's going on. Maybe the cat feeder needs a little training. Ask, "You know where his food is, right?" or "Is opening the can too hard for you?" Offering help when needed is not the same as doing it for her.

An hour later, if the cat still isn't fed, go to Megan and remind her of her role and the responsibility it carries. "I really feel sorry for Kitty. He looks so hungry. He's depending on you, because you're the cat feeder this week." It's not manipulation; you're pointing out that to keep the family pet healthy and happy, he needs to be fed every day, regardless of whether Megan is busy or tired or just doesn't feel like it.

Don't expect overnight conversions. Family members will often want something different from what you want—that's a given in family life. You don't always have to agree. Your partner or child doesn't always have to like what he or she sometimes has to do in order to keep the family afloat. It also helps to admit what *you* don't like to do!

Given the chance, children—whether they say so or not—like to play by the same rules as adults. It makes them feel grown-up. With time and living in an environment where it's normal to pitch in, most kids (and partners) get it. And when everyone is a stakeholder, not only does the family run better, but you will all be better equipped to handle change—the subject of our next chapter.

FYN Your Stumbling Blocks

How far have your chore wars progressed? The questions below are designed to help you look at whether your own attitudes and beliefs are standing in the way of everyone becoming a stakeholder.

- Are you and your partner in sync—coordinated—much, if not most, of the time? If not, do you take responsibility for your part, or do you just bitch and blame? If you feel a need to be in charge or that you do enough, take a second look at your answers to "Why I Do Most of It" (page 45) or "Why I Don't Do More" (page 45). Then apply the TYTT mantra (page 87) to get "unstuck."
- Do you regularly reevaluate and, if necessary, tweak your routine? Does it accommodate the needs of the **I**s as well as the **We**?
- Do you believe that children should have a real role in running the family?

Notes on Chore Wars

NINE

EXPECT CHANGE
Summoning Your Sage Brain

Learn from yesterday, live for today, hope for tomorrow.
The important thing is not to stop questioning.
—ALBERT EINSTEIN

Arlene Borden, age forty-four, a computer scientist who moved up in the ranks of a huge tech company, finally attains her career dream: an executive-level job at a well-financed startup. The only downside: She has a longer drive to the office. Also, her coworkers, mostly men without families, think nothing of staying until midnight. Although she doesn't work as late as some, she spends more time away from her family than she ever has. Harold, her partner, is supportive of the change. He knows Arlene loves the work and deserves the new position and the pay, which will help them with some long-overdue bills. He leaves his real estate office earlier than usual, telecommutes when he can, and gets dinner on the table most nights before Arlene returns. As partners, they're in sync; as parents, they're loving and consistent.

Still, Maya and Carter, ages eleven and eight, feel their mother's absence. They argue more, fight over possessions. The house is louder than usual. When Carter's teacher sends home a note saying that he seems "distracted" in class, the Bordens realize that although they are "handling" their new circumstances, the whole family has to adapt to the change.

Every family is part of an ecosystem in which the Three Factors converge—the individuals, their relationships, and their context. Ripples in the family ecosystem always require attention. The Bordens have been through transitions and tough times before and have learned from each of them. They plowed through their recent home renovation with minimal hassles, for example. Knowing that the construction would disrupt their daily routine, they budgeted to eat out more and made other simple adjustments, such as setting up a mini-fridge in the garage with snacks for the kids.

But that ripple was mostly an inconvenience, made bearable by planning and creative problem solving. Change is harder to deal with when bad news comes seemingly out of nowhere, as it did when Harold's father died, a man who hadn't been sick a day in his life. It took everyone by surprise, plunged Harold into depression, and brought a great deal of sadness into their lives.

The best the Bordens could do in that case was react in a way that nurtured each **I** and acknowledged how their **We** had changed. They allowed time for everyone, especially Harold, to heal. They made sure that Grandpa Borden was remembered. At Thanksgiving, they shared memories of him and talked about what he'd taught and given each of them. Maya suggested that telling stories about Grandpa and other people they loved should become a "new Thanksgiving tradition."

Families can't control what happens to them; they can only make choices and pay attention to what happens next. A few months after Grandpa's death, Arlene starts her new job, and Carter comes home with the note from his teacher. Once again, the family has to deal with change. If there's anything that this past year has taught them, it is that if any one member is in trouble, the whole family will feel it.

After speaking with Carter's teacher and brainstorming together, Harold and Arlene call an emergency check-in. They acknowledge how hard it has been for everyone—first the renovation, then Grandpa Borden's sudden death, and now Mom changing jobs. Just talking about it out loud puts the kids a little more at ease, because it makes them feel as if their parents are taking care of it. Arlene and Harold also tell them that Dirk, a neighborhood teen whom they've known for years, will come every afternoon to hang out and help.

Make no mistake, this family still has to adjust, no matter how much thought they put into it. Adapting to change takes time, and it's often taxing. Even positive change upsets the family ecosystem, which is why the widely-used Holmes-Rahe stress scale also includes events we celebrate, such as marriage, pregnancy, and gaining a new family member.

For the Bordens, things are shaky at first. It will take a few months for the adults and children to get used to the "new normal." But at least everyone recognizes this as a transition the family has to weather. They see what needs to be done—they have to protect the **I**s and preserve the **We**—and they do it together.

The Anatomy of Change

If there's a given in life, it is change. In families, nothing stays the same for long—not the individuals, not their relationships, not their circumstances. As you can see on the opposite page, there are at least fifty ways to send ripples through the family ecosystem. (You can probably add more, based on your own family.) We constantly bump into one another's **I**s and must deal with whatever family members bring home.

Family changes don't necessarily come in with a bang. Some slip under the radar, barely noticed. They creep up on us—a child changes schools and a year later becomes withdrawn. Some you can see coming, which at least gives you time to figure out what to do next. And some, like Grandpa Borden's death, come without warning and require more adjustment.

Even when you see the wrecking ball headed in your direction, there's no way of knowing how it will hit each member. For example, it's a given that your child will at some point become an adolescent or that you and your parents will age, but you have no idea what such developmental passages will be like or how they will feel (to you or them) until they happen. Even transitions you joyfully anticipate, such as a move or a new baby, are impossible to know beforehand. It's not just because you've never been there before. It's also because every person goes through life in her own way. Each new situation or challenge requires something different from us. How we are affected depends on who we are and how everyone around us handles the change.

It's not always clear at first whether the impact or outcome of any change will be good or bad, minor or major, or whether it will be the last straw, one thing following a series of small changes that dangerously tips the balance.

> *You can't stop change. You can't get around it. You can only go through it.*

Why is change so hard? It's a scary prospect to face situations beyond our control. We have no idea how this unfamiliar challenge will affect us and our future. So, we become anxious.

50 Ways to Send Ripples through the Ecosystem

What sends ripples through the ecosystem? Below is a list of common everyday situations and stressful events that force family members to adapt, even in small ways. It is in no particular order and by no means all-inclusive.

1. A new neighbor moves in next door.
2. The school makes drop-off a half hour earlier.
3. Someone goes on a diet.
4. One of the partners inherits money.
5. A child leaves home.
6. Someone new joins the family—a baby, new partner, stepchildren.
7. A child doesn't understand his homework.
8. Someone is diagnosed with [autism, dyslexia, diabetes, depression, cancer, or another life-changing condition].
9. Someone has an emotional or financial setback.
10. Someone learns a new skill.
11. Parents decide to separate.
12. A parent and child lock horns over [homework, eating, screen time, friends, clothing, curfew].
13. Someone (hopefully, not one of the kids) gets pregnant.
14. Siblings squabble over shared turf.
15. The family moves to a new community.
16. Something new is brought home or added to the house (home office, desks for homework, video game, toy, exercise equipment).
17. A parent is laid off.
18. The family plans a vacation.
19. Someone takes up a new sport or hobby.
20. A new childcare aide is hired.
21. A stock-market decline shrinks the 401(k).
22. A child changes schools.
23. A favorite teacher leaves in the middle of the year.
24. A parent changes jobs (or careers) or takes on more responsibility in the current one.
25. A child gets into a fight.
26. Someone becomes a vegetarian.
27. Someone starts spending more time away from the family.
28. A child or adult is home sick.
29. Someone starts a new exercise program.
30. Someone starts/stops smoking or drinking.
31. A family member dies.
32. The community passes a curfew law.
33. Someone makes a new friend.
34. A child repeats a grade.
35. One of the adults retires.
36. A parent reunites with a long-lost friend.
37. The family home is renovated.
38. A child tries out for a team.
39. A parent looks for a new job.
40. A grandparent or other close relative falls ill or has a health crisis.
41. A childcare aide is fired or quits.
42. A parent is transferred to another city/country.
43. The family attends a new house of worship.
44. Someone gets an award.
45. The holiday season starts.
46. An ex-partner/co-parent moves to another locale.
47. The family takes out a loan.
48. A close friend dies.
49. It's back-to-school time.
50. The family gets a new pet.

Being scared summons our "lizard brain," the oldest part of the brain, which acts automatically when threatened and tells us we'd better fight or flee. This sense of vulnerability spills onto our partners and kids, the people closest to us. Eventually, everyone's lizard brain kicks in, and the whole family is miserable, afraid of the change and too agitated to deal with it.

Change, in and of itself, isn't bad.
It just is.
What matters is how we handle it.

The secret of dealing with change is first to admit it's happening, and to realize that your lizard brain wants to take charge. Summon your "sage brain" instead.

Your Sage Brain in Action

Your sage brain is what we've referred to earlier as your "best self" or "higher self." It's responsible for what psychologist Daniel Kahneman calls "slow thinking"—observing, analyzing, and problem solving. Unlike your lizard brain, your sage brain mulls things over. It doesn't simply react.

Darlene Fournier refused to let her lizard brain take over when she was diagnosed with breast cancer. On a list of potentially bad changes, a serious medical issue ranks among the highest. It shifts the focus to the one and is a scary prospect for the many. There's nothing you can do about it except summon your sage brain.

Naturally, Darlene's lizard brain kicked in when she first heard the life-threatening news. The doctors were "hopeful"—she was relatively young—but she was looking at months of debilitating treatment. As a medical writer, she already knew that chronic illnesses affect the whole family. Caregivers can get sick themselves; children often begin to have behavioral problems or trouble in school. In worst-case scenarios, the "well spouse," drained and tired of giving, becomes angry and leaves.

"All three of my aunts on my father's side had breast cancer, and one died from the disease. But as much as I worried about myself," Darlene recalls, "I was more worried about how it would affect Harry and the kids."

Thinking about others and realizing that she needed to problem-solve instead of panic tells us that Darlene was tapping into her sage brain. She was then able to ask herself how they could best handle this as a family.

The sage brain also knows when it needs help, so Darlene turned first to the other adult in the household, her husband, Harry. Together, they discussed how they would break the news to the children, Patrick and Christine, who were ten and fourteen at the time. Once the parents had an initial plan of action in mind, they then shared it with the kids, not to burden them or ask their approval but to show them that the situation, though scary, was under control. The idea was to present the information, to get the children's reactions and input, and to help them all process in a way that engaged *their* sage brains. They would have several discussions like this over the coming months.

Darlene and Harry also made a list of relatives and friends to call on and to keep informed. They put in a great deal of thought about contingencies: Who'd stay with the children the nights Darlene was in the hospital with Harry at her side? What kind of help would they need to accommodate Darlene's postsurgical condition? Their sage brains helped them come up with a practical plan, and their large network of relatives and good friends enabled them to carry it out. One offered to stay overnight whenever they needed her. Another came over to declutter the front porch so that Darlene would have a pleasant place to recuperate. Several others chipped in to pay for a house cleaner, a masseuse, a yoga teacher, and other body workers who helped her get through chemo and radiation.

Before Darlene and Harry actually sat down with the kids, they had much of this plan in place and had rehearsed what they were going to say. "One of the things I love most about Harry is that he's an incredibly empathetic man. But he's also not good at hiding his feelings, so I warned him not to have his 'sad face' on when we told the kids." Then they had a family check-in. "We told them that I had breast cancer, that I was taking care of it, and that the treatment might make me feel very sick, but I'd get through it. *We* would get through it. And no, they couldn't catch it."

Being REAL—conscientious and careful about how they told the kids, seeing it from their perspective, talking about cancer with age-appropriate honesty, and appealing to the best in everyone—made a difference to the whole family.

Even as she was facing a mastectomy, a potentially painful and debilitating ordeal, Darlene found ways to create positive moments of connection instead of allowing the family to get infected by negativity. Harry accompanied her to doctor visits and treatment; at home, the partners gave each other the space each needed. Although both worked at home and normally shared household responsibilities, Harry stepped into some of Darlene's roles.

She had postsurgical "dates" with each child, watching reruns of *Dr. Who* with Patrick and catching up on the first two seasons of *Downton Abbey* with Christine. "We often use TV time to settle in and cuddle. I knew I wouldn't be able to do much with them after the surgery, so it was perfect."

Whether it was all the love and support or the fact that she elected not to have reconstructive surgery (an option that greatly reduces healing time), Darlene has had an amazingly successful recovery. She was at Christine's tennis match two weeks after her surgery. She saw Patrick participate in his first debate. She's still in mid-treatment at this writing, but her prognosis is good—and so is the family's. Both kids are appropriately concerned about their mother and more helpful than usual, but they're still involved with their friends and in their various activities. "I wanted to include them and listen to their ideas," says Darlene, "but I didn't want life to change for them—and, thankfully, it hasn't."

One reason the Fourniers were able to deal with Mom's cancer with only minor disruption to the family was that Darlene was able to summon her sage brain, rather than allow the lizard brain to take over.

Which Brain Is in Charge?

Given its ancient programming, the lizard brain, with its limited repertoire—anger (fight) or absence (flight)—can make a bad situation worse, whereas the sage brain sees what's needed to take appropriate action. When the sage brain is summoned, everyone is more careful and observant and less reactive.

In short, the lizard brain reacts; the sage brain reasons. Depending on which brain is in charge, each new situation or challenge will be regarded as a reason to panic or as an opportunity for growth. It can be hard, in the thick of the moment, to make a conscious effort to summon your sage brain. However, with practice, you can at least figure out which brain is holding forth.

The more you and other family members exercise your sage brains, the stronger you become. You get better at seeing (through 3-F glasses) the

Managing Your Brain

Your lizard brain is probably calling the shots if negativity prevails in any of the forms in the left column below.

By summoning your sage brain, you can combat the negativity with . . .

accusations/interruptions	nonjudgmental listening
stinginess and emotional withholding	generosity
mean-spiritedness	kindness
secrecy and alliances that exclude	openness
lying, covering up, denying	authenticity
grudges	forgiveness
arguments	conflict-resolving skills
disconnection	loving connection
isolation, withdrawal, stonewalling	thoughtful engagement
distraction	being present
moral lapses (stealing, bullying, bias)	good deeds that reflect the higher self
physical or mental illness, a child's problems in school	all of the above, and living a healthful lifestyle that feeds mind, body, and soul

bigger picture and controlling—or at least dialing down—the negativity. Your sage brain allows you to choose a better approach than your lizard brain.

With practice,
   Self-control and
   Awareness
   Get
   Easier.

The rest of this chapter is devoted to helping you and your family summon your sage brains. When we asked you to "rise above" your imaginary family in chapter 6, we prompted you to engage your sage brain, which gives you a different, more detached perspective. It allows you to observe whether the **I/We** is balanced and, if it's not, to figure out what else is going on. Ideally, it's best to rise above before negativity sets in.

Change through 3-F Glasses

Change invariably involves a combination of the Three Factors, each affecting the other. But it starts with one of them. Something happens to one of the individuals. A girl entering puberty suddenly worries that she's getting fat, and she starts dieting. A parent gets sick. A teen gets a tattoo. Or it could be that one of the relationships is shifting. Siblings become more distant because one enters junior high and has a new best friend. One of the partners drags the other into therapy. Change also can be forced on a family by the third factor, context. When the U.S. economy tanked, it almost brought the Hightower family (page 38) down with it.

Regardless of who or what initiates a change, its course is always unpredictable, a complex mingling of all Three Factors. For example, seven-year-old Bethany, whose family you'll read more about in chapter 10, has a profound hearing loss, more than 50 percent in both ears. She is sometimes taunted by insensitive peers, a problem for her as an individual. But how Bethany fares in the face of bullying will also depend on whether her parents, Ruby and George D'Angelo, are a solid team and good executives and what kind of family they've designed. Bethany's reaction will also hinge on her relationships with her parents and her two-years-younger sister, Sheri. Her context also matters: How Bethany's school deals with name-calling and aggression and whether the administrators and teachers discuss and tolerate difference can make the problem more or less difficult for Bethany and her family.

The beauty of a well-functioning family ecosystem is that regardless of what's thrown at one member of the family, the rest of the family can help manage the change before it festers into something bigger, as long as everyone feels like a stakeholder. "I tell each of the girls, 'You're a card-carrying member of this family, and you have an obligation to play your role,'" Ruby says. "This family works best when everyone is pulling their weight."

Because Bethany trusts her mother—a sure sign that a family is working well—she immediately asked Ruby what to do. "I told her to ignore the bully rather than give the girl fuel. If that didn't work, she can tell the girl, 'If you touch me again, I will talk to the principal.'" Bethany absorbed the lesson, and when she later had a problem with a boy in class, she wrote a letter to the school principal, lodging a complaint. "That's very much her personality—to take matters into her own hands. And Sheri takes cues from her: She's OK as long as Bethany is."

In the chart below are some of the most common issues that cause change in a family. We present them as a way of looking at how change happens, not because we expect you to tease out the reasons. Even family researchers admit that it's hard to disentangle the various elements that make waves in family life.

The Family Notebook questions that follow will help your sage brain see what changes might be happening in your ecosystem right now. Also, keep your ears open for what you or others say about your family. Off-handed remarks, especially from good friends, such as "You're not being

Change: Through 3-F Glasses			
Where is the change coming from?	**Individuals** (adults or children)	**Relationships** (partners, parent-child, siblings, extended family)	**Context** (the family itself or any of the various worlds that it is part of)
The possibilities (What might be going on?)	A developmental leap; new friends, new job, or other intellectual challenge; new interest; physical or mental illness; disappointment, disillusionment, or sense of failure.	Growing distance and disconnection; a sense of betrayal; infidelity; unhealthy alliances—a duo or trio excludes or gangs up on another member; parents take sides or play favorites; a death; stress from the extended family, an out-and-out family feud.	Change in family structure (a new baby, a divorce); problems in school, work-place, or the community that affect home life; circum-stances beyond the family's control (bad news, a crisis, economic downturn, or natural disaster) stress the system and affect family resources and security.
First signs (What might be said?)	"He's out of sorts." "She's not being herself."	"We're/they're having a rough time." "We/they seem discon-nected." "The honeymoon's over."	"You can cut it with a knife." "We can't seem to get out from under." "Nothing's the same around here."
If left to chance (What might you see?)	Crankiness; hostility, anger, or aggression toward others; eating or sleeping habits have changed; erratic mood swings; poor performance at work or school; lying; hurt feelings; withdrawal; lack of joy; depression.	Misunderstandings in-crease; one or both parties snaps at or blames the other; resentment festers; arguments escalate and take a predictable—and polarized—course.	The household feels tense; family members rarely have fun together or laugh out loud; problems overwhelm; difficulty in decision mak-ing; inability to imagine options or alternative scenarios.

yourself," or "Mickey kept falling asleep at my house this afternoon," or "It seems like the honeymoon is over," along with comments from teachers, coaches, and colleagues, should spur you to take a harder look at whether your family is dealing with the change or not.

FYN Change Is Always a Family Affair

Read "Change: Through 3-F Glasses" on page 221. Then, ask yourself:

- What's going on with each person in our family? Are one or more individuals having a hard time?
- What is the state of the various relationships? Don't forget to consider relationships with people outside your household.
- What else is happening to the family as a result of forces outside it?
- Have we been here before? If so, it's time to get your head out of the sand.

A Delicate Balance

Change doesn't lead to conflict as long as the sage brain is behind the wheel, reminding you to tell yourself the truth.

At the first sign of change, apply the TYTT mantra to the change.

Look around. Acknowledge what you see happening.

Tell yourself the truth. Think about how the change will impact the **I**s and the **We**. Are the **I**s getting their needs met? Does the family, as a unit, have a sense that we're all in this together and that we'll do what we have to do to get through it?

Move on. Take action; make good choices. Some change will shake up the ecosystem for a time. For example, in the Fournier household, Darlene's **I** dominated when she was first diagnosed. But even when someone is seriously ill and, for a time, necessarily gets more of the family's attention and other resources, it's important to keep the balance from tipping too much or staying there for too long.

It's often hard to reckon with change, especially those happening inside *you*. Know that whatever it is—a job change, a sense of discontent—it can take time to work up the courage to share what you're contemplating. Your lizard brain might try to crawl under a rock or strike out, making everyone wonder what's going on. At some point, if the struggle inside you becomes so difficult to live with or if one of your relationships or the context forces your hand, you'll have a *Whoa!* moment. You will finally have to tell yourself the truth and *do* something.

"I had a nagging feeling that I was in the wrong place doing the wrong thing," says Lanie Allen about her part-time job. Being at a private school where staff members paid a reduced tuition seemed like a fair tradeoff when her four children started school. But years later, as they grew up and Lanie became more interested in pursuing writing as a career, the job wasn't working for *her*. "Although I loved my students and the challenge of engaging them in the classroom, my life was slipping by me. I honestly feared that I was going to miss out on my true destiny. But my children were very happy and getting a top-rate education."

Lanie sat on that quandary for nearly two years. "I went through periods of mini-crisis over those years when I felt panicked and trapped." Then the school offered her a full-time position, and she was forced to consider the alternatives.

"Not accepting the job meant leaving a stable income, and my kids would have to transfer to public school. I was worried they'd be afraid, miss their friends," Lanie explains. "Staying meant I would continue to feel trapped and cut off from what I felt was my true calling—to write and to give talks. I had to get over the guilt of saying, 'This is just for me.' But I also hated the idea of telling my children that their lives would change."

When she finally shared her private hell, first with Bill and then with the kids, Lanie found out that the *fear* of facing change is often much worse than what happens when you finally take action. "I thought I'd get tears and crying and begging and pleading to stay at that private school," she recalls, "but it wasn't like that at all. My second oldest said, 'I thought you were going to tell us

---

Common I/We Imbalances

When the **I/We** balance tips too much, a family can get caught in one of these unhealthy patterns:

*The **We** swallows up the **I**.* Individual recognition is rare, and family members aren't accepted for who they are. In the face of change, the **We** does things a certain way, and too bad if you don't fall into line.

*One **I** saps all the resources of the **We**.* The family showers all its resources on a member seen as gifted or on one who has special or oversized needs. Adults sacrifice, and children have to go along for the ride.

*Only the children's **Is** matter.* A generational imbalance, the needs of the children overshadow the adults' needs. "Family time" is all about entertaining or nurturing the kids. The parents' own relationship suffers; siblings fight.

*The adult's **Is** overshadow the children's.* Common in earlier, less child-focused eras, variations on this theme can still be seen in dual-career or very affluent families who outsource childcare and home maintenance to professionals. Also, in some postdivorce families, parents are distracted, and the kids' **Is** don't get enough attention.

someone had died.'" For Lanie, the experience was a learning moment: "I didn't know that I was more afraid of the change than they were."

Of course, there are times when no one welcomes a change, and to complicate matters, every I seems to need something. The question is, who gets that something first, especially when there's not enough to go around? Families often deal with multiple issues and need some sort of triage to help them decide which issue to tackle first. So while you're telling yourself the truth, decide if it's time to rush in or to wait and see. The matter might be:

- *Urgent:* a crisis that has to be handled immediately.
- *A nip-it-now situation:* a small problem that, if not handled now, could become much more serious.
- *Important:* something that belongs near the top of the list; put it on the agenda for your next check-in.
- *Ongoing:* not new but worrisome or annoying; think about it.

Beware: Your lizard brain can perceive anything that's new or unfamiliar—and therefore scary—as urgent, which can hamper your ability to tell yourself the truth.

Remember how Greg Perlman complained about Sadie acting "rude and spoiled" after watching *That's So Raven* and other tween-target TV shows? That story isn't just about the dangers of TV programs that portray sassy teens and clueless parents. Sadie's newfound attitude set off an alarm in Greg's head. Like many fathers of preteen daughters, Greg panics, which summons his lizard brain ("Oh, no, I'm losing my little girl; next thing you know, she'll be sneaking off with boys, and I know what *they* want"). He's ready to fight.

Fortunately, Greg is a very conscious dad. He will eventually summon his sage brain and realize that his "little girl" is a preteen and that she is experiencing changes in her mind and body that she doesn't necessarily understand (and he might not be ready to accept). Greg has to put her behavior in perspective. When Sadie watches TV—a window into the culture—she gets ideas. *Oh, this is how a "cool" kid talks and acts.* Because her I is searching for ways to play out the changes that are happening inside her—changes, no doubt, that she also sees in her peers—she "tries on" a new, much sassier persona.

Instead of trying to stop the change and slam Sadie down for asserting her I, Greg has to see her sassiness as a sign. She's growing up. She *is* becoming more mature—good about homework and other responsibilities—*and* she's also asserting her independence. If he allows his lizard brain to dominate, it won't stop the march of Sadie's adolescence. But it will disrupt their relationship. At worst, Sadie will feel resentful and misunderstood and, possibly, get into real trouble.

But if Greg can summon his sage brain, instead of fighting with his preteen, he'll ask himself, "What can I do to keep Sadie safe, sustain our connection, and at the same time gradually give her more room to explore? How can I tend to her I without letting it dominate the family?" By telling himself the truth, reacting but not overreacting, and making sensible choices that take Sadie's growth into consideration, Greg will right the imbalance before it becomes chronic.

At the first sign of imbalance in your family, do whatever it takes: Have more frequent family check-ins, tweak the routine, spend extra time dealing with it all. The goal, always, is to right the balance. That doesn't mean that the change goes away or becomes easier. It just means that your family has adapted successfully—until the next sign of change comes along.

FYN Checking Your Balance

Think of a recent change your family had to deal with. Ask yourself how your family handled it:

- Did we acknowledge what it was? Did one or more individuals have a hard time? Did we take each I into account when dealing with the change?
- What is the state of our various relationships since the change? Did it have an impact on relationships with people outside our household?
- What else is happening in the family as a result of forces outside it? Are we still pulling together as a team? Is the atmosphere more negative than it was before?
- Is our family short on any resources since then? Do we suffer from a lack of time or money? Is the adults' attention diverted? Does the family have relatives or a support system in the community that they can count on? Have any other problems drained energy from our ecosystem?

The Danger of Runaway Negativity

In an earlier book, we warned about "runaway emotions," an escalating cycle of feelings that children are powerless to stop. In families, a similar phenomenon, "runaway negativity"—anger, fear, shame, guilt, sadness, contempt, embarrassment, and disgust—can travel like an unstoppable and highly contagious virus.

Negativity is a powerful and potentially destructive force. Minor incidents of disrespect, tattling, arguments, hurt feelings, mean words, and other negative interactions infect the whole family. Bad is stronger than good, many studies conclude. Negative emotions also stay with us longer. They flow from husbands to wives more often than the other way around and, not surprisingly, from parents to children. Babies and children of depressed mothers are burdened by their mothers' sadness. In homes affected by alcoholism or where one parent is a rager, children often suffer the aftereffects well into adulthood. Even in far less dysfunctional households, when parents argue, children feel it. They're often still reeling even after the adults have kissed and made up.

Of course, emotions are part of life. Few couples with children can claim that they never argue in front of their child, despite their sensitivity or good intentions. But at least if you understand the danger, you can buffer the effects. You can be authentic—acknowledge that it happened. You can say "I'm sorry" or "It was wrong." And, as Corbyn and Larry Hightower do, you can make up in front of the children, so that they witness both the resolution and the fight.

Negative feelings serve a purpose, especially fear, which helped our ancestors know when to run from danger. Disgust prevented them from eating rancid meat. But too much negativity narrows our options.

Food For Thought: Positive 3, Negative 1 = A Better Life

To study the effects of emotions on overall happiness, a team of psychologists offered subjects a list of 20 positive and negative feelings. Surprise was not included, because it can be negative or positive. Participants were asked to indicate on a scale of 0 ("not at all") to 4 ("extremely") which emotions they'd felt in the last 24 hours. Those who had a ratio of at least three positive emotional experiences to one negative experience were more likely to "flourish"—to be the best that they could be.

amusement	anger
awe	contempt
compassion	disgust
contentment	embarrassment
gratitude	fear
hope	guilt
interest	sadness
joy	shame
love	
pride	
sexual desire	

Source: "Positive Affect and the Complex Dynamics of Human Flourishing," by B. L. Fredrickson and M. F. Losada, *American Psychologist*, October 2005.

You don't get much out of life or feel very well if you're always in fight-or-flight mode or any kind of "bad place."

Positive emotions, in contrast, open us. They allow us to be more flexible, see more choices, and be more creative, intuitive, and attentive. They strengthen mind and body, making us more resilient and happier. Predictably, when researchers look at the everyday lives of individuals who flourish, positive emotions outweigh negative ones by three to one.

So while it's important to honor all our emotions, we can't allow negativity to infect the ecosystem, because it changes everything and works against your family's ability to withstand and adapt to change.

FYN A Quick Negativity Check

Is a change occurring in your family or is something happening to your family right now that seems to be affecting your positive-to-negative ratio? Answer with your whole family in mind. Copy the list of emotions (positive and negative) from the sidebar, left, into your notebook, leaving space after each one.

Then set aside 8 to 12 hours to record the positive and negative emotions that pervade your household. Every hour, look around you. What is the dominant mood? Put a check mark next to the feeling (or feelings) that best describe the emotional tone of your family at that moment. Some families vent negative or positive emotions more often and more intensely than others.

- How does your family compare with the one you grew up in? Are members afraid of or discouraged from expressing feelings?
- Do positive emotions outweigh negative ones by at least 3 to 1? If so, you probably don't have much runaway negativity. If not, read on; there are things you can do.

Sticky-Bottle Solutions: How to Dial Down the Drama

Family trouble often has a tinge of been-there-tried-that familiarity. That's the good news. As philosopher George Santayana famously said, "Those who do not learn from history are doomed to repeat it." So the next time you're caught in or witness a negative interaction, take time to reflect and learn from it. How have you dealt with similar circumstances in the past? What worked, and what didn't? Isn't it wiser not to go there again?

For example, you reach for the salad dressing in the fridge, and your hand sticks to the bottle. You rush to the sink, annoyed and ready to blurt out, "Can't anyone in this house ever wipe a bottle off?" You're furious, but it's probably not about the sticky bottle. It's about your needs—and you take it personally. *They do it on purpose. They're trying to provoke me. No one cares about me. How could they not remember?* At that moment, you're on a slippery slope made all the more treacherous because your company is downsizing, and you're wondering if your head is next on the chopping block. Before you start to rant and accuse, summon your sage brain to help you stop and think.

Yes, your partner probably could have wiped off the jar, if he had thought about it. But he didn't. His mother put bottles back in the refrigerator and paid no mind to the crust that built up. So he doesn't think it's a big deal. It doesn't even occur to him. Your nine-year-old could have wiped the bottle off, too. He had a friend over. Chances are, he won't think about it much, either—until he's married and he and his partner have to deal with their own sticky-bottle problem.

There are countless sticky-bottle problems like this in family life, potentially angry moments that you can defuse by remembering that they mean nothing, unless *you* bring meaning to them. Wiping off the jars makes you feel like an efficient homemaker. But to the rest of the family, a sticky jar is just a sticky jar. When they take it out of the refrigerator, they don't think about how it got that way. They just wipe off their hands. You, on the other hand, go ballistic.

Or not. Instead of ranting, you can summon your sage brain. Bring up the sticky-bottle problem calmly at a family check-in. Let them know it bothers you, explain why ("This was what my mom taught me" or "I hate it when my hands get sticky"). And ask for help. If your children are young, read *The Little Red Hen,* in which no one helps the hen bake the bread, but all are eager to eat it. Be realistic, too. They won't ever be as vigilant as you are. But at least you have averted a potentially disruptive and negative moment.

Negativity is hard to stop. Overtaken by the lizard brain, we say and do things that we can never *unsay* or *undo.* Let's say your partner is nasty, or your child lashes out. Even though you are angry, take a deep breath, and try to summon your sage brain. This doesn't excuse their behavior, but it does dial down the anger. You might say something along the lines of, "Wow, you must be really upset to talk like that to me. But I don't deserve to be your punching bag. I don't have to stand here and listen. It's not only hurtful, but I don't want to say something that *I'll* regret. So I'm going to my room. When you've calmed down, we can solve this problem together."

Always ask yourself, what's best for the relationship at this moment?

If your lizard brain kicks in, and *you* are about to dole it out, think before you speak. When you judge, criticize, insult, or berate, you push the other person away and poison the air between you.

It's one thing to express how you feel—in which case, start your sentence with "I," as in "I am worried about how tired I am." This leaves the door open so that you can admit you're feeling vulnerable and ask for help. It's quite another to accuse ("You never help me!") or to act as if your I is smarter and always knows better ("Just give it to me—I'll do it; you'll never get it done"). And it's not just the words you use. Subtle gestures, glances, eye rolls, tone of voice, throat clearing, pauses at particular moments, and how you hold yourself during a conversation convey meaning to the other person.

If you or any family member is in a bad mood or having a temper tantrum about some new wrinkle in family life, pay attention—to yourself as much as to them. Notice what runs through your mind and what's happening in your body. If your pulse races and you start to feel as if you'd rather be anywhere else or you want to somehow shut that person up, your lizard brain is probably taking over. Listen to what you're about to say before you say it. Witness your behavior. How would you feel on

What You're *Really* Saying

I told you so/I thought that would happen.
I'm smarter than you.

You did it again/There you go again.
This isn't the first time—and I'm counting.

I'm right/You're wrong.
I win this one.

It's your fault.
I did nothing to deserve this—it's all on you.

I don't mean to be critical, but . . .
This is what you do wrong or badly. I can do it better.

I've asked you a thousand times.
You're shirking your responsibilities.

I can't listen to this.
You're giving me the same old excuse. You're lying.

You drive me crazy.
You don't do/say what I want.

You are too/You never/You always . . .
I judge you to be a flawed, one-dimensional person.

I have nothing to apologize for.
You're bad/wrong.

I'm outta here.
I'm not willing to do the hard work of sustaining this relationship.

the other end of it? If the answer is "not good," lock your lips and do something kind instead. Try hard; remember that your goal is to better the relationship. If you can't be charitable at that moment, however, walk away and take a PTO (personal time-out). You'll be a better partner and a better parent if you do.

One of you—if with a child, it will always be the adult—has to start talking to the other in a more mindful, compassionate, and respectful way. In REAL families, members apologize quickly and sincerely and make restitution if necessary. Negativity doesn't have to spiral into something more serious or become chronic. Although you can't really know what's going on inside other family members' minds and hearts, these are the people you know best. You've been here before. You can make an educated guess *if* you tell yourself the truth. And unless the other person's lizard brain has taken over completely, you can also ask.

In the face of change, family members can experience a smorgasbord of unpleasant emotions:

- Sad ("I can't believe the summer's over").
- Disappointed ("Why did the community center stop having movie night?").
- Guilty ("If only I had studied more").
- Shocked ("What do you mean the new job requires you to travel for business?").
- Angry ("Look at this report card! I told you to pay more attention to Mrs. Grundy").
- Disillusioned ("I thought we agreed to consult each other before making this decision").
- Jealous ("Why does Timmy get to play baseball?").
- Betrayed ("You told your assistant this news before you told me?").

How you deal with a partner's or child's emotions is often a matter of what you've learned about negativity in the past. Amy Perlman, for example, never saw her parents argue, so when Greg raised his voice, she didn't think it was normal. His anger frightened her. Another person, with a different history, might have met Greg's anger with even more anger.

Figuring or finding out "where" a person is makes it more likely that your response will be what his or her I needs at that moment. John Hedley, for example, didn't know that twelve-year-old Brittany was having girl-friend conflicts at school. When he announced to the family that every-one was invited to the company picnic, she stomped out of the room, but not before she announced, "I hate the people in your office!" John was dumbstruck but remembered that earlier that morning, Brittany also went ballistic because he'd eaten the last banana.

He needed more information. His wife had it: "Brittany feels as if everyone at school has turned against her—and her life is *over!*" John, pained for his daughter and remembering his own social dilemmas as a kid, immediately offered her advice about dealing with "those girls." Brittany rolled her eyes and barely listened, which made John furious. Instead of stopping the negativity, John unintentionally escalated it. "Listen, missy," he shouted at her, "I'm trying to help you!" His angry response only made the situation worse and the drama more difficult to dial down.

The problem was, Brittany was in mid-change, still stuck in bad feel-ings. Her lizard brain was not ready for a solution. John offered her ad-vice, which was what *his* I might want under similar circumstances, but it wasn't what *she* needed. A better approach would have been to ask Brit-tany what was going on—and not to assume or judge. Talking to her, John might have realized that his daughter needed him to listen and reassure her that she had a reason to feel so rotten, that he was there for her, and that it's OK to feel bad at times, because some times *are* bad! Once she calmed down, then maybe they could work together on a solution to, or at least a distraction from, Brittany's social woes.

Do the Right Thing

You always have a choice. (Now we've said it three times.) To be sure, when negative emotions overwhelm you, it is harder to be mindful, to be kind, and to remember that other family members have their own Is. We are all naturally less resilient in the face of disruptions to our routines, less able to muster empathy and self-control. With effort, though, you can remind yourself that you have a choice. You don't have to go down the road of negativity.

Family life is filled with button-pushing moments, many of them

Why REAL Families Do Better with Change

All families must deal with change and the tension and disagreements that often accompany it. But some are better than others at handling change. In such families, everyone strives to be REAL.

Responsible: To the best of their capability, everyone makes a conscious and sustained effort to keep the family on an even keel and to right it when it's not.

Empathetic: Family members listen to one another with compassion and without judging, criticizing, or denying.

Authentic: They are not afraid to say what they really feel. They might argue the facts, but they accept one another's emotions and perspective.

Lead with love: Although it's harder during and right after arguments, family members reach down inside themselves for a kind response. They also assume that the other is coming from a loving place and has the best intentions.

spurred by change that we haven't yet recognized. Little Freddy kicks your chair *again*. Maybe it's time to question if anything new has happened with his sister or in school. Your partner keeps calling back, even after you've tabled the subject. What's pushing her anxiety level so high? The kids won't stop fighting over whose turn it is. Is this business as usual, or is there some new challenge one or both of them have to face?

We'll say it a fourth time: You *always* have a choice. You can stick your head in the sand or tell yourself the truth. You can want to win—establish that your way is better—or you can step back and figure out what's best for everyone. You can steamroll or be empathetic. You can groan in dismay (*Oh, no, the same old song*) or catastrophize—fear that you want something the other person won't or can't give you. Or you can summon your sage brain, get REAL, and say to yourself, *This is worth it. I can do it.*

FYN How Good Are You at Summoning Your Sage Brain?

Set aside a time when you can be alone without interruptions. Make a list of the children and adults in your family, including your parents and siblings. For each person, do the steps below. If you have only small patches of free time (or a very large family), do this exercise in several sittings. Start with a family member with whom you most frequently lock horns.

1. Think of a recent negative interaction with that person.
2. Take a deep breath, close your eyes, relax, and summon your sage brain. See the interaction from that person's point of view.
3. Open your eyes. Stay in character. Continue to "be" the other person, and answer the following questions as if you are him or her:

   ° *What kind of past experiences did I bring to the situation?*
   ° *What did I feel and think?*
   ° *What was easiest for me? Hardest?*

4. Write down any other insights that come to you. Psychologists call this "perspective taking"— you're putting yourself in another's shoes.
5. Wait a week (sooner if you have another not-so-great moment with that person), and reread what you wrote. Do you have a new understanding or appreciation of the person? Is it a little easier to accept who he or she is? Can you now find it in your heart to apologize, forgive, and/or do something nice for that person without expecting anything in return—just because you want to better the relationship?

Don't expect miracles. The point here is to exercise your sage brain. As they say in TV commercials, results may vary. Some old hurts are more difficult to deal with. It may take years to forgive, and you might never forget, but at least you can accept and understand.

Notes on Change and Negativity

TEN

SIB WRANGLING
Dealing with the Most Demanding Is

*We were a strange little band of characters trudging through
life sharing diseases and toothpaste, coveting one another's
desserts, hiding shampoo, borrowing money, locking each
other out of our rooms, inflicting pain and kissing to heal it in
the same instant, loving, laughing, defending, and trying to
figure out the common thread that bound us all together.*

—Erma Bombeck

"When Tina was born, our son Jamie was fine about having a new baby sister," Kara Guarini recalls of her two older children. "He was in day care, with a family, so he was used to sharing the spotlight. But when I was pregnant with Robyn, Tina, who was then four and a half, said to me, 'I told you we don't need another baby.' A few months later, when Tina's kindergarten class talked about adoption, she came home and said, 'I know what we can do with the baby.'"

No matter how much Kara and her husband, Barry Suskind, tried to coax and cajole their middle child to be nice to baby Robyn, Tina, as her mother puts it, "never adored her." The situation worsened after they found Tina sitting in a closet with a blanket over her head—one of the early signs of her anxiety and depression. She was nine.

From then on, Tina's I dominated the family. Kara and Barry, both doctors, dealt with and sometimes argued about their daughter's mental health. Most often, they disagreed about whether she should be taking medication. Jamie, the easygoing older brother, took on a caretaker role. Baby sister Robyn got progressively angrier. From her perspective, this sister, who wasn't particularly kind to her from the day she was born, was now draining her parents' energy. Robyn quickly learned to defend herself against her four-years-older sister and gave as good as she got.

"They fought like cats and dogs as kids," says Kara. Robyn often instigated. It was usually over simple things, such as what to watch on TV. It was the little digs—she knew just how to get to Tina."

In any household with more than one child, this is a familiar story. Many parents know what it feels like to spend a good part of the week "sib wrangling." One of our interviewees described it as "herding cats." At times, your kids might be getting along extraordinarily well (say, on a vacation or at someone else's house). Then they start in again. You probably alternate being annoyed by, tired of, or worried about the jealousy and jousting. As one summary of sibling research noted, "How children get along with their siblings is the most frequent source of conflict in middle school, and is reported by parents to be *a chief child-rearing concern*" (emphasis ours).

The rivalry varies in intensity. Siblings don't always demand, grab, challenge, refuse to cooperate, sneak around, conveniently forget, and want everything the others have. But they certainly inspire one another's lizard brains. Every family creates its own unique drama, sometimes drawing on scripts that have been in play for generations. Partners don't always agree; the kids get mixed messages. Insults are hurled, someone is ignored, someone retreats, someone cries, someone rages.

Sibling battles punctuate the drama of daily family life and try the patience of millions of parents. It's a given in many households. How could it be otherwise? Tracy often asked mothers who were impatient with their firstborn's jealousy, "How would *you* feel, luv, if your husband brought home another woman?" Brothers and sisters keep track. At any moment, they know who's more likely to be given in to and who gets what—attention, air time, new sneakers, a special date with Mom or Dad.

It's not the same in every family. In some households, siblings happily do things together, mostly cooperate with one another, and sometimes or rarely fight, and when they do, they work it out. In other homes, siblings' Is juggle and joust with one another constantly—in some families, up to *eight times an hour.*

However, sibling issues are not just about the children. Whether brothers and sisters vie for the spotlight or cleave together for support—or both—tells us a lot about the family: how feelings are expressed, how conflict is viewed, and to what extent there's a healthy **I/We** balance. Siblings are a lot less likely to battle when they're seen as individuals and when they also feel that they're part of a family that needs them.

Siblings: Powerful and Ever-Present

As we pointed out in chapter 5, the sibling relationship is the most enduring of all family bonds. Barring tragedy or a serious rift, your children will be in one another's life long after you're gone. As Abby Porter repeatedly tells her two sons, who are two years apart in age, "Your brother is more important than anyone in the world."

Sibling relationships are powerful and ever-present. Children spend more out-of-school time with their siblings than anyone else, sharing free time and family time. No wonder brothers and sisters have a major impact. Positive sibling relationships offer support and protection, a buffer against a harsh environment. Sibling conflict, on the other hand, can leave scars that last a lifetime on both the individuals and the family.

Sometimes both happen. A nineteen-year-old twin, looking back on how much he teased his brother, now has regrets. "I was a dick," he admits. "And now I try to make it up to him." The Guarini girls, now fifteen and nineteen, have reached a similar détente, even though Robyn sometimes still resents Tina's lifelong pull on the family. Circumstances change, and sibling relationships change with them. Tina is in college, so the girls are no longer living under the same roof. Robyn is old enough to know that Tina has an illness she can't control. She can also look back at times when various childcare providers were hired and fired. This parade of strangers taxed their young lives, but they had each other.

How your children's Is mesh is not entirely in your control, any more than how they turn out is solely a function of what you do as a parent. Sibling relationships depend on the same Three Factors mix that influences all intimate connections.

> ## Sibling Statistics
>
> - Kids today are more likely to grow up with a sibling than with a father. Nearly eight out of ten children live with one or more siblings—the majority with one or two, 16 percent with three or more.
> - Most siblings are related by blood, but 11 percent live with at least one half sibling, 2 percent with at least one stepsibling, and 2 percent with one adopted sibling.
> - Sibling conflict occurs up to eight times per hour. Physical violence (from mild to more serious hitting, biting, punching, and the use of weapons) takes place in 70 percent of families, a rate higher than either child or spousal abuse.
> - Most sibling fights end without clear resolution or with one child's victory over the other. Fewer than 12 percent of these battles, from toddlerhood to adolescence, end with compromise or reconciliation.

Make no mistake, though. You can't control your children's relationships, but you do make a difference. The way you interact with your partner every day and how you treat your children when they're not fighting matter. How you react when they fight and whether you teach them how to manage their conflicts matters. In short, you have a huge impact on sibling relationships from early childhood through adolescence.

Your fairness toward them—as perceived by siblings—is critically important. It's not that you have to treat them the same. You will interact differently and have different relationships with each child. How can it be otherwise? Each of them co-creates a unique relationship with you. However, different is not necessarily better or worse; it's just different.

Besides, it's appropriate to treat children differently. It means you're tuned in to their needs. For example, when Candace Holder allowed twelve-year-old Marcus to quit basketball camp, his older sister, Nina, objected. "You never let *me* quit anything." Candace calmly reminded her daughter that she and her brother were "built" differently. Nina was the kind of kid who never wanted to quit; she was a fighter. Marcus, who wasn't a natural athlete, had tried to tough it out at basketball camp, but he sat on the bench most of the time. The other boys, who'd been playing for years, called him "kid"—no one even tried to know him. Letting Marcus quit was a compassionate act. Candace explained to Nina that she supported her in other ways, such as when the school threatened to disband the girls' soccer team. "I stick up for you, too," she reminded her daughter, "but only when you need it."

Below we offer some secrets of "sib wrangling," ideas to keep in mind when your children fight, as they inevitably will. (Some of these might apply to your adult fights, too.) A lot is at stake. What children see around them and how they experience relationships in the family set the tone for how they will fare as partners and parents in years to come.

Managing Your "Cubs"

Why siblings argue is both simple and complex. At its core, sibling rivalry is an evolutionary thing: Getting what you need—food, water, and connection—is a basic biological drive that enables living creatures to survive. Next time your kids go at each other, imagine them as baby bears. They are almost as primitive! Each one wants as much as she can get. They don't care whom they have to push out of the way as they scramble to get hold of Mama Bear's teats.

Unlike animals, though, it takes a long time for human babies to become fully self-sufficient. Long after they're weaned, they still vie for family resources, and there's just so much attention, energy, time, and material possession to go around. It helps to keep it all in perspective and remember that the sibling dance is quite natural. It begins the day you bring that second child home, although you might not realize it at first. Most first children, at least for the first year of the second child's life, are happy to *become* brothers or sisters. When the older one realizes that the new kid is actually staying, his primitive **I** kicks in. That's when you're likely to hear, "Can't we give him back?"

Here are some ideas that can help you apply family-think to sibling relationships:

Understand what it's like from their point of view. Interestingly, Tracy fielded more calls from parents whose *second* child suddenly developed "behavior problems" after the birth of a third child than from parents worried about a firstborn's reaction to the new baby. Most parents take pains to prepare their firstborn. They are aware that it's important to carve out special time with the older child. But they aren't quite as vigilant when the third comes along and displaces the middle child. Next thing you know, little Joey is writing on baby Thad's forehead with a marker.

When siblings squabble at any age, ask yourself what basic need isn't being met. Are one or both children hungry, tired, bored, feeling left out?

> **Children need to feel seen and heard. Many sibling battles are a bid to get noticed or rescued.**

Particularly when a child or the family itself is under stress—a tough day at school, an argument with a friend, a disappointment, problems between the parents—a sibling is an easy target. Be empathetic, so the child feels seen, but let him know that it's also not permissible to abuse a family member ("Oliver, I know you're upset, but taking it out on your sister is not OK").

Be attuned: Look for little ways to nurture each child. In harmonious families, siblings tend to have a strong sense of who they are as individuals—they know they matter and, at the same time, feel connected to one another. Constant battles between siblings, on the other hand, are like a message from the ecosystem: "Someone needs attention!"

In today's busy family life, it can feel overwhelming to keep track of who's getting your attention (unless you're a sibling). But even ten minutes a day, to share a bit of positive one-on-one time with each child, can make a difference. It could be a cuddle, an activity you both like, such as a puzzle or a quick game, a walk or bike ride around the block. As children get older, engage them in conversation. Keep abreast of their interests and ask about them.

Note how you and your partner behave toward each child. We've never met two parents who treat their children the same way. It's impossible; you're two different people, and each child is different. One partner is usually more lenient than the other or more conscious of eating or more easily upset by sibling squabbles and possibly more reactive. Who is more likely to invite a child to play a game of frisbee, watch a sports event or a talent program on TV—and which child is usually invited? Talk about this with each other; say your preferences out loud ("I really enjoy watching baseball with Izzy." "I love to shop with Jen.") What strengths do each of you want to impart to your children? What interests do you want to share? We strongly advise one-on-one time with children. But watch the other children's faces. Do you see jealousy? Disappointment? Does one child feel left out? If both adults are at home, is there another way to involve the one who isn't invited, or doesn't want to participate?

Talk about their feelings toward one another. Ask how they feel about their brothers or sisters, what's the best thing about the sibling (or each sibling), what's the worst thing. Really listen when they volunteer information. Don't try to talk them out of their feelings ("But you love your sister"). In other words, open the door so that you stay up-to-date about the relationship, not just the individual.

Keeping tabs on their feelings is especially important when one or more siblings are going through transitions, such as a new school ("What will you miss when Eric no longer rides the bus with you?"). A younger child might depend on an older sib; an elder might enjoy the role of revered one. When circumstances change, as we pointed out in the last chapter, it can trigger fears that morph into fights.

Show them how to be "with." Kids don't come in knowing how to be part of a family. Some are inherently better than others at getting along, but most need help sharing the spotlight. Start early, if possible. Studies suggest that parents have little effect on sibling issues by adolescence.

All children squabble. Those who are taught and whose parents model civility and cooperation usually squabble less. Often, in fact, it's not what you *say* to a kid that matters; it's what you *do*. Even if you argue, as long as you and your partner respect and are kind to each other and are careful not to wound each other and to apologize when you do, it shows them that disagreements can be worked through.

Be proactive. As obvious as this seems, let your children know that you care about how they behave toward one another. Decide with your partner what you won't tolerate—physical violence of any kind, cruelty, emotional battering, invading someone's privacy? And make sure you tell them what kind of behavior you expect before fights erupt. Use your family check-ins to reinforce your ground rules and, if necessary, to renegotiate space and property. When they fight, refer to the rules. "In our family, we don't [talk that way to one another/hit/bite/scream/tattle]. In our family, we help one another."

Give them responsibility—not busy work but real jobs that the family needs done. Intentionally design family rituals and create roles that encourage children to work together. A three-year-old doesn't have the same capabilities as an eight-year-old, but she can, for example, help her older brother pull weeds. Kids who are busy being part of a family feel competent. They get to be part of a team and to step into new roles; they gain confidence as stakeholders. Reading to your little brother or helping a big sister wash the car makes a child feel more grown-up.

Kara Guarini, like so many parents of twenty-somethings, regrets that she didn't ask her three children to do more. "We were bad about giving them jobs to do," she admits. Among other reasons, many responsibilities were relegated to the *au pair*. "The kids cleared their dishes after eating without being asked, but that was it. When they went off to college, I had to teach them how to do their own wash."

Know where your I goes when they fight. It's fascinating to watch cubs wrestle with their litter mates on Animal Planet. But in your own living room, it can bring up memories of an annoying brother or sister who shut you out or lied about you. Or you might flash on a sibling whom one of your parents seemed to favor and hold to a more relaxed standard. It doesn't matter whether your recollection is the truth; such memories of the past are painful to you and will color what you see in the present. On the other hand, if you were extremely close to your siblings and have nothing but fond memories or if you grew up in a family in which no one fought, watching your kids go at it might baffle and even scare you.

Ruth Striker, a thirty-seven-year-old teacher and mother of two, identifies sibling rivalry as "our family's biggest difficulty—it divides us." Dory is eight, and Christopher is five. Both are Spirited children raised in the baby-whispering tradition. "The kids are each other's best friend *and* worst enemy," says Ruth. "If we are all at home for a day, they can't stop interacting with each other, but that quickly turns into an argument." Ruth has trouble believing that this is normal.

Brothers and sisters tend to be most involved with each other during middle childhood—they're no longer toddlers and not yet teens. Spending so much time together often leads to conflict, as in the Striker household. Ruth's husband, Percy, is likely to ignore the kids when they spar, among other reasons because he fought with his sister until he turned thirty. No big deal. Ruth, in contrast, is an only child. That is not to say that she is imagining her children's battle, just that it gets to her more. When she feels her own stomach tie in knots as the children fight, Ruth has to tell herself, "This is normal. My reaction is not."

Consciousness helps. Warren Davis, for example, might have gone ballistic when his son Wyatt, age eight, spanked his three-year-old sister, Ariel. Warren grew up with domestic violence, and when his daughter cried that day, it triggered very old feelings. But Warren is aware of how his childhood affects his parenting. He also has a vision of what he wants his family to be. To yell at his son or punish him physically would be to replicate the harm that was done to him as a boy. So he sat Wyatt down and calmly explained, "Women are life givers, and we need to treat them well. You, as a big brother, need to protect your little sister. Besides, we don't hit one another in our family." He knew from the look in his son's eyes that the boy understood. That moment led to a deeper connection between father and son, which also helped Wyatt make room for Ariel.

Don't overreact. When David Sargent-Klein clopped his little brother Seth on the head or grabbed a toy away from him, his parents wisely kept the focus on what they wanted for their family. Stephen recalls, "We never said, 'You have to love Seth. He's your brother.' It was about the fact that in this family, we take care of one another. You can't tell people how to love one another." David, now nineteen, has a great relationship with his three siblings. In fact, all of the Sargent-Klein siblings are incredibly close and supportive of one another.

It's tiring, sometimes tedious, to teach the same lesson again and again, to have to intervene. It's a tall order. On occasion, Stephen admits, he lost his temper. But most of the time, he was able to stop himself from overreacting. He'd talk calmly to David and remind him about the family they were building together.

With parents' help and an environment that encourages responsibility, honesty, cooperation, caring, compassion, forgiveness, apology, and mutual respect, children tend to interact with one another and with friends in a respectful way. They feel as if they're part of a team, as opposed to cubs scrambling to survive.

Expect changes as the kids get older. Abby Porter considers herself "lucky," because Zane and Levi, two and a half years apart, rarely fight, but she wisely adds, "so far." She knows that as her boys change, so might their relationship. Especially in cultures like ours that value independence over interdependence, siblings tend to grow apart when one reaches adolescence. Their interests diverge, and they spend more time out of the house.

Elena Rivera, age fifteen, and her brother Julio, eleven, recently reached such a point. On a typical day, Elena verbally assaults Julio, mimicking and mocking him, in front of his friends and family. In turn, Julio responds by poking her and physically invading his sister's space. Elena is at an age when she's struggling to separate. She also might feel that Julio, who is very precocious and articulate, is more "competition" now than he was as a cute little brother. Julio probably misses his big sister's companionship. And maybe he also feels abandoned.

Look at the whole family. It's no accident that Elena and Julio have been at each other more since their mother was diagnosed with diabetes. Although Camilla and her husband of twenty years, Alvaro, have taken steps to change the way the family eats and to educate the kids about the disease, the adults are understandably more stressed out and tired these days. Despite their best efforts, there is less attention and energy to go around.

Food for Thought: Whose Is It?

"It's mine." "Get out of my room." "Dad gave that to me." Siblings often fight over possessions and territory. But their scripts are also dictated by their family's notion of ownership. An interviewee who grew up "dirt poor in Jackson, Mississippi," had a shoe box with her "private things" that she hid from her siblings, because individual property was not recognized or respected in her household. Another, an identical twin whose parents "forced" her to dress like her sister until age twelve, had no sense of having anything of her own. And a mother of eight explains that her children *can't* have privacy or their own space; the house simply isn't big enough. "My kids don't fight over stuff," she says, "because they know they have to share. That's just the way it is."

What are the explicit or unspoken rules of ownership in your household?

Things are what they are. Siblings fight. Parents get sick. However, the Riveras have good coping skills. They've been here before. "When Elena was around five," Camilla recalls, "Julio would toddle over and wreck whatever she was meticulously setting up. She'd go nuts. So finally I designated a table as her space. Anything she wanted away from Julio, she had to put on that table." Now that the kids are at each other again, Camilla suggests a similar approach to give them more "space" from each other. The difference now is that Julio is old enough to take responsibility, too.

"Elena has a 'Keep out!' sign on the door, and both kids understand the rules," Camilla explains. "Julio has to be invited in before he enters. But Elena has to tell him ahead of time what he can't touch. If he doesn't listen, instead of screaming 'Maaaaaa!' she tries to stay calm and say, 'Julio, you have to leave now. I need my space back.' He doesn't always leave right away, and sometimes she yells at him. But Elena is also starting to realize that treating Julio nicely encourages him to respect her belongings."

In light of Camilla's recent diagnosis, the parents have also taken steps that help the whole family. They're keeping up their everyday routines, making as few other changes as possible. They have talked with the kids about adjustments they all make "to support Mom," eating earlier and healthier and figuring out ways to exercise every day as a family.

When to Intervene?

A perennial parenting debate pits the "let 'em work it out" advocates against those who say, "intervene." A family whisperer takes the middle road. It's important that children learn to "work it out" on their own. For one thing, constant refereeing drives parents crazy. For another, using words instead of fists is a valuable life skill. However, let's get real. Children don't learn conflict resolution on their own. The sensible middle ground is to intervene until they have the skills and maturity to work it out together (which takes a while). It's also important to know what each child is capable of developmentally. A two-year-old who writes on his sister's drawing doesn't grasp that he's ruining a treasured piece of art. A five-year-old does.

"We didn't let things get too much out of control when our kids were little," recalls Nancy Sargent. "It seemed to be really important to address conflict. So if there was a squabble between, say, Seth and David, we'd get in the middle, asking each one, 'What did you say? What did you do?' I found that it never works to let them be. They didn't have the tools. Now, as teenagers, it's a different matter. But when you're five and your eight-year-old brother abuses you, you need help."

Research bears out the Sargent-Kleins' approach. You don't have to act like a cop or become a twenty-four-hour referee. You do have to know the difference between an attention-getting whine and a real scuffle that requires adult intervention. Where quarrels over property and space can be handled in family check-ins, more serious battles that involve physical, emotional, or sexual assaults have to be handled in the moment. As a rule, parents should stop the action, as the saying goes, before someone gets hurt.

Think restitution, not punishment. Conflict is a signal that something needs to change in the relationship. That's the theory behind "restorative justice," an enlightened practice used, among other applications, in legal systems to help heal victims of sexual assault or families involved in domestic violence. The principles of restorative justice, or RJ, also provide a fresh way of handling sibling disputes.

RJ facilitators "view conflict as a gift—an opportunity for growth," explains Kris Miner, executive director of a program in western Wisconsin. The parties are brought together, they listen to one another, they talk about what happened, and, together, they come up with a course of action that "seeks to repair harm rather than punish."

The same goal applies to siblings, which is why it makes sense to adopt the spirit of RJ in your household.

- Set aside a time and place for them to process the incident *with* you. Say explicity. "We're going to take a few minutes to talk about this." If they're too agitated, tell them, "I want each of you to go to [different places in the house or yard]. Take some deep breaths and think about what just happened and come back here in [x] minutes." Define the cooling-off period according to their ages and personalities. Five minutes can be an eternity to some kids.
- Give each child a chance to explain what happened. If they're too agitated to listen to one another, use some form of "talking stick," an object that guarantees that the speaker will not be interrupted as long as she is holding it (see page 168).
- Believe both of them. Their different stories are true in their eyes, and how each perceives the incident affects what he or she feels. A

teenager, for example, who believes the worst of a sibling, as in "He did it just to be mean," will see their entire relationship as negative.

- Restate both sides' perspective and emotions. "Vern doesn't like it when you come into his room and touch everything. It gets him angry." "Barbara doesn't like it when you close your door. She feels lonely and left out."
- Seek alternatives. You might ask, "What could you do differently so that next time, no one gets hit?" or "What can you do better the next time one of you wants something that the other has?"
- Ask about restitution. "What can you do to feel better about each other—make it right between you?"

The principles of RJ are similar to asking them to use the TYTT mantra, which is good advice for any couple conflict, too. Look around you to figure out what's happening, tell yourself the truth, and move on. By all means, make suggestions, but let them do some thinking, too. Ideally, they will arrive at a sensible and joint solution for moving on.

Even if you secretly identify with one's plight more than the other's, muster empathy for both of them. Stephen Klein, for example, understood that David, his second-born, had good reason to be jealous when his parents brought home spotlight-stealing twins, one of whom was a boy. And whenever David unleashed those feelings, Stephen was able to put his son's behavior in perspective. "When David would do something that would make Seth cry," Stephen recalls, "I'd calmly say to him, 'You need to go into your room and figure out a way to make him happy again.' It wasn't a punishment. It was about making sure he knew I needed his help to make the family work. It also acknowledged that he could make Seth happy in a way I couldn't."

If you're in the thick of sibling skirmishes, know that someday they will become a distant memory, if not fodder for a humorous memoir. Granted, some siblings become lifelong enemies, and their battles can bring the entire family down. But most manage to find new footing at least by middle or late adulthood. It also should be of some comfort to know that although all siblings fight, most maintain regular contact throughout life. A survey in 1992 found that more than half of all adult brothers and sisters see and/or contact one another at least once a month. Given email and smart gadgets, which weren't available then, it's even easier today for siblings to stay in touch.

Coalitions: Family Subcommittees

Sometimes siblings are in cahoots—two or more join forces. Like stockholders in a corporation who combine their shares, they become more powerful than they would be on their own, a subcommittee of sorts. Social scientists refer to alliances within a group as "coalitions." They can also be formed by two adults or an adult and a child or can include members of the extended family—for example, Grandma aligns with a particular child. In-law problems are often the result of a parent-and-adult-child coalition that effectively excludes the partner and makes him or her question a mate's allegiance. This sorting into pairs and sometimes trios can happen in any family, even one headed by a single adult. One of the children, for instance, might align with the parent.

Coalitions can be beneficial or damaging. Brothers and sisters can help each other weather the everyday hassles of family life or shelter them in the wake of a storm (parents' conflict, divorce, serious illness, death). One reason the four Allen children took the news of their mother's new job in stride, no doubt, was that they were a close-knit group to begin with. When siblings are mutually supportive, as in the Allen family, it softens the impact of any kind of family change, because they have one another.

With some sibling alliances, though, a child might feel left out or ignored by brothers and sisters who exclude him. Or two younger children might align themselves against an older one whom they perceive as more powerful. In blended families, "blood" siblings sometimes bond against a stepsibling. You can't control how coalitions form, but what you say and teach definitely matters. Lanie Allen recalls that when Peter, her oldest, was two, and his brother Kyle came along, "I encouraged them to be 'best brothers,' so they'd feel cohesive and connected and forge that bond. When Tom was born, he was immediately part of being a best brother. And when Hannah arrived, it was their job to watch over her." The four of them have their sibling moments, of course, many of which Lanie defuses with her characteristic humor, but they are clearly there for one another.

Regardless of which family members band together, coalitions tend to shift as change occurs—a career move suddenly allows a parent to be home, or children grow and spend increasing time outside the family. A middle child who once taunted her baby sister might gradually realize that she gains power by aligning with the youngest against their domineering older sister. As we saw in the Rivera household, Elena's starting high school has weakened the coalition with her younger brother Julio. She now spends more time with friends her own age, and he, as a result, feels abandoned.

Coalitions always affect the whole family, for better or for worse. In-law problems can be inflamed by a parent-and-adult-child coalition. Sherman is extremely close to his mother, for instance. His wife, Gayle, often feels excluded, which makes her question his allegiance to their marriage and affects how she feels about her mother-in-law.

A strong parent coalition is generally beneficial to children. As a rule, it's best for the adults to be a strong team that sets ground rules and at the same time is open and flexible enough to allow children to feel that they have some say in things. The kids feel held and heard and are less likely to go at one another. And when the chips are down, each one feels comfortable seeking a parent's support. But when parents coalesce "against" the children in an authoritarian way, the children can't align with either parent. They feel powerless and unseen and, therefore, might be less inclined to step up for the good of the family.

If there's no parental coalition—say, one parent's I chronically dominates or is absent a lot ("married" to work or having an affair)—you might see a strong bond between the oldest child and the weaker or more present parent. The remaining siblings form their own cabal and gang up against the seemingly favored child.

Needless to say, there are many possible scenarios. Perhaps you are already aware of the coalitions in your family. If not, do what social scientists do when they study coalitions: Pay attention when a decision that affects the whole family has to be made. In the Family Notebook section below, we explain how.

FYN Analyze Your Family Coalitions

Here's a hypothetical situation that researchers use: If your family had to decide how $100 would be spent, who would be most likely to get his or her way or have the most influence (power)? Try posing that or a similar question at your next check-in. Or just pay attention to whatever happens to be on your family agenda that involves everyone, such as a family vacation or a group project.

- Who calls the shots? Do the children dominate? Do the parents? Does one parent?
- Are everyone's suggestions listened to? Supported?
- Are there obvious sibling coalitions?
- Do you—the parent(s)—really consider children's input, or do you automatically dismiss their ideas, even though you act as if you're listening?
- When one child makes a suggestion, who usually backs him or her up? Supportive statements often indicate a coalition. At the same time, words don't always tell the whole story. In one study where many families identified Dad as the main decision maker on paper, videotapes indicated something else: Mom was listened to and supported more often than Dad, which actually gave her the final say.

Notes on Siblings and Family Coalitions

ELEVEN

PARENT-CHILD CONFLICTS
The Wonder of Self-Control

You have power over your mind—not outside events.
Realize this, and you will find strength.
—MARCUS AURELIUS IN *MEDITATIONS*

I should say here, because some in Washington like to
dream up ways to control the Internet, that we don't need
to "control" free speech, we need to control ourselves.
—PEGGY NOONAN, IN *PATRIOTIC GRACE*

In the Grayson household, minor conflict is a daily occurrence, and everyone blames ten-year-old Quincy. He wears his parents down at home and repeatedly loses friends at school. "He's a difficult child—always has been," says Janet, his mother. "But I often wonder, how much of this is my fault? Most of the time I want to wring his neck—he's gotta know that."

"Quincy is very overbearing," his father adds. "He's happiest when he's calling the shots. After play dates at our house, many kids don't want to come back."

When Quincy is diagnosed with ADHD and put on Adderall, his parents are initially relieved. His concentration improves almost immediately and, for a while, so does his schoolwork. But the medication doesn't stop the tantrums or make Quincy a more likeable kid at school—problems that drive his parents, yet again, to seek professional help for their son.

The new therapist tells Janet and Orin what they were told when Quincy was four and acting more like a terrible two: Caving in to him is not the answer. The therapist suggests clear rules, consequences when

Quincy disobeys them, time-outs when necessary. But the Graysons weren't able to deal with his tantrums six years ago, and they're still having trouble now.

Meanwhile, their daughter Tiffany has a lock on the role of The Easy Child in this family drama. She is "incredibly smart" and "mellow" by comparison, her parents say. She also seems to need less than her older brother—or at least she is less obviously needy. Quincy, three when his little sister was born, played with Tiffany during their early years and for a while relished his status as big brother. Things changed when Tiffany started school. In certain subjects, such as reading, little sister zoomed ahead of Quincy, which delighted and amazed her parents but raised the sibling ante. Quincy became aggressive toward his sister, less eager to read, and more "addicted" (the word his parents use) to his many gadgets.

Today, both parents are frustrated, worried, angry, and in as much pain as their son. They thought ADHD was "the answer," but when they tell themselves the truth, they admit that little has changed. The Graysons are educated, caring, and concerned parents, but they're clearly "stuck." Why can't they make it better?

Janet and Orin need to switch from parent-think to family-think. Focusing only on Quincy, they see *him* as "the problem." They talk about getting *him* to yet another therapist and "trying everything" to make *him* "better," without realizing that what the family is experiencing right now isn't merely within one individual. Perhaps Quincy's brain *is* different; perhaps he was born with a difficult temperament. No doubt, he is bossy. But he has also been tempered by his family and by the larger environment. Proper medication helps him focus, because it gives him some control over his very busy mind. But in order for the conflict in this household to ramp down and for Quincy to feel better about himself and less defensive and demanding toward others, the whole family needs a remedy that can't be delivered in pill form.

The Graysons' story is a familiar one to anyone who has studied families. Out of guilt, pity, their own childhood dramas, and/or a misguided sense of not wanting to squelch a child's spirit, parents tolerate moodiness and emotional outbreaks in children who should be taught self-control. In greater and lesser degrees, similar scenes are enacted in households everywhere. The topic might be bad grades and homework, screen time and video games, lying or other misbehavior. There's no magical way to end conflict with our children, whether they're everyday hassles or big blow-ups. But we *can* change how we handle them. We can also view conflict as an opportunity rather than hope to eliminate it. When we handle it well, conflict can be a growth-inducing experience for both generations and for the whole family.

How *Not* to Respond

Many of us rely on a limited repertoire of responses when children don't do as they're told: *giving in* or *grandstanding*. Whether we favor one or swing back and forth between the two, neither actually works, or at least not for long.

Orin Grayson tends to give in. Most of the time, he pretends not to notice, because he cherishes his "good guy" image and tends to avoid conflict, a pattern he learned long ago in his "hippie" family. His pot-smoking parents were awash in positive emotions; no one was allowed to be sad or feel strong emotions. So when Quincy loses it, and Janet's not around, Orin takes the road of least resistance.

All parents give in sometimes. It seems easier than arguing, especially when you're busy. But as a steady diet, giving in is a form of accidental parenting that teaches kids how to be good negotiators. Blame it on the Las Vegas principle, or the strength of "intermittent reinforcement." Behavioral scientists train lab rats to push a lever for food by rewarding them every time. If the humans stop dispensing the pellets, the rats quickly learn that it's pointless to push the lever. But if the researchers reward the rats randomly, they act like gamblers waiting for slot machines to pay off: They keep trying, and the behavior becomes even more entrenched.

The same principle applies to kids. Consider how eight-year-old Bonnie explains the screen time policy in her household: "No games during the week, but I can play on my iPod on the weekends when Dad says it's okay." On a typical Saturday, her father allows her to play video games for a half-hour. An hour later, her father comes into the kitchen and yells at her to "turn that damned thing off and get dressed for soccer practice." When they come home from the game, Bonnie heads straight for her iPod. "Pleeeeeease, can I play for a little while," she whines. "I just want to ..." She then spews out a string of digital activities that Dad has said "yes" to in the past: "I just want to Face Time Grandpa."

The Demon Guilt

Although many parents in our child-focused times feel guilty about *something*, they are especially hard on themselves when their children have behavioral or learning issues. They worry: Do we spend enough time? Do we spend too much time? Is our household too chaotic? Too regimented? Even if some of those reasons are partially true, guilt is neither appropriate nor helpful.

In a nutshell: When you're burdened and blinded by guilt, it's hard to see that you have options, which makes it almost impossible to take positive steps toward a solution. A better approach? Instead of feeling guilty, look around you and tell yourself the truth about how your family got here.

"I only want to listen to music." "I need to look up something for school." Dad thinks, *What's the harm?* He needs to make a few phone calls anyway. So he gives in.

Parents are often unaware that they reinforce the very behavior they find objectionable. Janet Grayson insists, "I *never* give in. I used to. But now if, say, he has a meltdown after dinner because he wants to play video games, I put my foot down." The problem is, after all those years of appeasing Quincy, he knows that the slot machine pays off. At some point, one of his parent *will* give in. Also, although Quincy loves video games, what he really wants is Janet's attention. When nagging doesn't do it, a tantrum will. Janet might not hand Quincy his DS every time he asks her, but she keeps giving him the floor. They lock horns, Janet "puts her foot down," and the grandstanding begins.

Grandstanding can range from a mild rebuke to a tirade—anything that lets the child know that the adult is in charge ("I said so, and that's why!"). Sure, we all lose it now and then. We think we're teaching the child how to behave "right" or "be good." In reality, browbeating and trying to exert control teaches nothing, damages the relationship, and fills the household with negativity.

When Janet Grayson loses her temper, she refuses to listen to another word. The argument becomes loud and ugly. She hurls unkind words; Quincy says he "hates" her. She banishes him to his room.

"I definitely lose it a lot," she confesses. "It feels like I'm turning into my father. He was such a bastard. When I was sixteen and told him I'd gotten the lead in the play, he asked, 'How in the world did they pick *you*?' He meant it. When I cried, he told me to 'toughen up.' Sometimes I sound just like my dad. And then I feel horribly guilty afterward."

The truth is, whether Janet stays silent or stamps her feet, verbally abuses her son or beats herself up, no one wins.

You can't control your child's thoughts, feelings, desires, or actions. You can control your reaction.

Even as the chorus in Janet's head—led, no doubt, by her father–sings the familiar refrain, *I'm the parent and we play by my rules,* she needs to muster the self-control to ignore it.

Self-Control: Reining in the Is

As we have stressed throughout these last several chapters, there *is* an I in family. Each member is seen, known, and respected. However, family life also gives us many opportunities to rein in our Is and to unite as a family. We cooperate with and at times cede the floor to one another. We do favors and help out, even when we don't feel like it. We spend time and energy on others' needs, even when it doesn't benefit us directly.

Those who can rein in their Is when necessary are said to have self-control, a key predictor of personal and relational success. We touched on self-control in chapter 3, as one of the "muscles" an individual exercises in order to lead with love. But as we explain here, self-control also turns us into better people.

When psychologist Roy Baumeister gave various groups of college students self-control coaching in fitness, money management, and school-work, they were not only able to attain the particular goal—exercising regularly, spending wisely, developing better study habits—their self-control in other arenas also improved. Students with improved "willpower"—the term Baumeister uses—also:

> *. . . smoked fewer cigarettes and drank less alcohol. They washed dishes instead of leaving them stacked in the sink, and did their laundry more often. They procrastinated less. They did their work and chores instead of watching television or hanging out with friends first. They ate less junk food, replacing their bad eating habits with healthier ones. . . . Some of the people even reported improvement in controlling their tempers.*

Baumeister didn't actually put it this way, but it's not a stretch to say that the participants acted like responsible stakeholders. They could rein in their Is, when necessary. Willpower enables you to work toward a goal and to finish what you start. If you can wait your turn, delay gratification, manage your emotions, and listen while the other person is talking, you feel better about yourself and others want you on their team. Good self-control also makes you a better parent.

Granted, it takes consciousness, willingness, and work to rein in your I—more for some than others. But the payoff is well worth it. Adults and children who have high self-control are less prone to anxiety, depression, and obsessive behavior. They can entertain and satisfy themselves, instead of depending on other people or material things, like video games. They forge good relationships—among other reasons, because they also can restrain themselves from criticizing.

For example, going shoe shopping with her husband was once a painful and potentially explosive experience for Daria Wilkerson, who makes decisions quickly. Conrad would try on several pairs, finally gravitate to one of them, and after walking around the store for what felt like an eternity (to Daria), he'd tell the salesman he needed a few days to think it over. At that point, she'd explode: "You gotta be kidding! You say they're comfortable, they look good, and—come on—it's just a pair of shoes." Now, however, Daria reminds herself that Conrad's I is different from hers. And she manages to stop herself from criticizing or trying to change him.

It's possible to apply the same kind of thoughtful restraint to interactions with your children. For example, when her daughter's grades began to slip, Lila Locklear considered the situation from her child's perspective. Until now, Georgina has been an A–B student. At fifteen, she has more distractions than in the past. She's a popular kid who plays the flute and runs on the track team. So instead of threatening her daughter ("If those grades don't improve, we're going to take your cell phone away"), Lila engaged Georgina in a calm discussion: "What kind of student do you want to be?" she asked. "Are you happy getting Bs and Cs? If so, then fine. But if you want to be an A student, then whatever you're doing is not getting you there."

Hearing this story, we had to ask Lila, "Did you *really* mean that? Are you *really* OK with her getting lower grades? Or were you trying to guilt your daughter into studying?"

"I meant it," Lila answered. "I can't make her into a good student. She's out of the house way more than she used to be. I keep tabs on her; I know where she is. And she's basically a good kid. But I can't control her."

The discussion ended with Georgina promising to "think about it." Lila, wisely, left it at that, adding, as she'd done countless times in the past, that she was there if Georgina wanted to talk more about it.

Bear in mind that exercising self-control *doesn't* mean relinquishing your responsibilities as a parent. By all means, continue to direct, teach, and correct. Be a guide and a power of example. Introduce them to new ideas and experiences. Keep them safe as they're learning how to negotiate the world. Give them increasing responsibility. Encourage their talents. Allow them to falter and even fail. Help them learn from the experience. Revoke privileges, if necessary, but mostly as a last resort.

In short, stay in charge but give up the illusion of control.

Think of their childhood as a collaboration—your love and guidance and their raw materials.

Stay in your own skin; your child's life is hers to live. You cannot choose her destiny or tell her what to strive for. You *can* make self-control a family value.

First, Be the Solution

Every choice *you* make teaches your child. In a store or restaurant, you can be polite and congenial and introduce yourself or barely acknowledge the salesperson. Lesson taught. When another driver cuts you off, you can respond by saying "Wow, he must be in a hurry" or curse, lean on the horn, and call him an idiot. Lesson taught. At home, you can be conscious and careful about your tone of voice or lash out and lose control. Lesson taught.

When you lose it, your child reasons, *My parents rant, treat others badly, criticize, scream, and hit. Why shouldn't I?* But when you exercise self-control, that sends an entirely different message. Here are some other strategies to help you make better choices:

Admit that it's hard, at times, for you to exercise self-control. Role-model parents aren't perfect; they admit their faults and frailties. Talk about your childhood. "I always loved math homework, but I hated writing papers. I'd wait until the last minute, and then it was even harder." Explain that sometimes you *still* have to make an effort to think things through before reacting. Share your hot buttons—comments and situations that cause you to overreact. "I was so angry at the handyman for showing up two days late. I get so angry when people are late and don't call. I wanted to scream at him! But I took a deep breath instead and said to him, 'I hope nothing was wrong.' Then I gave him a chance to explain."

When you stick with a job and push through the hard parts, talk about the process out loud. Whether it's a report you need to finish or a garden-ing chore, acknowledge how hard or tedious or annoying some responsi-bilities are ("It seems like the grass grows back as soon as I cut it!"). It's okay to tell them you'd rather be doing something else or that you've *been* procrastinating until now. But don't forget to tell them how good it feels to finally complete whatever you've been putting off—that is, if it really does feel good. Otherwise, they're empty words—a lecture from a grown-up. Your kids will see right through you, and, worse, feel manipulated.

Take a breath when your child disappoints or even shocks you. When you make the effort to rein in your I, you're more likely to be fair, creative, and compassionate which, in turn, de-escalates the conflict and strength-ens the parent-child relationship. For example, over the course of several hours, Felicia Germaine repeatedly asks her twelve-year-old son, Lamont, "How's your homework coming along?" Each time, Lamont says, "Great, Mom, I'm working on it."

Hours later, when Felicia asks to see his math assignment, Lamont has solved only three problems out of twenty. He hasn't touched his other homework. Caught, he tearfully confesses that he spent the afternoon writing "fan-fic"—a spin-off narrative based on an internet site's charac-ters and situations. The idea is to then post your writing online, where other users read and comment on it. Felicia, who normally keeps a close eye on Lamont's online life, had no idea that her son had become so ob-sessed with this particular site.

She could have lost it. Her lizard brain was screaming, *That little liar!* And who can blame her? What parent wouldn't be enraged and perhaps even scared about her child visiting an unfamiliar "neighborhood" in cy-berspace? But instead of coming down hard on her son, yelling, threaten-ing, or shaming him for lying *again*, Felicia reined in her I and tapped into her sage brain. She also thought about what the school psychologist had recently told her: "Whenever a twelve-year-old boy moves his mouth, he's lying!"

"Show me what you've been writing all afternoon," said Felicia, in as calm a voice as she could manage. Controlling her own negativity allowed her to understand the situation from Lamont's perspective. The story was well-written and imaginative. Lamont had obviously applied himself, be-cause this was something he was willing to work for. It wasn't his home-work, but it wasn't all bad either.

Finally, she said, "Look, Lamont, the way I see it, we have two problems here. One, you didn't do the work you were supposed to do, so now you have to figure out how to manage your time so that you get it all done by tomorrow. Two, you lied to me, not once but four times."

Her tone was stern, and she didn't hide her disappointment or anger, which would have been inauthentic. She was honest but managed to lead with love. "The worst part about this," she added, "is that now you've lost my trust, and I don't know how long or what it's going to take for me to believe you again."

Because Felicia simply stated the problem, Lamont couldn't get defensive. There was nothing for him to defend against, because the ball was in his court. Regaining his mother's trust was *his* responsibility. That night, Lamont, a gifted child who is bored at school and often balks about homework, completed his assignments without further prompting. Like most kids, he wants his mother's trust.

Stop the action before <u>you</u> spin out of control, too. When you clash with an out-of-control child, and each of you wants it *your* way, calm your own **I** first. Then, reel both of you back into the relationship. Remember how Sara Green handled her daughter's "middle-school meltdown" (page 50)? She didn't grandstand and try to control Katy, nor did she give in, which would have allowed her daughter's **I** to dominate. Her compassion and kindness let air out of Katy's emotional balloon and reminded the tween of their connection. Katy went to her room, free to have her feelings without imposing them on others.

Prepare an exit speech. When you call "time out" to regain your own composure, it's important to do it in a way that doesn't leave your child feeling abandoned. Our suggestion is to plan ahead by writing and rehearsing an "exit speech"—measured, loving words that explain why it's not good for anyone to continue this conversation right now. That way,

Writing Your Exit Speech

Written and rehearsed in a calm moment, a good exit speech is a product of your sage brain. It's the right thing to do, because it will preserve the relationship. You don't have to say it exactly as you write it. But in the heat of the moment, you're more likely to remember your sage brain's advice if you've written it down. Below is a sample. (The phrases in parentheses could be included if this is not the first time.)

I'm very angry now, and I don't want to lose my temper (the way I usually do). You're probably angry, too. It's not good for us to talk when we're angry (because you yell, and I yell back). Both of us will feel bad if we fight. It's okay to be angry, but lashing out at each other hurts our relationship. So (this time), I'm going to my room to calm myself down. I suggest you figure out a way to calm yourself down, too. Then when we're not so angry, we can try again. We'll both try to listen better and to talk instead of yelling at each other (which is what tends to happen when we disagree). Even if we don't feel the same way about this situation, we don't have to be mean to one another.

you stop the action and give yourself time to recover. Before you exit, explain, "I'm going to [do yoga, meditate, listen to music, play the piano, take a walk/run, knit, read] to help myself calm down." Also, give your child something to think about. "You need to figure out what works for you."

You also might want to introduce this idea at a family check-in. It's a way for the whole family to think about how to *not* engage when tempers flare. Use the sample exit speech in the sidebar on page 259 to talk about what else might be included. Then write your own. Younger children can dictate to a parent or older sibling. At the very least, you'll gain insight into how each family member handles conflict.

Apologize when you lose it. This might sound obvious, but saying "I'm sorry" isn't just about owning up to bad behavior. Also acknowledge how painful or frightening it is to be on the receiving end: "I'm sorry, Carmine. I shouldn't have yelled about the dishwasher not being emptied. I know it's a little scary when I seem so out of control. I don't want our home to feel like a scary place."

Note: By apologizing, you're *not* lowering your expectations. Carmine accepted the role of dishwasher-emptier this week. You're not giving him a pass because he's "so busy" or because you lost your temper. You're apologizing for your lack of self-control. Next time, think of a better way to remind him that it's his responsibility, not yours.

Self-Control Doesn't Come Naturally

Mary O'Donahue had an epiphany when her then five-year-old son forgot to thank a friend who'd brought him an unexpected gift. Even worse, the boy didn't try to hide his disappointment when he opened the box to find a T-shirt instead of a toy. As he began walking out of the room, Mary writes:

> *I remember saying the all too familiar "Hey . . . what do you say?" and he had replied with a lackluster "Thaaaaaank youuuuuu" with barely a glance in our direction. Not much of a proud moment for me, but probably a familiar one for many parents.*

When Mary later thought about what had happened, she realized, "We'd never actually taught our son to be thankful. Not once. All we had ever done was *train* him to *act* thankful." Thereafter, she and her husband began compiling a list of values they deemed important and then set out to explicitly teach them—a project that morphed into Mary's book, *When You Say "Thank You," Mean It.*

Along with gratitude, Mary included self-respect, respect for others, integrity, compassion, forgiveness, a sense of joy, commitment, lifelong learning, and inner strength. Your list might be different from hers. But whatever life-enhancing and relationship-strengthening values you want to pass on to your children, they will need to develop self-control, and you will need to teach them.

The twelfth-century philosopher and poet Rumi wrote, "The intelligent desire self-control; children want candy." Teaching your kids to wait for their candy is arguably one of your most important jobs as a parent, no matter what else you believe in. How soon and how well they learn depends on personality and age. But they won't get it at all without your help.

Reining in their Is doesn't come naturally to children. We need to teach them, guide them, and give them opportunities to experience the rewards. Consider the following strategies:

Give your children practice. Telling children to "calm down," "wait your turn," or "share" means little unless you also help them understand why and what it feels like to exercise self-control. When your preschooler asks for a snack and you say to him, "You can have some Goldfish in a few minutes," he doesn't just learn to wait, he begins to see that he *can* wait. *Don't* give in if he whines. If anything, shorten the "few minutes" to one. Gradually increasing the waiting time as he gets older will build his tolerance for frustration. If you also suggest, "Why don't you color or play with your blocks while you're waiting?" he learns to distract himself, a key strategy for improving self-control at any age.

When your child exercises self-control, point it out, praise it, and discuss it. "Thanks, honey, for keeping a calm head when you couldn't find your baseball glove. I notice that instead of whining about it, you took a breath and retraced your steps. How did that feel?"

Don't reward tantrums. A tantrum is the opposite of self-control, and the quickest way to extinguish any behavior is to *not* reward it. That's why Tracy told parents to ignore whining, foot stomping, yelling, backtalk, even head banging. When parents react by giving in or grandstanding, or when they are frozen by guilt and do nothing, the child becomes chronically petulant and demanding. At the same time, Tracy didn't believe in time-outs for young children. Because they lack the skills to deal with strong emotions, in addition to letting them know you won't tolerate the behavior, you also have to help them manage their feelings:

If you're dealing with a young child, remove him from the situation. Go to another room or, in public, find a quiet place, even your car. Put him on your lap, facing away from you so as not to make eye contact. Even if you *think* he is too young to understand, say something along the lines of "I'm not going to talk to you until you calm down" or "I can't listen when you [whine/scream/cry/hit]." Then, say nothing. Don't try to reason with him. When he finally stops struggling and screaming, give him suggestions as to how he might have handled the situation. "That was Tommy's truck. I know you wanted to play with it. But next time, instead of grabbing, you have to ask him for a turn. And if he says no, you cannot hit him." Consider each incident as an opportunity to teach self-control. A toddler won't get it right away, but if you are consistent, he'll learn to ask (nicely), share, and wait.

Removing a child from the scene of the crime works with most young children, because they are easily distracted, and their short attention spans typically make for short tantrums. Unfortunately, in the Graysons' case, the parents didn't take these steps with Quincy at an early age. Today, pitching a fit is Quincy's go-to tactic for engaging his mother. Adderal helps him concentrate, but no pill can counteract years of accidental parenting or "right-size" a child who has been allowed to rule the roost. What can his mother do? Instead of feeling she has to "take it" or, worse, has to yell at Quincy and send him to his room, *she* can walk away until she regains *her* composure.

Tell it like it is. "He knows that the medication helps him concentrate. But we haven't specifically told him about the diagnosis," says Orin Grayson, in response to a question about how much Quincy knows about ADHD. "We think it's better if he doesn't label himself." The question is, would the Graysons hesitate if Quincy had a physical problem, such as juvenile diabetes or Long QT, a childhood heart ailment? Those conditions are affected by diet and activity and require a child to understand the risks. It's no different with ADHD.

Children, especially kids who have learning and/or behavioral issues, are more likely to develop self-control when you are honest with them, when they have clear-cut, attainable goals and immediate feedback about their actions. "By not telling them," says Lynne Hacker, a veteran speech and language pathologist in New York City, "it indicates shame, which is the one thing you want to avoid, as the kid probably feels enough of that already.

"The goal is to remove shame. If the parents act as if *they* feel shame, it's so much harder to convince the child that there's nothing to be ashamed of. These are the kids I usually don't end up working with."

Hacker has never met the Graysons, but she's seen enough children to say with authority that "most kids are relieved that what they have is legitimate, has a name, and means they aren't just stupid or willful." She adds, "What's important is making sure the child (a) doesn't feel defective, (b) knows there are strategies to help ameliorate the problem, and (c) has someone in his corner who understands."

Although Quincy's ADHD is not the only reason for conflict in the Grayson family, he *does* have trouble concentrating, and he *is* impulsive. Being the loudest, crankiest, and bossiest person in the room also affects his life outside the household. Someone needs to say to him, "You're getting older, and it's really important for you to learn how to find a better way to deal with your feelings when you don't get what you want. Otherwise, you'll keep pushing people away."

A boy like Quincy needs to know himself in order to start making better choices. Increasing his awareness will enable him to tune in, understand what's going on inside his brain, and allow him to see the consequences of his actions. Eventually, he'll learn to tell himself the truth, which will also help him exercise self-control. Playing video games doesn't.

Value doing good over being good. Doing for others and making sacrifices is one of the most rewarding forms of self-control. Look for opportunities to praise your children when they do a favor or extend themselves on another's behalf. Ask how they feel when they're generous—for example, when they share a toy, sit through a sibling's game or recital, or forgo a birthday party to visit an aging relative. Mention selfless acts and small kindnesses in everyday conversation: "Wasn't it nice for Carol to bring us dinner when she heard I had the flu?" "It was lucky that Dad was in the parking lot when poor Mr. York had to change that flat tire." Get them involved in your own good deeds: "Please help me make cookies to bring over to the Drapers' house when we pay a condolence call. It will make them very happy to know you pitched in."

Share stories about sacrifice. In the wake of Hurricane Sandy, for example, one mother made sure that her three sons were aware that hundreds of volunteers had left their families and the comforts of their own well-lit and heated homes to restore power more quickly in New York and New Jersey. She showed them newspaper articles about courage and bravery. This might seem like an insignificant act—it took only minutes of her time. It will take much more time for the message to sink in. But ongoing conversations about reining in one's I add up and remind kids that they're not the only ones who matter.

Technology and Its Impact on Self-Control

Today's children devote more than fifty-three hours a week to screen time, according to the Kaiser Family Foundation, which has been tracking children's media use since 1999. The proliferation of computers, tablets, cell phones, and electronic games has created what journalist Hannah Rosen identified in 2013 as "the neurosis of our age." Parents, writes Rosen, "are becoming more, not less, wary" of how technology affects children.

> *Technological competence and sophistication have created yet another sphere that parents feel they have to navigate in exactly the right way. On the one hand, parents want their children to swim expertly in the digital stream that they will have to navigate all their lives; on the other hand, they fear that too much digital media, too early, will sink them. Parents end up treating tablets like precision surgical instruments, gadgets that might perform miracles for their child's IQ and help him win some nifty robotics competition—but only if they are used just so. Otherwise, their child could end up one of those sad, pale creatures who can't make eye contact and has an avatar for a girl-friend.*

There's no doubt that there's a digital downside. However, when adults discuss technology, they often catastrophize. At worst, kids are positioned as criminals and parents as cops. That's not only inaccurate—adults of all ages are similarly seduced by their gadgets—it's also unhelpful, because it does nothing to help families manage screen time or alleviate the generational battles caused by it. A better approach is to help one another put tech into perspective.

Parse, don't panic. At this point in time, even the experts are mixed on whether interactive technology is "educational" or "dangerous." The digital revolution has certainly changed the way we play, think, and communicate.

But reading a book on a digital device, sending an email to Grandma, or searching the internet for information is not the same as playing a video game or watching "Charlie bit my finger" on YouTube for the hundredth time. Don't paint all things tech with the same brush. Instead, educate yourself (see box, page 266).

Be honest about your own struggles. If you're an adult who checks your cell phone regularly for work, plays games online, or visits social media sites, you understand the dilemma first-hand. There is no perfect solution for adults *or* children. Tech *is* tempting; managing it requires self-control. One mother asked her children to "bust" her whenever she reached for her cell phone in the car. A grandmother admitted to her grandson that she was playing too many word games online and had to quit for a few weeks in order to finish an important project. Also, remind them (and yourself) that managing screentime is not a new family dilemma. "My mother used to yell at me about watching TV all the time. She wouldn't let me have a TV in my room either, even though many of my friends did."

Become technologically "literate" as a family. Gather around your computer, and go online together. Calmly discuss the benefits and dangers. Help your children find forms of media that engage them and that you approve. Warn them about clicking on ads or unknown sites. Help them understand privacy issues and the downside of leaving a less-than-flattering digital trail. Let them give you tours of online places they visit and apps they use. Ask what they like about each one. Your goal is to develop what Howard Rheingold calls "digital literacy," twenty-first-century skills that parents *and* children need to become savvy and safe consumers.

Make explicit screen policies. Interestingly, according to the eight- to eighteen-year-olds surveyed by Kaiser in 2010, only one in three households sets specific limits on tech time. However, when the Pew Internet and American Life Project asked *parents* about limits, more than half said they regulate time spent on video games and have rules about time on the internet. Why the discrepancy? We suspect that some parents don't state their rules explicitly and others let them slide. The kids, therefore, think they have no rules, or at least that they're highly negotiable.

Rather than giving in when you feel like it and slamming them when you've had it—which epitomizes the Las Vegas principle—think it through. How much screen time are your kids allowed? How do you decide? Is it the same for everyone? When, if ever, do you relax your rules?

Educate Yourself

You can't force the technology genie into the bottle. But if you become "net smart"—a term coined by veteran tech watcher Howard Rheingold—you can at least guide your family intelligently. "Mindful use of digital media means thinking about what we are doing," Rheingold cautions, "cultivating an ongoing inner inquiry into how we want to spend our time." To decide what's right for your family, read books and articles and visit online sites that offer a balanced view of the research and the controversies. Here are a few to get you started.

Books: *Net Smart* by Howard Rheingold, *Now You See It* by Cathy Davidson, *Screen Time* by Lisa Guernsey, *Networked* by Lee Rainie and Barry Wellman.

Articles: "The Touch Screen Generation," by Hanna Rosen, *Atlantic Monthly,* 3/20/13, "Shooting in the Dark," by Benedict Carey, *New York Times,* 2/11/13, "Wired for Distraction: Kids and Social Media" by Dalton Conley, *Time,* 2/11/11.

Research: Pew Internet and American Life Project (http://www.pewinternet.org/); Children's Digital Media Center (http://www.cdmc.georgetown.edu/); Berkman Center for Internet and Society, Youth and Media project (http://cyber.law.harvard.edu/research/youthandmedia).

How consistent are you? Do *you* live by the same rules? Again, all parents give in *sometimes*. But when kids have explicit limits, Kaiser found, they consume nearly three hours less media per day than children who live in households without rules.

Make the bedroom a no-tech zone. One family we know, after catching their nine-year-old son playing video games under the covers well past his bedtime, designated a small wicker container as their "gadget basket." It sits on a kitchen counter, and every night, an hour before bed (some families set the cut-off time even earlier in the evening), family members deposit their smart phones, iPods, handheld games, and other small electronic devices.

Monitor their monitors. Making rules as a family doesn't mean that you relinquish your role as a parent. Just as you would authorize a particular route and make sure your child has the skills needed to negotiate a new neighborhood, you don't want them to roam in cyberspace without your forethought and supervision. Regularly check the history bar on your computer, which indicates sites visited. Find out whether and how they're interacting with online strangers. Keep a list of their passwords and let them know it's not okay to change them without informing you.

Join 'em. Consume media as a family. The online site Common Sense Media (http://www.commonsensemedia.org/) is an excellent resource for advice, age-appropriate family fare, and reviews. Watch movies together. Listen to tapes on long car rides. Find good stories, fiction and nonfiction, to share and discuss. Listening to narratives trains children to concentrate and give their undivided attention—an antidote to multitasking and attention-draining devices.

Devote a family check-in to technology. Search "family media agreements" on the Common Sense Media website, and download the one (or ones) that corresponds to your kids' ages (elementary, middle, or high school). Use it/them as a conversation-starter. Your children's opinions about what's "reasonable" will probably be quite different from yours, but listen anyway. Make your own lists of the pros and cons. Talk about how annoying and hurtful it is to be ignored because someone is busy texting or is glued to a screen. Children don't like it any more than adults do. You might be surprised at how honest your children are when they are not criticized for their opinions. They are also more likely to follow rules they help write.

Ask for their assistance. Most kids are naturals when it comes to tech tasks; many parents are not. Your child is most likely "the expert" when you don't understand on-screen directions or Nana has trouble opening an email attachment. Letting a child show a parent or grandparent how to do something the adult genuinely can't do is a great way to "bank" a positive experience—a sweet moment that says to the child, "You are seen and needed, loved and respected. You matter."

Does Homework Have to Be a Battleground, Too?

Getting homework marks the beginning of an increase in children's responsibilities to their first "employer," their teacher. They now have "work," just as the adults do—assignments that require self-control. One question is, whose job is it? In many families today, parents sit *with* their children as they complete their daily school assignments. In some households with older children, the entire evening is eaten up by homework— starting it, doing it, arguing over it.

Some parents don't feel as if they have a choice. Everyone does it; and many school systems expect parents to be involved. It's also a good way to keep abreast of what's happening in school. The problem is, homework hassles can erode the parent-child relationship and send serious daily ripples through the ecosystem. If homework is a battleground in your household, you owe it to the whole family to try to figure out why. Here are some questions that might help.

What form does your help take? Research is mixed on whether parents' help actually improves academic performance. It depends on the particular parent and the particular child. A parent's involvement can help a child practice skills and speed up the learning process, but if a parent jumps in too quickly and gives too much help, it can undermine the child's confidence.

Does your child need extra help? Gauge whether you actually have to sit with your child, or is it enough to be available just in case? If she needs help, is it because the work is too difficult for her, or are you overinvested in her performance? Children might not have the language or sophistication to express it, but they can sense when a parent's I takes over. Listen to yourself when you talk about homework; you might hear clues that homework help is about your I as much as hers. One mother rationalized, "I don't want my kids to hand in homework that's wrong." Another, recalling her "latchkey" childhood, said she wanted "to give my child more help than my mother gave me."

Do you hold back and listen? Your role as homework helper is to discuss, clarify when needed, and brainstorm, not to *do* the work *for* your child. Don't supply the answer; do tell him to have a second look ("I'm not sure this one is right"), and then it's up to him to correct it. Also, listen for clues about what works and what doesn't ("Mom, that's not the way Mrs. O'Grady taught us to do it").

Do you know the best way to help? Talk to your child's teacher and, if he has a learning issue, to his tutor. What you see at home might not tell you everything you need to know about how he is in school. It's important to understand his strengths and deficits and how best to get through to him. Especially if every homework hour is a battle, ask what you might do differently. Find out how your child learns best and when to back off.

Do you take advantage of other opportunities to discover what your child is learning? Homework is not the only way to find out what's happening in school. Read his assignment book or work folder to see what he's reading and studying. Ask questions, and discuss ideas at the dinner table, in car rides, or when cuddling at bedtime: "I see that your class is reading *The Mice of NIMH*. What's happening in the story now?" Share honestly your own learning experiences, too: "It took me much longer than my brother to learn how to read, but once I got it, I loved books," or "I still make mistakes when I add." If you were a straight-A student and your child isn't, you might tell him about a sibling's difficulties.

Have you considered an exit strategy? When do you *stop* helping? When does your child develop the self-control needed to slog through difficult assignments? The father of a twelve-year-old who is "trying to wean his daughter" off his help every night, laments, "Now she complains that she's 'lonely' if I don't sit next to her." He might have waited too long. Start as you mean to go on. As soon as your child is on the road to becoming an independent learner, back off. Pay attention when your child says something like "I get it, Dad, you don't have to show me." It's time to let him figure it out on his own.

If your child seems resistant to doing homework on her own, reduce your time in small increments ("Finish these problems, and I'll look them over"). Set up a space where *she* does homework. Don't help with tasks she can do on her own. Be direct—*don't sneak out of the room*—and be honest: "You're getting older now, and it's important for you to learn how to work on your own and to stick with it, even when it's hard. I have to [do my own work/pay bills/spend some time with your brother] now, but I'm here if you need me."

As a final note to this chapter, and a segue into the next, we remind you to question whether hassles over homework, screen time, and other garden-variety conflicts are symptoms of bigger family issues that you might need to address. Deal with them quickly rather than denying them. Use them as opportunities to get to know your children, to help yourself and them practice self-control, and to deepen your relationships. But keep them in perceptive and don't overreact. You'll need your energy and wits when something truly disruptive comes along.

FYN How Do You Handle Conflict with Your Child?

In a calm moment, take the time to reflect on the common conflicts in your household and how you handle them.

- What leads to hassles and arguments in your family? Make a list and, next to each category, write down how you usually respond. Do you mostly give in to avoid the argument or do you grandstand and try to control your child? Do you feel guilty? All of the above?
- When trouble erupts, do you take a whole-family view, or do you tend to blame one particular family member? If the latter, consider the Three Factors, and see how each plays a role in this latest drama. (It might also be helpful to ask the "essential" troubleshooting questions in Appendix II, page 301.)
- How do you measure up when it comes to mustering self-control? If you haven't already taken the test on page 63, do it now. What are your hot buttons? In what kinds of situations and at what times of day are you most likely to lose it? How hard is it for you to regain your composure? What might you do to help yourself?
- Have you explicitly taught your children to exercise self-control? Do you know which child or children need the most help? Run through your daily routine, and ask yourself if the policies in various zones—especially when it comes to screen time, homework, and household responsibilities—are helping your kids develop self-control or working against it. If the latter, try to find ways to help your child stop, slow down or wait, and do for others.

Notes on Conflict and Self-Control

TWELVE

FAMILY "GRIT"
Handling Hardship and the Unexpected

One of the secrets of life is to make stepping-stones out of stumbling blocks.
—Jack Penn

Every family is subject to winds of change that cause ripples in the ecosystem. Some turn into big waves. How you face and handle hard times is a measure of how tough and together your family is.

Bad things happen to good families, to all families—cancer, mental illness, addiction, disability, depression, a suicide attempt, death. REAL families weather such storms because they give a great deal of thought, time, and energy to good "familying." They are creative and courageous and somehow manage to stay the course. They acknowledge that there are times when life is overwhelming and hard and that some days, they just can't rise to the occasion. But for the most part, they do. They're in it together. It doesn't kill them; it makes them stronger.

You've already met some families for whom this happened and who have learned from their hardships. Darlene Fournier stared cancer down, refusing to let it disrupt her family. The Hightowers faced a dramatic change in their standard of living and have learned how to get more out of life than they ever imagined possible. The Guarini-Suskinds, who spent most of their twenty-five-year marriage dealing with their middle child's depression, somehow managed to maintain a sense of "being a unit," despite their ongoing difficulties.

"The children are now close to one another in their own ways and keep in touch outside of Barry and me," Kara explains. "They also go out of their way to come home, and when they're not, they want to Skype with us and talk with us. That connection is very strong.

"If you had interviewed me ten years ago, I would have told you, 'I'm not sure I'm doing the right thing,'" Kara admits. "But part of the reality of family life is change. In the big picture, it all worked out." In many ways, this family is fortunate; they have had the resources to get good advice and medical care, but it has been challenging nonetheless.

"I think it's important for people to read this," says Kara when thanked for her candor about a situation that other people might not want to reveal. "Not everyone has their kids perfectly dressed or has perfect childcare, nor are the kids perfectly well behaved. Yet we survived, and so can they. As I look at where we have been and where the kids are currently, I figure we got some of it right."

Indeed, they did, because they hung in for the long haul. A single strand runs through the Guarini-Suskinds' and other families' stories: We think of it as "family grit."

The Lowdown on Grit

The dictionary tells us that grit is a personal quality: "indomitable courage, toughness, or resolution." Researchers, studying grit in individuals, define it as "perseverance and passion for long-term goals." Not surprisingly, it's a key predictor of success in life.

Why shouldn't grit be applied to families?

Families with grit are able to join in a mutual goal: building a solid family. They accept that it won't always be easy or without daunting problems and unanticipated roadblocks. But they are willing to work hard, be patient, and, when necessary, adjust their expectations.

How does a family get grit? In some cases, it's the power of everyone pulling together. In others, grit is inspired by one member who has enough stamina and determination to keep everyone else afloat. A single parent living in a rough urban setting who is determined to protect her brood from the mean streets. A divorced partner who somehow musters the maturity to cooperate, even when the other is too injured or angry to act civilly. A child with a disability or serious illness who seems to have wisdom and acceptance beyond her years and whose spirit buoys everyone else. In each of these cases, the one inspires the many to have grit.

As a life-shaping trait, grit is more important than actual talent or IQ. The very gifted don't necessarily become the stars of their professions, studies show. More often, it's the determined, the goal-minded, and the hard workers who more dependably rise to the top.

The same applies to families with grit. They know that having the smartest or most talented members only takes them so far. What the family stands for is more important than whether they stand out. In the long run, it is the *meaning* attached to their achievements that matters to them, not the medals. Trophies on the mantel represent sportsmanship, not just individuals' talents. Money in the bank is the result of having passion and working hard, not a measure of being better. And no matter what is happening to them or around them, family members always feel connected to something larger. Together, they can withstand hard knocks.

A sense of integrity—a code—guides these families and gives them a collective strength. Greg Perlman alludes to this aspect of grit when he says, "We are a family that is committed to trusting our own values and not worrying about what other people do."

Lanie and Bill Allen, parents of Peter, sixteen, Kyle, fourteen, Tom, twelve, and Hannah, ten, remind their children constantly, "You have a responsibility not only to uphold yourself and your actions but also to uphold the family." The Allens have always had a clear picture of what they want their family to be, and their collective grit enables them to keep reinforcing the lesson. "I constantly remind the kids," says Bill, "that we value integrity and doing the right thing."

Families with grit can see their greater whole. They know who they are as a family and are therefore less likely to be tripped up by distractions or difficulties. They view the family itself as something valuable and worthy of protection.

In short, families with grit have:

- *Strength and solidarity.* Members have the right stuff—good coping skills—and communicate clearly and honestly, so no matter what their context throws at it, the family has a strong spiritual core.
- *Determination.* Their collective strength and stamina enable them to push past disappointment and other hurdles.
- *Good "management."* The co-op has a board of directors whose "policies" ensure that the ecosystem stays balanced. It doesn't matter whether the household has one adult at the helm or two.

- *Family-consciousness.* They rarely lose sight of the power of family. They lean in to be there for one another *and* they reach out to expand their own borders.

Families with grit aren't immune to hard times. To be sure, their honesty, closeness, resilience, and persistence help everyone dig in. But sheer will cannot conquer illness or incapacitation or prevent a marriage from unraveling or make a hostile community more accepting. Consciousness alone can't replenish resources spread thin when a family is under stress. But at the very least families with grit tell themselves the truth.

Family grit is a form of *resilience*—"positive adaptation under adverse circumstances." Some of what we know about resilience is fairly obvious. For example, some families have more than others. But resilience doesn't necessarily look the same in every family. It depends on who its members are, what they're dealing with, and what resources they have at their disposal. A New Zealand family scholar, who reviewed what science knows about resilience, concluded that it is "one of the enduring mysteries that confronts those who work with families and children."

And yet we usually know grit when we see it.

Listen for grit as you read the following stories. The situations are quite different, but in each case, the members unite as a family. Their grit, like the little pig's bricks, enables them to stop the wolf from blowing down their house.

Strength and Solidarity: The Burbanks

When the individuals have good coping skills and their relationships are healthy, it creates a sense of solidarity and connection. Regardless of what life throws at them, they have faith. As we pointed out on page 64, a family's spiritual life might or might not have anything to do with organized religion. Still, members derive strength and hope from being part of something bigger—their family, the universe. In the Burbank family, faith is a three-way cuddle in Holly and Rob's king-size bed.

Holly, a five-time survivor of cancer, is now in her fifties. She and her husband, Rob, have always communicated honestly and appropriately with their son, Danny—about everyday life and about her condition. As he's gotten older, they've continued to explain the situation and help him understand his feelings. Recently, the three of them flew to Chicago for her recurring six-month checkup.

"Danny was in the room when the doctor came in and said something about the clinical trial I was on being a good thing, because there's a strong possibility of recurrence. That was on a Friday, and the next day, we kayaked and had fun." That evening, Danny, whose nightly routine has always included brushing his teeth in his parents' bathroom, was noticeably absent.

"I went into his room and said, 'Hey, Danny, what's up?'" She didn't need an answer, because she understood the enormity of what he'd heard. "I asked him, 'Do you want to sleep in our bed tonight?' and he said, 'Yeah, that would be nice.' He hadn't been in our bed since he was a toddler. I knew he just needed it to be OK and for the family to be intact."

Holly can't promise that she'll be around forever, but she says Danny, who is now twelve, "knows that I'm doing everything I can to stay healthy." When Danny recently heard that an acquaintance was given an award by a health advocacy organization, he told Holly, "You deserve to be honored, Mom. You've survived cancer five times."

In earlier generations, the word *cancer* was whispered. Today, in some homes, discussions of illness qualify as dinner conversation. While there's always a fine line between burdening children and being honest with them, solid families trust that their children can handle reality. Danny will be no less sad if his mother dies young, but he certainly will be better prepared and more mature than a child who has been lied to or kept away from the truth because it's too hard.

Determination: The D'Angelos

Ruby and George D'Angelo are parents of seven-year-old Bethany and Sheri, her two-years-younger sister. Ruby describes herself as "the parent of a wonderful, energetic, and dynamic child who, incidentally, is hearing-impaired." She is also quick to point out that her enlightened attitude evolved over time and with considerable struggle at first—a common pattern among parents who have to deal with a child who is different and whose experience they might never fully understand.

Bethany failed the hospital hearing test when she was born. "I cried like a baby. The thought of my child being deaf was devastating. I was panicked. I've often thought of life as a series of hallways and doors representing different opportunities and experiences. The moment it was suggested that Bethany couldn't hear, I imagined the doors slamming shut. Would they be locked forever? Would she ever enjoy music or be able to hear the sound of my voice? Time would tell." Although Bethany passed a subsequent hearing test two weeks later, Ruby admits, "I always knew in the back of my mind that something still could be wrong."

Bethany was an active, curious child. "She spoke at nine months, had a terrific vocabulary and a great personality." But there were also signs in between, easier to recognize in retrospect. She didn't always look up when Ruby called her name. "Sometimes she'd pull my face toward her, and I'd think, *I'm so cool and interesting*," Ruby confesses. "Turns out she was actually trying to read my lips." Then baby sister Sheri came along. By age two, when Sheri began to acquire language skills, Ruby realized that the littlest D'Angelo already spoke more clearly than her older sister, who was then almost four.

New tests confirmed that Bethany has a 55-decibel loss, less than 50 percent hearing in both ears. It has probably been there since birth, genetically derived from both parents. "Once again, the doors in the hallway of life slammed shut," Ruby recalls, "but this time, we faced the challenge head-on."

Acceptance is difficult. When you're first told, or you observe, that your child is suffering or somehow not like other children, it's almost always a devastating blow. It takes maturity *not* to overreact and grit to hang in. This is *your child* they're talking about. But if you don't tell yourself the truth, you will not be able to give him the answers and help he needs. You will not be able to find or listen to other parents and professionals who can support and help you. And by not facing what *is*, you will not be able to see what *can be*. Whether the problem is physical, emotional, psychological, or intellectual, many children not only live with serious problems, but they thrive.

"Wrapping our heads around her hearing loss," Ruby adds, was also somewhat easier because they had already gotten to know Bethany *as an individual*. "At four, she was quite obviously a person in her own

When Your Child Needs Help

The prospect of a child getting sick or becoming disabled is every family's nightmare. It doesn't matter whether one diagnosis seems more serious than another—for example, deafness versus depression or autism versus ADHD. When a child is diagnosed with *any* problem, this is what needs to happen so that the whole family can deal with the news and its aftermath:

- The parents tell themselves the truth.
- The parents tell the child the truth.
- All family members—the child who is sick or disabled, siblings, parents, even extended family members—get help in order to learn how to cope with the new reality.
- The situation is periodically reevaluated to accommodate change.

right. We already had so many other labels for her—dynamic, outgoing, smart, bossy, a wonderful kid. 'Hearing-impaired' was just another label."

This is not merely a matter of political correctness. Advocacy organizations advise parents to refer to their child as a person *with* a particular condition rather than calling her a "deaf child," because language frames our perceptions. Furthermore, those who deal effectively with a child's (or an adult's) disability know that no one's I can be described in only one word. As Ruby realized with Bethany, we are all made up of many selves—multiple identities that we step into depending on where we are and whom we're with. These various aspects of your I don't necessarily land in the same place on the capability/inability spectrum—no one is great at everything. An adult or child might be described as "smart" or "a good athlete" or "deaf," and all three can be true.

Once Bethany was school-age, Ruby also had to deal with her older daughter's context outside the family. Getting Bethany the tools and services she needed to attend public school, Ruby says, has been "a frustrating and exhausting process." It meant developing relationships with everyone involved and tempering her own anxiety. "When I went into it all emotional and a mess, it wasn't helping her. Now when I walk into a meeting, I'm not Bethany's mother. I'm her advocate. I don't make it personal. I walk in with a list of minimum requirements, and I present them in a very businesslike manner." That the school administrators and teachers see how much effort and time Ruby puts into her child probably makes them more willing to go to bat for Bethany. "I will never ask someone to work harder for her than I am willing to work myself."

By the time Bethany was in first grade, thanks to a number of factors—among them Ruby's determination, George's patience, Bethany's spirit, and little sister Sheri's support and companionship—Ruby had stopped worrying about closed doors. "Bethany has shown us that she controls her future. She will open her own doors and prance right through them."

Good Management: The Martinez-Garlands

Roberto Martinez and Allison Garland split up in 2005. "Everyone always asks, 'Who ended the marriage?'" says Allison. "I did, but whoever walks out the door is not the villain. It's never for one reason, and it's always complex. I had a tremendous amount of guilt," she admits. "Neither of us was the product of a divorced home. And I was only thirty-five, the first in all of my social circles to end a marriage."

They had been married for seven years. Roberto admits that he was surprised and hurt: "I felt like the wheels were falling out from under me when she first told me. I was concerned about how we'd make it work for the kids and how much time I'd be able to spend. She made clear that she didn't want to put me out of their life." Eli and Mimi were then eighteen months and four years old.

"I spoke to friends whose parents had split up and asked what had worked for them and what didn't," Allison recalls. "The worst thing was to see their parents fight or to lose a parent altogether."

Allison wanted to separate in a way that wouldn't hurt the children and, just as important, would help the adults heal. "I didn't want it to get ugly," she says. "I wanted us to be like Bruce Willis and Demi Moore. I needed to be able to look at myself in the mirror."

She suggested using a mediator, rather than each hiring a divorce attorney who would argue the case for one party and view the other side as the enemy. A mediator, on the other hand, acts as coach and legal adviser, an advocate for the whole family. Accordingly, when Allison or Roberto was "being spiteful," the mediator would ask, "What's your motivation?" a question that reminded them of what they both wanted: to build a new, different kind of family.

Talk about needing grit to get through a change! Divorce is nothing less than a total overhaul of the family. Parents relocate to new homes, possibly with new partners. The adults have to be mindful of the kids' needs and at the same time willing to start seeing their relationship differently—no longer as partners but forever as co-parents. Unless the adults can keep their own insecurity, hurt, and anger in check, the children inevitably get caught in the middle. At worst, they feel they have to take care of their parents.

"It took work," Roberto says. "But all of us worked hard. Thankfully, the open communication was always there. That laid the foundation." Although Roberto lost a wife, he gained his children. He had been a "hands-on" father before the divorce, but with Allison tending the homefront, he often put his work first. "Getting divorced made me a stronger parent. I do a lot of driving them to activities, waiting for them—like a soccer mom! And in the car, I have time to talk one-on-one. It's very good."

His advice to other divorcing dads: "The more involved you are with your children, the better the relationship you're going to have with them and the more you'll enjoy them. It's tiring, but you have to push through that."

When Roberto and Allison talk about "my family" today, they mean everyone—the children, who are now eight and eleven, and *three* adults: Allison, Roberto, and his new wife, Sophie, whom Allison calls her "wife-in-law." Sophie and Roberto began dating a year after the couple's separation, adding a new level of complexity to the parenting arrangement.

The kids now spend half a week with each parent. The schedule works because all three adults are aware of what's at stake. Whenever a problem comes up, they all muster the courage to communicate honestly, the empathy to see where the other is coming from, and the self-control to keep their lizard brains from taking over. "We all try to communicate our way through the gray and the messy," Allison says. "I am very proud of our modern family. The kids are thriving and have a very open mind to the idea of family."

Family-Focused: The Montana-Porters

"I look at us as a family often," says Matthew Montana. "I dreamed about it for so long." On his twelfth birthday, as he blew out the candles, Matt, now thirty-four, wished for a child. "And every birthday after that, it was the same. I knew I wouldn't live my fullest life if I didn't have kids."

But the wish also made him sad. In his twenties, even after he came out as a gay man and began making a good living as a designer, he couldn't picture himself adopting on his own. Then he met Gavin Porter. Matt immediately knew he could share his life with Gavin. They had similar backgrounds and ideas about life. But there was no point in continuing to date Gavin if he wasn't at least open to the idea of having children "someday."

"It was such a priority for him," Gavin recalls of their early conversations. "Raising a family always appealed to me. I didn't know other gay parents at the time, but I was open to it."

Arguably, gay men who become parents *have* to be more conscious of family. As one researcher concluded, "their daunting routes to parenthood seem likely to select for more strengths than limitations." Also, the process of adoption requires prospective parents to put their intentions in writing. "The agencies force you to consider your vision, your desires," recalls

Gavin, "and to think about church, discipline, and what your parenting strategies are."

Let's be clear here. We are not telling this story about family grit because Matthew and Gavin are gay. They don't have a problem or a dread disease. They are bright, conscientious men who love each other and have made a family together. They are also living in enlightened times: As this book was going to press in 2013, the Supreme Court handed down a landmark decision recognizing gay marriage. But regardless of politics or pride, some people will continue to view gay parents as "nontraditional" or worse. And when a family's context—country, city, town, neighborhood, school system—is not hospitable, the partners and their children need grit on a daily basis.

Matthew and Gavin are fortunate. They've been together for seven years and have a solid, honest, loving relationship. They're like Brian and David, the TV couple portrayed on *The New Normal*. Each has work that engages him. At the same time, family is a priority to both men, who find deep comfort and pride in their union and in the careful decisions they make. They were together at their son Gaylen's birth in 2009, and, at this writing, are already making plans to adopt another child. Luckily, they also live in a community where there are other same-gender couples, and they have a generous circle of family and friends who support them.

For now, and let's hope forever, no serious stuff is looming. But the two men are consciously building skills and putting memories in the bank that will help them thrive as a family, no matter what happens in the future. When faced with something new or difficult, they'll get through the anxiety and be able to sustain the effort, because they will be able to hold in their minds and hearts the bigger image of what they're trying to create. They have family grit. Gaylen is young, so he's not bringing much to the table yet, but that's appropriate and good. His fathers' job is to gradually and lovingly make Gaylen part of the whole—by getting to know him, listening and soliciting his ideas, and teaching him how to be a stakeholder. It's a tough mission, but to a family with grit, it's far from impossible.

"Family life helps me to see what is really important in my life," says Matthew. "When you are caught up in work or other personal issues, if you take a moment to look at your family, you know that everything is going to be OK."

Gavin agrees. "If things are good at home, everything else can fall into line."

Grit Required: When Bad Things Happen to Good Families

We never know what's in store for us, and it's impossible to predict how we'd handle a tough situation. The most difficult situations are when a family member becomes ill or disabled. Whether your partner is about to have heart surgery and is facing several months in recovery, or you've just found out your child might be limited in some way, you need grit to get through. Here are a few rules of thumb to follow:

Do it now. The real tragedy of children or adults with problems is that we tend to wait too long. Accept what is, and take action. The longer you delay, the more difficult it will be for everyone.

Educate yourself. Read; find other families; become part of a support network. Contact organizations whose advocacy applies to the diagnosis—for example, Children and Adults with ADD (CHADD), the National Alliance on Mental Illness (NAMI), Autism Speaks, Advocacy for Patients with Chronic Illness. Ask lots of questions. Each case is different, but you need to at least learn how to talk about the condition with other adults and how to have age-appropriate conversations with children.

Find the right kind of help. Look for people who have considerable experience with the issue and who can work directly with the child or adult and help you understand what to do at home. A good diagnostician will take a thorough history, administer tests, and review your routines and activities. Seek a second or, if necessary, a third opinion.

Coordinate your efforts with whoever else is in the child's or adult's life. If family members (or those in the extended family) can't reach a consensus, ask the professional for a best course of action, and stick with it. Don't undermine each other or the treatment.

Be honest. Accept that your child or partner needs extra help and perhaps different care from what he or she has been getting. Speak openly about it. As we pointed out on page 262, children with any kind of issues do better when their problems are labeled. The same is true of adults; we can only accept and work with what we understand.

Treat the person normally. Understand his or her limitations, but don't baby, pity, or exempt that person from family responsibilities. If she's an only child, treating her as "special" will retard her progress. If she has siblings, they might resent it. And if it's your partner, you might eventually resent him or her.

Maintain, monitor, and get feedback. It's not enough to delegate treatment to an expert. Find out what you can be doing at home. Address the issue at your family check-ins.

Be prepared to make adjustments. As their bodies change, children usually need to adjust medication types or dosage. So might an adult who gains or loses weight. Also, when people age, illness and disability manifest in different ways—for example, going into a new grade or leaving home might present new hurdles for children; pregnancy and retirement change adults' lives.

Don't "catastrophize." Strike a sensible balance between being realistic about how far and how fast the person can go and, at the same time, not rush the proccess. Have faith in the power of practice and persistence—and the love and support of family.

Sustain a whole family view. Make sure that you don't abandon the **We** for the sake of one person's **I**. Observe how everyone takes in this new information. Has it changed your various relationships? Ultimately, having a strong set of others to come home to and feeling that she's a stakeholder who matters to the family will do as much for the person as therapy.

If your family is going through a difficult time, and one or more of you feel guilty or have trouble accepting what's happening, it's important to address the issue with honesty and compassion. Help each other live with the ongoing stress. Be sure to read the Family Notebook exercise below.

FYN Do You Apply Family-Think to Hardships?

If you've dealt or are dealing with a loved one's diagnosis, do you see it as a *family* issue? Are you "stuck" in guilt mode? It's never too late to switch to family-think. Ask yourself:

- How many of the "Grit Required" rules of thumb have I followed? Why am I having trouble with certain ones? You might need to do the TYTT mantra to find out why and to help yourself move on.
- Do I have regrets—about a decision, the way I reacted and behaved, something I said, or a decision I immediately made? What caused me to do it that way—guilt? Fear? A desire to keep peace?
- What can I do differently the next time or (if it's an ongoing condition) from now on? Be specific. Does the person need more attention? Does your own relationship need tending? Do you have to be more assertive in whatever environment you are part of (school, a medical practice, your workplace), to get what you need?

Notes on Inspiring Grit

SHELTER FROM THE STORM

Lean In and Reach Out

Given the scale of life in the cosmos, one human life is no more than a tiny blip. Each one of us is just a visitor to this planet, a guest, who will only stay for a limited time. What greater folly could there be than to spend this short time alone, unhappy or in conflict with our companions? Far better, surely, to use our short time here in living a meaningful life, enriched by our sense of connection with others and being of service to them.

—The Dalai Lama

Coming together is a beginning; keeping together is progress; working together is success.

—Henry Ford

"Where's the line between being supportive, and suffocating? Between connecting joyfully, and clinging?" professor of journalism at New York University and mother of three Mary W. Quigley asks on the "About" page of her blog, *Mothering 21*. Mary designed her blog to act like "a GPS for the new terrain" of postcollege parenthood: "We're aging and our offspring have come of age in a rapidly changing social landscape, making intergenerational relationships all the more precious and challenging."

To that end, Mary and her contributors regularly churn out "news, views, and advice on family matters ranging from the everyday to the life-changing." But on November 6, 2012, that changed. As Mary explained, "Mothering21.com doesn't usually deal with natural disasters but to not do so this week would be ignoring the elephant in the room."

Mary first details her own experiences as Hurricane Sandy, aptly called "Frankenstorm" and "the storm of the century," goes "from media hype to all-too-close reality." Huddled together in their home on Long Island, one of the hardest-hit areas of the Northeast, Mary, her husband, and her daughter watch helplessly as trees fall and sparks fly. She tries calling her two sons, who no longer live at home, but is unable to get service, "bringing back eerie memories of the last time that happened, the morning of 9/11." A text comes through from NYU's emergency system. The downtown Manhattan dorms are without power, and students are ordered to stay put. Mary feels the pain of the "hundreds of parents unable to contact their college students stranded in dark dorms."

As day breaks on Tuesday, the Quigleys are spared serious damage, but many of their neighbors are not so lucky. One bemoans that his daughter, her husband, and their two sons had made extensive repairs to their home after Hurricane Irene last year. Now their home is destroyed. They have to start over.

As the week wears on, Mary, who is keenly attuned to interactions between the generations, sees the aftermath through a *whole-family* lens:

> On my block alone, half dozen families were either helping their adult children cope or vice versa. That young couple who lost their house is now living with her parents for the foreseeable future, and the 60-something grandma is off with the two boys in a double stroller several times a day to keep them occupied while the parents make plans for another round of repairs. The neighbors next door are sheltering their adult daughter, her husband, two small children and a baby born last Thursday. . . . The family ties become stronger during times of crisis . . . and helpful.

Mary goes on to describe other acts of family kindness and generosity. An older couple goes to live with their daughter in an adjoining town. A friend opens her house to her niece and her five young children. A neighbor takes in relatives from Long Beach, a seaside community consumed by an angry and uncontrollable ocean.

It isn't easy to give shelter to traumatized relatives, especially when there's no end in sight. It "could be months," Mary learns, before that family from Long Beach can repair their own home. The displaced relatives are clearly there for the long haul.

"But it's family," says Mary's neighbor. "That's what you do."

You Don't Have to "Family" Alone

Natural disasters tend to inspire the best in people, in part because calamity brings us together. For example, in the winter of 2011, a snowstorm knocked out electric power in the Northeast town where the Sargent-Klein family lives. The unexpected blackout affected the entire downtown, including supermarkets and convenience stores. Families had to raid their own cupboards. On the first of what would turn out to be a four-day outage, the twins, Seth and Rachel, took a walk around the neighborhood and began to knock on doors. They had shared a paper route and had worked for various neighbors since they were thirteen, doing yard work and other odd jobs. With snow and ice blanketing the area, no one had to tell them that there were driveways to be shoveled and fallen branches to clear. After the heavy lifting was done, they went home for a cup of hot chocolate, and together with some of their peers (juniors and seniors at the local public high school), the kids cooked up another way to help their neighbors.

Rachel and her friend Ashley went door-to-door again, this time with a clipboard. "We're taking orders for coffee and donuts tomorrow morning," they offered. "Would you like something?" Back home, Seth was making sure he had all the ingredients he'd need for the donuts. From the time he was in middle school, Seth had been the family baker, a role he cherished. The wood-fired oven he and his dad had built didn't require electricity, so he was good to go.

The next morning, armed with thermoses and freshly baked cinnamon donuts, the kids, up since dawn, made good on their promise. They had perceived a need and reached out on their own. It was natural and rewarding to them, because from early on, they had grown up in families that valued hard work and perseverance. They had been taught to care about another's misfortune.

Lanie and Bill Allen also taught their kids to reach out to other families. They've all worked with McDuffie Mission, a local church-affiliated project. "They go around for a week and do labor," explains Bill, who traveled with his oldest boy to Michigan to help rebuild a house destroyed in a fire. "It made my son feel great." Closer to home, his thirteen-year-old helped build a wheelchair ramp. Even a child without skills can help out, says Bill. "After the tornado, the boys and I went to clear debris, and our youngest helped make sandwiches."

Such lessons pay off, often in surprising ways. Bill, who coaches his oldest son's soccer team, recalls a recent game in which their team was ahead, 9 to 0. Peter, who is very competitive and talented—often the best player on the field—could have easily sunk another goal himself. Instead, he passed the ball to a weaker player. "Giving one of the less experienced players a chance to score was good sportsmanship. I didn't tell him to do that," says Bill. "He did it on his own."

When children or adults are good citizens and are willing to do *for* another person, it not only builds character, strengthens self-control, and opens their hearts, but it also makes *them* happier and healthier. Scores of studies on volunteers, for example, confirm the restorative and healing power of giving others a helping hand or standing up for those who can't do it on their own. You actually live longer.

Recent research conducted by psychologist Phillip Zimbardo, professor emeritus at Stanford, who's currently on a quest to figure out what inspires people to "do good," found that people who volunteer are *three times more likely* to perform heroic acts when the opportunity presents itself. Like the teens who delivered donuts and coffee after the storm, they look for opportunities to help others.

Fortunately, over the last decade, many internet venues have been developed with families in mind. Volunteer Family, for example, was launched in 2003 by Heather Jack, a Boston-based attorney and mother who wanted to help families "find opportunities that they can do together." It is now a national phenomenon, having already placed more than 20,000 family volunteers. Heather has counterparts everywhere who connect families with those in need.

You don't necessarily have to go through an organization to offer time and talent. One of you might give a free class in yoga or mentor writers at a community center. A teenager who's a great athlete might offer a catching-and-throwing clinic for parents and children. A child who usually gets paid for baby-sitting could offer it *as a favor* around the holidays. It's a way of thanking his regular clients for hiring and trusting him. These are simple ideas that feel good and stay with us. You care about connection, are more open and giving, and you cleave toward the positive, rather than living in negativity.

Families Need the Village

Brea Heron, a hairdresser in her mid-forties, takes her parenting seriously but also believes that it does, in fact, "take a village" to raise her son, Troy. Some people are baffled by Brea's on-again, off-again relationship with Anthony, Troy's father; others assume she's a single mother. Brea doesn't see it either way. "I have a child *with* someone. Do I do a lot of things on my own? Absolutely. But that doesn't mean I'm a—quote—single mom. How can I be if there's always someone else to consider? We're a family, no matter what. Even if other people come into our lives, we're still a family."

As for Troy, she adds, "It's all he knows. I've explained to him that adults sometimes need to be in different places from one another, but no matter what, we're a family."

Brea chose a profession that makes it easy to expand the boundaries of her family. Her shop (like many beauty salons and barbershops) is like a friendly town square. Located in a tree-lined city neighborhood and decorated with bits of fun and kitsch, along with photos of Troy at different ages, the shop has been like a second home for her son. As a baby, he was passed around the salon, a smiling bundle that everyone took turns holding. Growing up, he became a familiar fixture, lying on the little banquette near the sinks, playing video games, doing homework, occasionally looking up to answer an adult's question.

Over the years, Troy has gotten to know those adults—his mom's friends, coworkers, and longtime clients. He isn't as frequent a visitor these days—he's fourteen, and now the family lives in the suburbs. But the cast of characters at the salon will always be part of his village. He feels held and loved by a special few, members of the tribe who have became his unofficial "aunts" and "uncles." Brea sometimes hears him "talking" to Seth, one of the hairdressers, whose untimely death a few years ago shook the boy ("He loved him, and they were very close"). And when Toni, another coworker, was pregnant, Brea recalled, "he'd point to little baby things and say to me, 'Let's get that for Toni.'" Now, he's an unofficial uncle and loves the role.

Brea is happy for the bonds Troy has forged with other adults. "Each of these people gives him *something*. It could be something as simple as a remark that then puts an idea into his head," says Brea. "I don't believe in home-schooling, because children don't get that kind of interaction. Kids need to be around people. They learn how to talk, to listen, and to be there for others."

Increasing numbers of parents consciously create social networks to extend their family's boundaries. In the rush of everyday life, it can be challenging to coordinate your family members' schedules, let alone those of other families. But as Ruby D'Angelo puts it, "amazing things can be achieved by small people in great numbers." Ruby teamed up with the Hearing Loss Association of America (HLAA) and continues to participate in the annual Walk4Hearing to support hearing impaired families.

Neal and Andrea Gorenflo included in their wedding vows their intention to reach out: "We wrote a shared mission statement," explains Neal, publisher of Shareable.net, a cutting-edge online magazine that focuses on new social and political ideas. The Gorenflos themselves walk the walk. "We wanted to be an outwardly directed family, a family engaged in society." By exposing their son, who just turned four, to many different kinds of people, they're already giving him more social experiences to draw on, which reinforces the empathy "loop":

You care about others, they are grateful, they care about you, and you begin to see that human connection is better than any material reward. That inspires you to be even more empathetic, courageous, and caring.

The Gorenflos are part of a network of families that share ideas and resources. Neal and his wife adore their son but don't put him at the center of their universe—he's part of a larger whole. "You can't connect families together if they're all child-centric," says Neal. He and Andrea share a nanny with three other families. It took some doing, but they managed to make it work by finding others who think the same way.*

"Nanny sharing," says Neal, "has been the best family thing we've done so far collectively. It saves us a ton of cash, and we've created a little

---

*The many issues that have to be ironed out are covered on Shareable in "How to Share a Nanny." http://www.shareable.net/blog/how-to-share-a-nanny.

village for our family, socially speaking. If Andrea and I want to go on a date, friends will stay while Jake is sleeping."

Gorenflo, whose magazine often highlights new ideas and arrangements that benefit families, says, "I think we have it backward in modern society. Family should be the priority, compared to profit and economic growth, work, or money. After all, families reproduce and spawn the next generation. Anything we do should enhance that, not work against it."

Your Family-Whispering Project

As we said at the outset of this book, family is where it all begins and ends. It's where intimacy is learned, where we all learn to "read," respect, and relate to each other. It's where adults hone their emotional intelligence and self-control and where children learn how to manage—not stifle—their feelings and monitor their own behavior. It's where everyone learns to sacrifice for the greater good. Family *is* shelter from the storm.

This book was conceived to help you look at your **We**—to make sure everyone's a stakeholder; to put relationships above all else; and to be conscious of the welfare of each **I**, especially when new ripples flow through the family ecosystem. We've offered stories, reminders, and strategies— information that, we believe, will help your family produce happy, generous, and willing adults and children—good citizens.

It's a lot to digest! Take from it what works for you. Consider it your "family-whispering project," an idea akin to Gretchen Rubin's "happiness project," which she defines as "an approach to changing your life." Her bestselling book of the same name, Gretchen points out, is the story of *her* happiness project. It is based on her experiences, what she's tried and learned, her values and interests. "Your project would look different from mine."

The same is true of a *family-whispering project,* which is an approach to changing your family life for the better. But as we've said repeatedly, every family is unique, as different from one another as snowflakes. Even the well-run families we've highlighted in these pages haven't necessarily figured it out, nor are they doing everything amazingly right. It's about hanging in and doing the best you can.

All families are full of mess, joy, pain, disappointment, love, resentment, and sometimes tragedy. No family is immune, and none is perfect or ideal. Each one is a work in progress.

To conceive your own family-whispering project, sift through the information and ideas in these pages to see what's applicable. Take the Whole Family Test (pages 299–300) to gauge how family-focused you are. Decide how much time and energy you want to invest in your family-whispering project. It might entail no more than reading this book and changing your perspective from parent-think to family-think. That, in and of itself, will better your family life. Your family-whispering project might start and end by looking at your routine. It might be inspired by a particular change in your family that requires all of you to adjust. It might be a response to trouble that's been brewing, which you've been too overwhelmed to handle. Or it might be a last-ditch effort to solve an ongoing problem by taking a more family-focused approach.

You might also want to join others—individuals and/or couples—to study family whispering *together*. Commit to reading a chapter a month—a manageable goal given everyone's busy schedules. Over the course of the year, meet at a community center, a coffee shop, or at one another's homes. There's strength in numbers and comfort in knowing you're not alone in your struggles. Being together will also make it easier to see through 3F glasses and to sustain family-think. Once you get to know one another and digest some of the basic ideas in this book, you might widen your circle. In the fifth month, for example, when you read the chapter on "Adult Family Ties," invite parents or adult siblings to join in the discussion. Depending on the age of your children, you might also include the younger generation, especially when you talk about family check-ins. And for your last meeting of the year, you can celebrate yourself for putting so much thought and energy into strengthening your families. (You'll find more ideas about family-whispering groups online at www.familywhispering.com.)

However you conceive it, your family project should *not* cause you to ruminate on the past. None of us can know what would have happened if we had done things differently—been more attentive, understanding, proactive, or consistent or taken better care of ourselves or our children. Other people and events beyond our control can change a family's trajectory. Besides, we can't undo the past. So why spend time beating ourselves up? "We don't know how much time we have together," Tracy once wrote in her diary. "What's really important is happening to me today."

Any kind of family project, we hope, will help you *now* to make mindful decisions about your own family and inspire you to have conversations with other parents about what they want for their families. It's a constant balancing act, to be sure, between nurturing children's talents and helping them see themselves as part of the many; between protecting children and letting them explore on their own; between meeting your own family's daily needs and reaching out to help other families.

None of it is easy, but achieving balance is more likely if we think of ourselves as part of a global family. As an old African saying goes, "If you want to go quickly, go alone. If you want to go far, go together." If we all put thought and energy into our own family projects, we believe it will bode well for the world.

Imagine what life in general would be like if *all* adults, not just parents or grandparents, felt like stakeholders in the global family. Imagine if teachers, therapists, lawmakers, entrepreneurs, corporate big wigs, health professionals, divorce attorneys, spiritual advisers, politicians, policy makers, and anyone else whose work affects families and children got REAL. Imagine what might happen if they based their decisions and everyday interactions on a sense of **R**esponsibility to *all* families and came up with realistic, respectful ways to educate and support them. Imagine if they mustered the **E**mpathy to understand what mothers, fathers, and children must deal with on a daily basis. Imagine if they were **A**uthentic and admitted the enormous challenge of helping families in need. And imagine what a better place the world would be if they—and all of us—consistently **L**ed with Love.

With awareness comes change. More than a decade ago, when Tracy Hogg introduced the notion of baby whispering to a new generation of parents, she exhorted mothers and fathers to slow down and calm down. Just as she advised you then to take a deep breath and figure out what your child needs, family whispering begins when you apply the same kind of wisdom and consciousness to your whole family. Lean in to your family. Figure out what *it* needs. Be aware of what you do and mindful of how your words, behavior, and pace affect those around you. Start as you mean to go on. Realize that it's not just between you and your child. Make *all* your relationships a priority. And know that your family isn't alone in the struggle.

BABY WHISPERING: THE LEGACY

Remembrances from Sara Fear Hogg

I cannot forget my mother.
She is my bridge.

—ROBERTA WEEMS

Los Angeles, California, January 2013. Anyone who ever met my mum thought she was the most welcoming, warm, loving lady they ever met. No one was left out when my mum was around. She would always encourage family discussions that got everyone involved. When my sister and I argued, as siblings do, she tried—to the best of her ability—to get us to see things from each other's perspective. She taught us that conversation and communication were keys to any successful relationship.

My mum believed that having a strong, caring nuclear family was imperative to a thriving child. Although she took care of mostly babies and toddlers, she knew it was also crucial to pay attention to the delicate, intricate world of the family. Family was always of the utmost importance to her teachings. She wanted not only to "fix" problems but also to help create a loving and nurturing environment that allowed everyone in the family circle to have a voice and to be heard.

Tracy knew that we also create "family" wherever we are. Nowadays, as our extended families are spread far and wide, we reach out to what we call our families of choice—friends we take in and other relationships we build in our communities. But no matter how far away we go from our roots, she said, home is always where the heart is, even if it's six thousand miles away! Home is where we feel grounded. It's where we develop relationships built on love and trust with people who nurture us, help us grow, and give us a secure foundation and a sense of belonging.

One of the things my mum often said to me when I was a child was, "When you have a family, you will understand." As I have grown into my own shoes and my career, I have had the pleasure of experiencing what that means. I'm not a mother yet, but I hope to be one soon. In the meantime, I have the privilege of witnessing parents doing whatever it takes to make things work for the sake of their families. When children and adults are given a voice and recognized for who they are, it makes a world of difference to their souls and their beings.

Today, my sister and I are very proud of the work Mum did and the teachings she left behind. It is wonderful to see how her ideas have helped so many families—and that her voice lives on.

I am happy that so many people recognize Mum's wisdom and still use her techniques. Baby whispering is a timeless tradition. Mum would be so very proud of the family book. She wanted it written, and it's a great finale to her fantastic series of books.

—*Sara Fear Hogg*

ACKNOWLEDGMENTS

When we become more fully aware that our success is due in large measure to the loyalty, helpfulness, and encouragement we have received from others, our desire grows to pass on similar gifts. Gratitude spurs us on to prove ourselves worthy of what others have done for us. The spirit of gratitude is a powerful energizer.

—Wilferd A. Peterson

My deepest gratitude is reserved for the late Tracy Hogg, whose spirit will always be with me. Baby whispering is her legacy. She taught it to me and trusted that I would find ways to apply it to the whole family. She never used the phrase *family whispering*, but I suspect she'd love the idea.

I want to thank members of Tracy's family who also lent their support: Sara, her elder daughter and star pupil, and her younger sister, Sophie, who is a mother herself; Tracy's siblings, John Hogg and Michelle Gleadhill; her mother, Hazel Dixon; and most of all, the indomitable matriarch of the family, Tracy's "Nan."

In our last phone conversation, in November 2004, I assured Tracy that *her* "mums" all over the world wouldn't let her die. And they haven't. They share her tips on Facebook and on www.babywhisperer forums.com, the chat boards that survived Tracy's original Baby Whisperer website. These mothers (and a few fathers) have created *community* in the truest sense of the word. Some of the daily posters have been there for more than a decade, showing up to help new mothers even as their own kids are inching toward adolescence! They're like loyal ambassadors, teaching and living the core principles of baby whispering. Tracy would have wanted to thank them for carrying on her work—and so do I. While writing this book, I had illuminating conversations—online, by phone, and via Skype—with many of them.

Thank you also to Tracy's former clients who were willing to reminisce and to the mothers, fathers, and teenagers in other families who allowed me to peek into their lives over these last two years. I hope I have done justice to your stories.

I am personally blessed to have a wide network of friends and professionals (sometimes one and the same) who shared their enthusiasm about this project and their insights about family. Their comments, ideas, and research inform this book.

Every writer needs a team. I must (again) thank my "New York agent" of more than twenty years, Eileen Cope. She resurrected this project, kept it going, and has always supported my work. I am also grateful for Greer Hendricks, who is not only a superb editor but also a friend who shared stories of her own family; Meghan Stevenson, who provided enthusiastic and invaluable editorial insights and direction; and Sarah Cantin, my go-to person at Simon & Schuster. And on the days I needed it, Jill Parsons Stern, fellow writer and most excellent sounding board, talked me off the ledge!

As always, but especially for this book, I thank my **We**—family members and close friends who feel like "home." You know who you are. Your love and caring light my way, and wherever I am, you are in my heart.

—*Melinda Blau*
Northampton/Manhattan/Miami/Paris

APPENDIX I

THE WHOLE FAMILY TEST

The hero in my family IS my family because of who we are together.
—"MANNY" ON *MODERN FAMILY*

Families *should* be our first priority. Making families strong makes society strong. All the better if we create networks of families, linked by geography, interests, and need. But the work begins at home.

To help you gauge how family-focused you are or have become, we hope, as a result of reading this book, we leave you with one final quiz: the Whole Family Test. In addition to giving you a "score," it will also serve as a reminder of what you've read in these pages.

It might be fun to make copies of this test—and actually take it with *the whole family*. (It can be a great way to introduce the idea of having family check-ins; see pages 164–69.)

On a scale of 1 to 5, with 1 meaning "not at all" and 5 meaning "almost all the time" (no one does anything *all* the time), rate yourselves *as a family* on the following items.

1. We pull together as a family during hard times. ____
2. We respect and support one another as individuals. ____
3. We are family-centered, not child-centered. ____
4. We listen to, and learn from, one another. ____
5. We see problems as opportunities to figure out how to manage better next time—*not* to assign blame. ____
6. We don't argue with reality—we accept who each of us is and tell ourselves the truth about what's happening around us. ____
7. We encourage children, not just adults, to assume roles that help keep the family running. ____

8. We have regular, predictable routines and rituals that bring us together as a family. _____

9. We keep track of and document our good memories. _____

10. We accept that people argue and that bad things happen, but we try not to let negativity overwhelm us. _____

11. We take on projects as a family. _____

12. We know that each of us is different and believe that makes us stronger as a family. _____

13. We know what we stand for as a family. _____

14. We are all willing to work hard—and know that it's everyone's job—to keep the family ecosystem in balance. _____

15. We see our family as part of a greater whole, both in our community and as part of a larger global family. _____

16. We put our heads together to look for solutions, because it's never just one person's problem. _____

17. We try our best but don't necessarily have to *be* the best. _____

18. We call on relatives and people outside the family when we need help. _____

19. Even as we pursue our individual goals, we are grateful for the support that comes to each of us through the family. _____

20. We try to reach outside ourselves, to other families and to our community, to support those who have fewer resources. _____

If you racked up between 80 and 100 points, you already embrace the whole family idea. You're on a path that benefits all of you.

If your score is between 0 and 20, you might inadvertently be focusing more on your children than on making your family strong, or perhaps you've recently been hit by a string of changes and haven't quite recovered.

Most likely, your family will fall somewhere in between—and there's room for improvement.

THE TWELVE ESSENTIAL TROUBLESHOOTING QUESTIONS FOR THE WHOLE FAMILY

In our book on solving baby and toddler issues, we explained that troubleshooting is like an investigation. When parents insisted that a baby's or toddler's behavior had "come out of nowhere," Tracy would answer, "No luv. You just haven't asked the right questions."

Below are "The Twelve Essential Questions" from our previous book, rewritten so that they apply to the whole family. So whether the problem is between the adults, warring siblings, disputes about screen time or homework, or any other disruption to your everyday routine, ask these questions *first*.

1. Is a child or adult approaching a developmental stage that might be contributing to a change in him or her or to our relationship? (Reader: Does this new stage and the new behavior jibe with your expectations? clash with your personality?)
2. Has our daily routine changed, giving us more or less time together?
3. Has an adult's or child's diet or sleep patterns changed?
4. Is anyone doing any new activities at home or outside? If so, how is it affecting our **We**?
5. Have any of us changed jobs or schools or experienced a problem at work or school, such as a social problem or increased workload?
6. Has the family, or one of our members, been away from home more than usual, taken a trip or family vacation?
7. Is anyone recovering from surgery, an illness, or an accident (even a minor one)?

8. Has anyone been exceptionally busy, or going through an emotionally difficult time?

9. Is there anything else going on within our household that might affect the rest of us and our relationships—adult or sibling arguments, a new housekeeper, a job change, a move, a death in the family?

10. Have we been REAL with one another or have we been accidentally reinforcing negative patterns of behavior that affect the whole family?

11. Has our family been influenced by an outside relationship—say, a member of the extended family, a friend or group of friends?

12. Has something in our context—our immediate household, the school system, the neighborhood or community, the country, the world—affected us directly or indirectly? Have changed circumstances forced our family to deal with our environment differently or changed our understanding in some way?

APPENDIX III

WHAT WE READ

If one reads enough books one has a fighting chance. Or better,
one's chances of survival increase with each book one reads.

—SHERMAN ALEXIE

We've drawn from many sources—relationship scholars, journalists, and researchers who study and report on the family, along with authors who have written about their own experiences as family members. If you'd like to read what we read, here are a few books and articles we like by authors whose ideas and words have informed these pages.

Baumeister, Roy. *Willpower: Rediscovering the Greatest Human Strength.* Penguin Books, 2012.

Bronson, Po, and Ashley Merryman. *Nurture Shock: New Thinking About Children.* Twelve, 2009.

Clarke, Jean, Connie Dawson, and David Bredehoft. *How Much Is Enough?: Everything You Need to Know to Steer Clear of Overindulgence and Raise Likeable, Responsible and Respectful Children.* Da Capo Press, 2003.

Covey, Steven. *The 7 Habits of Highly Effective People.* Free Press, 2004.

Cowan, Carolyn Pape, and Phillip Cowan. *When Partners Become Parents: The Big Life Change for Couples.* Routledge, 1999.

David, Laurie, and Kirstin Uhrenholdt. *The Family Dinner: Great Ways to Connect with Your Kids, One Meal at a Time.* Grand Central Life & Style, 2010.

Davidson, Cathy N. *Now You See It: How Technology and Brain Science Will Transform Schools and Business for the 21st Century.* Penguin Books, 2012.

Druckerman, Pamela. *Bringing Up Bébé: One American Mother Discovers the Wisdom of French Parenting.* Penguin Press, 2012.

Duke, Marshall P. "The Stories That Bind Us: What Are the Twenty

Questions?" *Huffington Post,* March 23, 2013. http://www.huffington
post.com/marshall-p-duke/the-stories-that-bind-us-_b_2918975.html.

Feiler, Bruce. *The Secrets of Happy Families: Improve Your Mornings, Rethink Family Dinner, Fight Smarter, Go Out and Play, and Much More.*
William Morrow, 2013.

Gibbs, Nancy. "The Growing Backlash against Overparenting." *Time,*
November 30, 2009. http://cdn.optmd.com/V2/62428/415005/index
.html?g=Af////8=&r=www.time.com/time/magazine/article/0,917
1,1940697,00.html.

Gottman, John. *Ten Lessons to Transform Your Marriage.* Three Rivers
Press, 2007.

Guernsey, Lisa. *Screen Time: How Electronic Media—from Baby Videos to
Educational Software—Affects Your Young Child.* Basic Books, 2012.

Hendrix, Harville, and Helen LaKelly Hunt. *Making Marriage Simple.*
Harmony Books, 2013.

Hightower, Corbyn. *When Life Gives You Crabapples, Make Something
Somewhat Palatable.* Kindle Books, 2011. http://www.amazon.com
/dp/B004TNGLFM.

Hochschild, Arlie. *Time Bind: When Work Becomes Home and Home
Becomes Work.* Holt Paperbacks, 2001.

Honore, Carl. *Under Pressure: Rescuing Our Children from the Culture of
Hyper-Parenting.* Harper One, 2009.

Johnson, Sue. *Hold Me Tight: Your Guide to the Most Successful Approach to
Building Loving Relationships.* Piatkus Books, 2011.

Kahneman, Daniel. *Thinking, Fast and Slow.* Farrar, Straus and Giroux,
2011.

Kashdan, Todd. *Curious? Discover the Missing Ingredient to a Fulfilling
Life.* William Morrow, 2009.

Kohn, Alfie. *Unconditional Parenting: Moving from Rewards and Punish-
ments to Love and Reason.* Atria, 2006.

Konigsberg, Ruth Davis. "Chore Wars." *Time,* August 8, 2011. http:
//www.time.com/time/magazine/article/0,9171,2084582,00.html.

Koslow, Sally. *Slouching toward Adulthood: Observations from the Not-
So-Empty Nest.* Viking, 2012.

Langer, Ellen. *Counterclockwise: Mindful Health and the Power of Possibility.* Ballantine Books, 2009.

Lareau, Annette. *Unequal Childhoods: Class, Race, and Family Life.*
University of California Press, 2011.

Lerner, Harriet. *Marriage Rules: A Manual for the Married and the Coupled Up.* Gotham, 2012. *The Dance of Connection: How to Talk to Someone When You're Mad, Hurt, Scared, Frustrated, Insulted, Betrayed, or Desperate.* William Morrow, 2002.

Levine, Madeline. *The Price of Privilege: How Parental Pressure and Material Advantage Are Creating a Generation of Disconnected and Unhappy Kids.* Harper Perennial, 2008.

Marano, Hara Estroff. *A Nation of Wimps: The High Cost of Invasive Parenting.* Harmony Books, 2008.

Milardo, Robert M. *The Forgotten Kin: Aunts and Uncles.* Cambridge University Press, 2010.

Mogel, Wendy. *The Blessing of a Skinned Knee: Using Jewish Teachings to Raise Self-Reliant Children.* Scribner, 2008.

Moret, Jim. "Still the One on Our 30th Anniversary." Huffington Post, May 22, 2012. http://www.huffingtonpost.com/jim-moret/still-the-one-on-our-30th_b_1536867.html?ncid=wsc-huffpost-cards-image.

Morgan, Jay. *Fingerpainting in Psych Class: Artfully Applying Science to Better Work with Children and Teens.* iUniverse, 2010.

Newman, Susan. *The Case for the Only Child.* HCI, 2011.

O'Donahue, Mary. *When You Say "Thank You," Mean It.* Adams Media, 2010.

Pennebaker, James. *The Secret Life of Pronouns: What Our Words Say about Us.* Bloomsbury Press, 2013. *Writing to Heal: A Guided Journal for Recovering from Trauma & Emotional Upheaval.* New Harbinger, 2004.

Pink, Daniel. *Drive: The Surprising Truth about What Motivates Us.* Riverhead Books, 2011.

Pranis, Kay. *The Little Book of Circle Processes: A New/Old Approach to Peacemaking.* Good Books, 2005.

Quigley, Mary. "Surviving Sandy." Mothering 21, November 6, 2012. http://mothering21.com/2012/11/06/surviving-sandy/.

Rabinor, Judith Ruskay. *Befriending Your Ex: Making Life Better for You, Your Kids, and, Yes, Your Ex.* New Harbinger Publications, 2013.

Rainie, Lee, and Barry Wellman. *Networked: The New Social Operating System.* MIT Press, 2012.

Rheingold, Howard. *Net Smart: How to Thrive Online.* MIT Press, 2012.

Rosen, Hannah. "The Touch Screen Generation." *Atlantic Monthly*, March 20, 2013. http://theatlanticmonthly.com/magazine/archive/2013/04/the-touch-screen-generation/309250.

Rubin, Gretchen. *Happier at Home: Kiss More, Jump More, Abandon a*

Project, Read Samuel Johnson, and My Other Experiments in the Practice of Life. Harmony, 2012. *The Happiness Project: Or, Why I Spent a Year Trying to Sing in the Morning, Clean My Closets, Fight Right, Read Aristotle, and Generally Have More Fun.* Harper Perennial, 2011.

Savage, Dan. *The Commitment: Love, Sex, Marriage, and My Family.* Plume, 2006.

Schnarch, David. *Passionate Marriage: Keeping Love and Intimacy Alive in Committed Relationships.* Norton, 2009.

Seligman, Martin. *Authentic Happiness: Using the New Positive Psychology to Realize Your Potential for Lasting Fulfillment.* Free Press, 2003.

Skenazy, Lenore. *Free-Range Kids, How to Raise Safe, Self-Reliant Children (without Going Nuts with Worry).* Jossey-Bass, 2010.

Solomon, Andrew. *Far from the Tree: Parents, Children, and the Search for Identity.* Scribner, 2012.

Steiner-Adair, Catherine, Ed.D., and Teresa H. Barker. *The Big Disconnect: Protecting Childhood and Family Relationships in the Digital Age.* HarperCollins, 2013.

Stinnet, Nick, and John Defrain. *Secrets of Strong Families.* Little, Brown and Company, 1986.

Taffel, Ron. *Childhood Unbound.* Free Press, 2010. *Nurturing Good Children Now* (with Melinda Blau). Golden Guides from St. Martin's Press, 2000.

Tannen, Deborah. *I Only Say This Because I Love You: Talking to Your Parents, Partner, Sibs, and Kids When You're All Adults.* Random House, 2002.

Warner, Jennifer. *Perfect Madness: Motherhood in the Age of Anxiety.* Riverhead Books, 2006.

Weil, Liz. *No Cheating, No Dying: I Had a Good Marriage, Then I Tried to Make It Better.* Scribner, 2012.

Willet, Beverly. "Pause in the Name of Love." Huffington Post, December 3, 2010. http://www.huffingtonpost.com/beverly-willet/pause-in-the-name-of-love_b_790637.html.

Wilson, Timothy D. *Redirect: The Surprising New Science of Psychological Change.* Little, Brown and Company, 2011.

INDEX